RADIO POWER

International and Comparative Broadcasting

A Series Edited by Sydney W. Head

RADIO POWER

Propaganda and International Broadcasting

JULIAN HALE

Temple University Press
Philadelphia

Temple University Press, Philadelphia 19122

© 1975 by Julian Hale

All rights reserved. Published 1975

Printed in Great Britain by The Anchor Press Ltd
and bound by Wm Brendon & Son Ltd
both of Tiptree, Essex

International Standard Book Number: 0–87722–049–2

Library of Congress Catalog Card Number: 75–18694

Contents

Acknowledgments

I am grateful to Alexander Lieven, Anatol Goldberg, Keith Edwards, and other friends and former colleagues in the BBC External Services and Monitoring Service (here John Chadwick in particular); to James Monahan, and to helpful sources in Washington and Munich; and also to my wife for her constructive criticism throughout.

I must emphasize, however, that all the opinions in the book are entirely my own.

After all, what is a lie? 'Tis but
The truth in masquerade.

> Byron

For if the trumpet give an uncertain sound,
who shall prepare himself to the battle?

> 1 Corinthians xiv, 8

Introduction

Radio is the only unstoppable medium of mass communication. It is the only medium which reaches across the entire globe instantaneously and can convey a message from any country to any other. Combined, these qualities of radio ensure that it plays an indispensable role in international communications, and keeps its place as the most powerful weapon of international propaganda.

The printed word is clumsy to distribute and easily censored. Television's power is still purely national, although direct international communication by satellite, even when unsolicited, will soon be a technical possibility. When the Americans distributed Greta Garbo's film *Ninochka* to a politically wavering Italian audience before the crucial 1948 election, they did more to turn voters off communism than through any open attempt at persuasion. But films, though potent means of propaganda in the broadest sense, are, like books and newspapers, defenceless against the censor. And unlike advertising, to which it is also compared, radio propaganda does not identify itself as selling a product; its influence is deeper and wider.

In the twenties and thirties, when radio was a novelty, exaggerated claims were made—in Germany, America and Britain especially—for its power to influence men's minds. Hilda Matheson, a senior BBC executive, wrote of one of the dangers in 1933, declaring that 'broadcasting is a huge agency of standardization, the most powerful the world has ever seen'. But it was the Nazis who first saw, and then developed, the use of radio as a means of international propaganda designed to act as an extension of diplomacy—in Goebbels' view virtually as a substitute for diplomacy.

The widespread use of radio propaganda during the war established both the power and the limitations of the medium. The war was a testing ground for the principles of psychological warfare, for the claims of 'white' (overt) against 'black' (covert and misleading) propaganda. It pitted the two extremes of propaganda against each other: total, opportunistic, offensive (in both senses) Nazi propaganda against the BBC's policy of telling the truth in good times and bad, risking charges of insipidity and hypocrisy in order to establish a reputation for credibility in the long term. American and Soviet radio propaganda, operating on the middle ground of more or less single-minded commitment to their respective ideologies, had also established by the end of the war broadcasting patterns which have lasted ever since.

International radio propaganda has stood the test of time because it can do things which other means of persuasion, education, and information cannot do. It can flash news, and reaction to it, across the world quicker than any other medium. It can convey the original sound of the human voice, the sounds of people making news, getting angry or happy about it, reproducing political styles and moods as well as the substance of the message. Television completes the picture visually later on, whenever film is available, which is far from always, and it can stage grand spectaculars like the landing on the moon. But radio is first across national frontiers with the unexpected news as it is with the day-to-day events. In some countries where censorship limits the coverage of the domestic media, foreign radio is the only source of a large part of people's information about things that happen outside their immediate locality and their closed society.

As an instrument of persuasion, radio has some psychological advantages over its competitors, which, although more apparent in pre-television days, are still real enough. Whereas cold print appeals to the reason, radio can also appeal to the emotions. Hitler used it deliberately as a way of inducing mass hysteria. There is no reason to suppose that it cannot be used in the same way again wherever in the world the quantity and variety of the local media have not yet induced satiety and scepticism. In specific conflict situations, as there was for example in pre-independence Algeria, radio is a potent revolutionary force. The Voice of the Arabs has been a powerful incitement to Holy War. Radio Free Europe was believed by many Hungarians to have brought people out into the streets in 1956.

On the other hand, radio, except when relayed through some kind of public address system, can easily be switched off, and, being ephemeral, its message can be corrected or denied by more permanent sources—one reason why the Nazis repeated to the point of saturation things they wished the audience to retain. But in totalitarian and closed societies, the elusive nature of radio signals can be an advantage. In Nazi Germany, listening to foreign stations was a symbol of the right to think for oneself. The message becomes that much more intimate and urgent. Wherever there is censorship today, listening to foreign stations is regarded as that much more precious. The very fact of making a special effort to tune in predisposes the listener to pay more attention to, and believe, what he hears. This is radio's particular advantage.

Jamming, which is one form of censorship, is rarely totally disruptive, and in fact it encourages listening where it is ineffective or partial rather than discourages it. Natural hazards to short-wave signals present more serious problems to the broadcasters. Most international programmes are carried on short waves which, by bouncing up and down off earth and sky, can cover the entire globe in a fraction of a second, but mysterious holes appearing in the ionized layer which reflects the waves back to earth, electrical storms, magnetic currents, sun-spots, are only some of the factors which can reduce the most powerful signal to a maddening buzzing jangle which fades and reappears like an early Marconi experiment. The surer medium-wave signal travels relatively small distances and therefore relies on a network of relay stations and transmitters which are not only expensive to erect but depend on the political goodwill of the host. The Voice of America, for instance, had a medium-wave relay in Iraq before the 1958 revolution. When the Americans most wanted it, it was removed.

Interference also comes from other sources. Today, even when a listener prefers to tune into the Voice of America or the BBC or Moscow Radio, he is more and more likely to find some unwanted station straying on to the wavelength because it has been allocated a place on the frequency spectrum so close that a lack of special attention results in interference. While international organizations vainly struggle to put order into the allocation of wavebands, the babel of sound on both short-wave and medium-wave frequencies becomes less and less comprehensible. Distortion as a result of overcrowded airwaves is perhaps a more widespread problem than deliberate distortion of the truth.

In Britain and North America in particular, listening to other countries' radio programmes is a minority habit. Many people who are well aware of the number of national newspapers, and television and radio channels at their disposal, are quite unaware of the hundreds of international radio stations whose signals can be picked up in the more esoteric areas of the frequency range. Although the British and Americans are no less likely to own sets which can capture short waves than people in other parts of the world, they have no tradition of listening, nor any immediate incentive to listen to foreign programmes. Perhaps also they lack curiosity. Radio Luxembourg, on which pop music is the bait for advertisements aimed primarily at young listeners, is the only foreign station with anything like a mass audience in Britain. In the United States a small number of people tune in to the BBC's World Service for a highbrow antidote to the cacophony of local commercial stations, and an even smaller number tune in to Moscow Radio for a political antidote.

But, on a global scale, cross-frontier broadcasting is a part of mass communications. The BBC and the VOA claim a minimum of fifty to sixty million for their regular worldwide audience. The number of short-wave voice broadcast transmitters in the world rose from 385 in 1950 to 1,365 in 1972, of which 185 had a power of 200 kilowatts or more. There are about nine hundred million radio sets now in the world: * one for every four people—men, women and children. About a third of these sets can receive programmes on short waves.

In 1939, twenty-seven countries had international foreign-language services; in 1945, fifty-five countries; and in 1974 there is hardly a single country of any size that does not have some rudimentary External Service. Many new national stations have been established during the seventies—from Brazil and Chile to Zambia and Uganda —bringing the total now to almost a hundred, and this does not include the many religious and clandestine or semi-clandestine operations all over the world. The longer-standing External Services, apart from the French, are constantly expanding their output.† Each week about 17,000 hours of monitorable international programmes go out on the air, almost a third of them accounted for by the United States, the Soviet Union and the People's Republic of China; and this figure takes no account of all the domestic programmes which are audible, often deliberately made audible, across national frontiers.

While an international radio station is in some sense a prestigious luxury, like a marble palace, its cost does not compare to that of the installations necessary for television. Radio is an example of low technology which can pay educational and social dividends for a modest outlay, and the international extension of the medium, if limited in scale, need not break the exchequer of even quite a poor country. It is also easier and cheaper to rebroadcast radio programmes, or send pre-recorded tapes from one country to another, than it is to exchange television programmes. Different technical systems, the danger of misuse—for example alterations being made to the commentary to someone else's pictures—the problem of performing rights, all these factors hamper international television cooperation, even where formal agreements exist, as between Eurovision and Intervision.

It is radio's special function to penetrate even where it is not wanted. All the first seven international broadcasters in the world league table, from the United States to Albania, are primarily concerned with reaching audiences whose governments would rather they were not reached. Radio propaganda is an arm of diplomacy. In particular, it is an important negotiating card in the struggle to define and institutionalize east–west détente, because broadcasting reaches, and in a sense can create, a public opinion which questions the single-

* see Appendix A
† see Appendix B

minded assumptions of governments claiming a monopoly of the source of news and information. The Nazis, whose methods and goals are now almost identified with the term radio propaganda, provided a model of propaganda diplomacy to future generations of broadcasters, even if none since has harnessed the medium to such aggressive political and military objectives.

The use of radio to further national ambitions is universal, even when the slogan is 'Nation shall speak peace unto nation' and the techniques used are quite different from those developed by the Nazis. UNESCO, which has as much of a duty to be blandly optimistic as any other agency of the United Nations, published a report on international broadcasting which said:

> There seems to be general agreement among nations that ideally the purposes of international broadcasting are a) to present the best of the culture and ideas of the broadcasting country; b) to present world news objectively; c) to explain the broadcasting country's viewpoint on important world problems; and d) to promote international understanding.[1]

The key word here is 'ideally'. Dostoevsky had written in 1880:

> We are assured that the world is getting more and more united and growing into a brotherly community by the reduction of distances and the transmission of ideas through the air. Alas, put no faith in such a union of peoples.

He doubted ahead of time the self-interested optimism of Marconi:

> Communication between peoples widely separated in space and thought is undoubtedly the greatest weapon against the evils of misunderstanding and jealousy.[2]

Professor Briggs's cautionary gloss that 'the greatest spur to international agreement about the use of radio was not idealism but self-interest' provides the clue to why Dostoevsky proved more accurate in his prediction than Marconi.

It is not radio propaganda's fault that there is still not peace throughout the world. But, taking the positive with the negative, its overall effect is more disruptive than constructive; disruptive, that is, of the forces of reaction as well as of progressive forces. What this means in political terms is something we shall be examining throughout this book.

As a generalization, however, it is true to say that even when it is overt and official, international broadcasting is essentially subversive. In the case of Moscow Radio, the Voice of the Arabs, Radio Free

Europe, the Voice of South Africa, and most other radio propaganda operations, no secret is made of the fact that many of the programmes are directed at 'enemy' countries. Among this majority are, of course, included the External Services of countries whose foreign policy tends to play down or disguise their aversion to alien ideologies—Spain for example. But there are also radio 'wars' going on in Indochina, Korea, the Middle East, southern Africa and elsewhere; and all clandestine and black radio stations are by definition subversive. In the case of government-sponsored but consciously inoffensive stations—the External Services of Holland, Canada, Japan, Brazil, for example—the idea of subversion merges into the vaguer concepts of national advertising, the spread of information, cultural or economic promotion, and so on, but it is not completely submerged.

Critics of the spread of American global power regard the total 'propaganda' effort, from satellites to Coca-Cola ads, as an imperialist hydra, of which overt radio propaganda by the Voice of America and the two American-financed stations in western Europe beaming programmes to the Soviet Union and eastern Europe is only one of the heads, and by no means the most dangerous. Radio Liberty and Radio Free Europe are, however, fundamentally different from the VOA. The Munich-based stations are staffed by émigré broadcasters operating under overall American control whose intention is to provide an alternative Home Service in the target areas and so weaken the communist governments' grip on public opinion. Their aim is to promote 'democratization'—in other words, to free the Russians and east Europeans from communist 'oppression', while avoiding, in recent years at least, 'even the implication of support for illegal and violent actions'.[3] Despite their disclaimers, both stations are anti-communist and, through indirect methods, are out to change the political situation in the target countries.

The Voice of America, like the BBC, has a less clearly defined role. Neither can claim to be as disinterested in political change as, say, the Canadian or Dutch External Services, but both fight shy of the idea of interfering in the internal affairs of foreign countries beyond upholding the principle of the free flow of information. The differences between them boil down to a greater American insistence on selling the 'western' concept of 'freedom' and a greater British insistence on balance (which includes telling the bad as well as the good news) in the long-term interests of establishing a reputation for reliability and truthfulness.

The BBC's line is to take as much of the propaganda element out of international broadcasting as possible. In 1964, the impact this approach was having on international communications generally was summed up by two stern critics of all propaganda:

There is some reason to believe that a new phase in the history of propaganda is in its early beginnings—a phase in which emphasis on facts begins to displace frenzy and invective. Undoubtedly the BBC deserves primary credit for this turn of events.[4]

Frenzy and invective are, however, still a feature of many international broadcasts, from Libya to Korea. But the major powers, with allowances for the more colourful of Radio Peking's ritual phrases, stop well short of the kind of violent and vicious propaganda purveyed by the Nazi External Services up to 1945.

This does not mean that the BBC's goal, to influence foreigners' minds in favour of the political principles it represents, differs fundamentally from that of any other External Service. It so happens that those principles are the minimally offensive ones of liberalism, moderation, and parliamentary democracy; and that the best way to promote them is through liberal, moderate means. The notion of ideological persuasion is not absent, it is merely tacit.

Countries with a more positive ideology to sell, notably the Soviet Union, regard the BBC's low profile as an example of hypocrisy and cunning. Indeed, the effect of the BBC's programmes on the Soviet Union is subversive. The BBC reflects political and class values which, if accepted by the Russian people, would make the Communist Party's task extremely difficult, if not impossible.

But, while the BBC does not pretend to be above the propaganda battle, it does represent one extreme of the propaganda spectrum: it rejects the idea of a conscious, 'scientific' propaganda. To the BBC, propaganda is like M. Jourdain's prose, something that you do by definition, but don't think about. In this sense, it is the very opposite of the calculated operation designed to promote specific political and military short-term goals, which was set up by Dr Goebbels to further the international ambitions of the Nazis.

Scientific propaganda by radio was largely an invention of the Nazis, who saw the potential of the medium more clearly than their enemies and used it with unequalled force. In the post-war years, the lessons that they taught have been learned and adapted, though to serve quite different ends, by radio propagandists all over the world. In the Middle East, especially, radio has been used as a weapon of war, both in the military and ideological sense. Propaganda by radio is studied as a part of the technology of war by both Arabs and Israelis. In the Arab world radio has been primarily responsible for the creation of nationalist feeling. Listening to radio, from sources local and foreign, government and clandestine, is a habit more widespread in the Middle East than in any other part of the globe.

Propaganda, however, is no more of an exact science than

politics itself. For many people, this only adds to its danger. Captain Liddell Hart wrote in 1938 that 'propaganda is concerned with persuasion, not with scientific investigation. Valuable as an agent of war, it is a dangerous ally for the cause of human progress.'[5] Such a view has been constantly echoed. Propaganda's basic function was well described by Eugene Ionesco:

> We know that existence means aggression. We know, too, that society is divided, that the different social categories war on one another. That each social unit has a clear conscience, since it is a collective unit. In an absolute sense, no social category has more reason to have a clear or a guilty conscience than any other. To destroy the clear conscience of a social category and strengthen that of one's own category is the aim of propaganda.[6]

Or, as Erik Erikson puts it in *Childhood and Society*, 'nothing can be more fatal in international encounters than the attempt to belittle or to argue another nation's mythological space-time'.[7] In other words, nations are best left alone to develop in their own way unless they are actively offensive towards any other nation. The trouble is that ideological disarmament is as much a pipedream as nuclear or any other form of disarmament; nations keep on trying to persuade other nations to adopt their own social and political patterns, or at least modify the ones they already have.

Radio propaganda is unusually easy to identify. And precisely because it is audibly propagandistic in a political sense, in the way that a comedy film or a novel or an advertisement is not, and because it is addressed to an audience whose other propaganda stimuli run counter to the message from abroad, many people argue that it is hard put to upset the status quo. Where it is not reinforced or reinforceable by more direct means of coercion, international radio is, in fact, often seen as a hit-and-miss affair. In the words of one American student of propaganda:

> If our persuasive communication ends up with a net positive effect, we must attribute it to luck, not science. The propagandist cannot control the direction or intensity of his message, if, indeed, he reaches his target at all.[8]

While some people conclude that the more extreme the propaganda, the more dangerously revolutionary it is, others regard all propaganda as ineffective or merely conservative. Aldous Huxley believed that 'the propagandist is a man who canalizes an already existing stream. In a land where there is no water he digs in vain.' But advertising techniques for stimulating public opinion and creating a unity of views among people who were unaware that they believed the same things, have proved Huxley's opinion too narrow. While it may be argued that a man can only be persuaded if he is persuadable, nevertheless if he latently accepts the proffered message, propaganda can introduce one particular set of ideas as opposed to many others which might have been equally acceptable. Governments neglect the impact of propaganda from abroad at their peril. In practice, when it strikes the right note in the right circumstances, propaganda can help create revolution and change. It can incite to violence, subvert, or whip up emotions, though for most of the time it is acting as a corrective to the ambitions of governments by reducing their influence over the people they govern.

It can be a conservative force. In particular, right-wing propaganda, where it is not being used to further aggressive ambitions, sets out to maintain the status quo. The South African international radio services, for example, are designed to make acceptable the policy of apartheid by a constant process of resisting change. Radio propaganda is also a conservative force in that listeners for the most part tune in only to the stations that carry the message they want to hear. A small minority listen in long enough to 'opposition' or 'enemy' broadcasts to be persuaded over to the other side. It is mainly communists who tune in to Moscow Radio (those of a Maoist persuasion to Radio Peking), and non-communists or anti-communists in the Soviet Union who reach for an alternative to their own Party-controlled media. The fact that the audience to foreign broadcasts is so much larger in the closed societies than in the open ones means that the number of non-committed or sceptical listeners is also large, but this does not necessarily increase the proportion of such listeners in the total audience.

Recognizing this, the major international broadcasting services admit to limited and general aims. It is left to the smaller services, particularly where local wars and tensions provide the fuel for radio polemics, to engage in the kind of psychological warfare that characterized the world radio scene between the late thirties and early sixties. Already in 1944, Kris and Speier could reflect that:

> The experience of the Second World War is gradually destroying the myth of Propaganda that arose as an aftermath of the first. Belief in the dark powers of propaganda is being replaced by a better understanding of its limitations and functions, which vary with the social order and the situation.[9]

Although the lessons had to be learned over again during the Cold War, the trend towards information and persuasion, as against agitation and proselytizing, is still observable.

This does not devalue the role of radio propaganda. On the contrary, it lends further weight to the long-term importance of the world's ideological struggles. As even the naturally isolationist Americans and Russians have discovered, foreign public opinion matters. No country can afford to ignore the effect its foreign policy will have, not just on states directly affected by it, but also on world opinion generally. In that sense at least, the world is a global village. The fact that almost every country has developed an international radio service is a reflection of this and a gesture of conciliation towards world opinion.

The problem is that the flow of information on the international airwaves is not an even one. The Russian complaint that they are the victims of hostile propaganda is spurious, since they give as good as they get, compared to the complaints of the smaller and poorer countries whose own feeble voices are drowned out by those of the rich and powerful.

The argument for a free flow of information appears reasonable when used in support of those frustrated by censorship in totalitarian societies; but it sounds less convincing when virtually all communication between the rich and the poor flows in one direction. Although the Americans are the largest single source of propaganda, in its widest sense, to the Third World, all the major powers compete to sell their political systems as well as their other, more material, products. Until the improbable day when the free flow becomes an equal flow, the Third World is bound to regard international radio as just another element of great-power imperialism.

The resources of the major world broadcasters, particularly their ability to put foreign correspondents in the field all around the world, ensure for the time being that they will continue to swamp the smaller stations, but even the most expensively produced programme, using every radio technique and resource, has to fight against the growing problem of the sheer profusion of competing signals. One group of listeners most involved in coping with this problem are the professional monitors. A large part of international broadcasting is done with these monitors in mind. It is through them that a political kite is sure to be visible and government thinking made public, even though not officially conveyed through diplomatic channels. Revolutionaries appeal for help over the radio because monitors ensure that their appeals are heard. Even the smallest clandestine station can reach a world audience if its message is considered important enough.

Radio signals are one of the principal sources of world news, generally the quickest and sometimes the only source, but propaganda is what international radio is really all about. It is a weapon of modern diplomacy neglected neither by governments nor by political activists and publicists. Only among the general public in the Anglo-Saxon west does it fail to make much impact.

Most international services are under the direct control, and act as the voice, of their government. What they put out is at least semi-official. But there are exceptions, the most important of which is the BBC. Although many people question the reality of the BBC's independence (and indeed it is only partial), its editorial freedom and tradition of credibility built up during and since the Second World War have made it a model for a number of international services based as nearly as possible on objective information. Yet even here the object of getting 'our audience to accept our view of events', in the words of former BBC Director-General Sir Hugh Greene, amounts to propaganda.

But the BBC provides a model of radio propaganda broadcasting that puts it apart from the American and the communist models, and at the other end of the spectrum from the Nazi External Service. In the first part of this book we shall examine these four models in terms of techniques, aims and effectiveness. Later, we shall see how they have influenced the propaganda battles being conducted throughout the world and pick out some of the special functions of international radio. At the end, we shall raise the question of the intentions and effectiveness of radio propaganda as such in the light of the success and failure of the numerous stations operating throughout the world.

1 *The Nazi Model*

In 1933, when the Nazi Party came to power in Germany, radio was a novelty. Its propaganda potential was virtually untried. Yet the Nazi leaders' faith in it was unbounded. Eugene Hadamowski, chief of German Radio, wrote in his autobiography:

> We spell radio with three exclamation marks because we are possessed in it of a miraculous power—the strongest weapon ever given to the spirit—that opens hearts and does not stop at the borders of cities and does not turn back before closed doors; that jumps rivers, mountains, and seas; that is able to force peoples under the spell of one powerful spirit.

And Hitler wrote of radio in *Mein Kampf*:

> It is a terrible weapon in the hands of those who know how to make use of it.

Goebbels at the opening of the 1933 Berlin Radio Exhibition declared that in the twentieth century radio would take over the role that the press played in the nineteenth.

Had television been available as a national propaganda medium in the thirties, there is no doubt that Goebbels would have welcomed the combination of sound and pictures. At a time when British politicians were less aware, even unaware, of television's political implications, Goebbels was telling one of Baird TV's directors how wonderful it would be for the German people to have Hitler and himself in every home.

But the war put a stop to television's development, leaving radio to lead the propaganda assault. Nevertheless, for all its peculiar powers and its leading role, radio was only one of an arsenal of propaganda weapons. It was part of a tightly integrated network organized and co-ordinated by the *Propagandaministerium*. The techniques and the media used by the Nazi Party so successfully in their bid for power in Germany were, after 1933, fitted in to the entire coercive apparatus of the state. As Zeman has written:

[Goebbels] interfered with the lives of the people to an extent un-paralleled in history. The news and even the comments in their papers were centrally supplied; a dissenting opinion could never take the form of the legally printed word. The films they saw and the broadcasts they listened to all carried an indelible Nazi stamp. The Party took care of their leisure time, their travel, their social activities; it presented newly married couples with copies of *Mein Kampf*.[1]

Under Goebbels' control was everything that could be used as propaganda: not just the media, but the organization of Party speakers and rallies, of tourism, literature, the arts in general, the cinema, and entertainment for the troops. Propaganda was perhaps the Nazis' one new contribution to the science of politics. Propaganda workers, whether in the Reich Chambers of Culture, the *Reichs-rundfunkgesellschaft*, or any of the other bodies which formed the pyramid of which Goebbels was the apex, were specially selected, examined and trained. All were compelled to belong to the Nazi federa-tions. Propaganda was regarded as a science, a mixture of politics, psychology and elocution. People who wanted to broadcast but were not on the RRG staff were tested by a 'microphone examination com-mittee' which formed part of the Reich Chamber of Broadcasting and issued certificates of proficiency.

One of the reasons why broadcasting was held in particular esteem in the Propaganda Ministry was the skill and enthusiasm for microphone addresses displayed by Goebbels himself. Even late on in the war, when the situation was obviously hopeless, troops and citizens in beleaguered Berlin would take heart when they heard the convincing tones of the Minister. Goebbels had always been at his most eloquent when talking about radio and its power.

Real broadcasting is true propaganda. Propaganda means fighting on all battlefields of the spirit, generating, multiplying, destroying, exterminating, building and undoing. Our propaganda is deter-mined by what we call German race, blood and nation.[2]

We shall return to the themes of German radio propaganda. The point here is the faith that was placed in the medium. It was a faith confirmed as early as 1934 by the evidence of a radio campaign to reincorporate the Saarland into Germany. Goebbels had set up a special office to co-ordinate the broadcasts, and cheap radio sets were distributed in the target area. The message was not one of political reasoning, but a frank emotional appeal to German feel-ings. In January 1935, ninety-one per cent of those who voted in the plebiscite opted for the return of the Saar to Germany. From this point on, the Nazi leaders felt they could achieve almost anything through the planned use of radio propaganda.

In retrospect it is clear that the effect was greatest within the confines of the Reich itself. Inside Germany, all the media spoke with one voice, obstacles were placed in the way of outside sources of information, and through intimate knowledge of the home audience the propagandists were able to adapt their psychological tools to fit the audience's fears, hopes and prejudices. The very nature of German propaganda required it to be both monopolistic and single-minded. As Hitler put it in *Mein Kampf*:

As soon as by one's own propaganda even a glimpse of right on the other side is admitted, the cause for doubting one's own right is laid.

The object was to create a captive audience which could be manipulated by the 'leader' and the army of propagandists whose job it was to interpret and to publicize his will.

Ironically, it was radio that presented the greatest danger to the Propaganda Ministry's monopoly. Although the BBC did not start its German-language service until 1938, and the Nazis succeeded in negotiating temporary non-aggression pacts with the Soviet Union and Poland which covered the use of mutual propaganda, the signals from foreign radio which penetrated German jamming, especially during the latter years of the war, were a constant worry to the Nazis. As for the German people, however, the vast majority were deflected not at all from a behaviour pattern dictated by the Nazi media and backed by the sanctions of physical power.

But the Nazi External Service, broadcasting from Zeesen, was in open competition with local information sources and the radio output of a whole range of hostile nations. The German answer was to concentrate on the foreign audience that they knew best—Germans living abroad. During the campaign against Czechoslovakia, for example, Nazi propaganda was directed solely towards the German minority, in the German language.

This is not to say that they ignored foreign-language broadcasting. On the contrary, Zeesen was putting out programmes in fifty-five languages by the end of the war. But the primary aim was to create a fifth column of convinced believers in the Nazi cause and to use them as a lobby to back up the work of the German embassies. (Goebbels himself would have preferred to have no embassies to compete with his personal control over the projection of Nazi Germany abroad.) During the war, of course, the emphasis in enemy countries had to switch to undermining the morale of the citizens as a whole. But even then the logic of an internal propaganda designed to rally a committed audience around the catchphrases of total fascist power spread into the sphere of foreign propaganda. There was no consistent attempt to understand the psychology of the anti-fascist foreign audience, little attempt to modify the hate-language and emotional racist appeals that characterized the RRG's output. When the tone sometimes lapsed into friendly chattiness, or into highbrow monologues on German culture, the intention was only to make more relevant and more respectable the uncompromising political message.

Although the treatment varied from country to country and from moment to moment, the themes of Nazi foreign propaganda were little more than an echo of the internal line: anti-Semitism, anti-communism, the superiority of the Aryan race and German nation, the wisdom and power of the Führer. There could be no positive message based on the ideology of national socialism or fascism.

> National Socialism was basically an open invitation to an elect nation to indulge in the pursuit and the worship of naked power. And propaganda was an instrument for its achievement. It carried no consistent doctrine, but only an amorphous and opportunist set of ideas.[3]

Goebbels' task was merely to reinforce the power of the state by the most effective means, whatever that involved. He was an admirer of all 'clever' propaganda, even if it came from the Bolsheviks. His deep commitment to Nazism was in part due to the scope that this particular political system allowed him for developing and displaying his talent as a total propagandist.

What did Goebbels mean by 'clever' propaganda? Above all, that it should be planned in every detail and designed to create or maintain specific emotional states. After the British propaganda successes in the First World War, the Nazi leadership had been obsessed by the role of propaganda, seeing it as the main cause of German defeat. The idea of a 'master plan' constructed according to his own theories of propaganda lay behind all Hitler's thinking on the subject. In Goebbels he found someone who shared this obsession.

In the first place, both men believed that propaganda should be aimed at the masses. The audience was no more than a manipulable crowd. Ideally the aim was to create a hypnotic effect, a mindless reaction. People who resisted the message would preferably be eliminated physically rather than persuaded round. To the committed, Goebbels would then supply the symbols of Nazi power. The radio would match the appeal of flags and swastikas. He would identify and attack the targets of hatred: the Jews, communists, 'Windsy' Churchill, and senile plutocrats. Goebbels saw himself as the high priest of Nazism, presiding over the rites and rituals, leading the hymns, extolling the godhead and reviling the legions of devils.

There was little room for reason in this approach, and no need to tell the 'truth'. Truth in Nazi propaganda was not even the subjective, ideological version of it that, for instance, communist agitators aim at in preference to 'bourgeois objectivity'. It was naked opportunism. What was true for one audience was not necessarily—unless exposure risked reversing the effect—true for another audience. What was true now may not have been true in the past, and might be something else again in the future.

Hitler was notoriously the advocate of the 'big lie', but he was not careless of the truth. 'Alongside Hitler's statement on lying one must place Goebbels' insistence that facts to be disseminated must be accurate.'[4] The lie was something to be used with discretion as a tactical weapon. The Nazis were not looking to the long term, as the BBC was, to establish a reputation for reliability, they were after short-term conquest. That was why they depended so heavily on military success to validate their propaganda. Nazi propaganda did not stand or fall by itself, and it was a weapon of war which could work successfully only when the audience was physically captive. Like all weapons it was neither gentlemanly nor reasonable. It was intended to hurt. As Hitler said to Rauschning: 'Mental confusion, contradictions of feeling, indecisiveness, panic—these are our weapons.' Just as for Clausewitz war was an extension of politics, so, for the Nazis, propaganda was inseparable from the functioning of the state, in war and peace. They drew no real distinction between the peacetime use of propaganda and its role as a weapon of war. Indeed it was often compared to an artillery barrage as a means of softening up the enemy before the troops go into the attack.

The clearest wartime example of a successful radio barrage was the Nazi campaign against France between the outbreak of war and the fall of Paris. Asa Briggs mentions five reasons for its success: the existing defeatism in France; a highly professional team of broadcasters led by their star, Paul Ferdonnet; French Anglophobia which split the Allies; the timing of the stages of the military Blitzkrieg to create maximum fear and terror; and the mixture of exaggerated and evasive French propaganda which could easily be discredited by the Nazi radio.[5]

Looking from across the Channel at the effect all this was having, Tangye Lean, a prominent figure in the BBC during and after the war, saw at the time that:

From the outbreak of war the German Radio built up a large audience of French listeners who had grown suspicious of the statements of their home press and radio. As the invasion began the weapon was already in contact with its objective.[6]

Lean compared German Radio with the praying mantis which, by separating its hind parts from its legs, so terrifies its prey that it meets with no resistance.

Yet Professor Briggs wonders whether the success of the propaganda campaign was more apparent than real, given the overwhelming role played by the army. An artillery barrage, like a propaganda barrage, can make no lasting effect on its own, nor is it intended to. This was proved by the German radio campaign to soften up the British for the invasion that never came. Certainly the British, including those in the European Service of the BBC, had been impressed by the French campaign, and feared that, when the invasion came, the Nazi propaganda directed at themselves might well prove to be no less devastating. J. B. Priestley said in one of his BBC talks that 'this idea of Nazi power, which their propaganda has encouraged, has done more good so far than all their dive bombers and armoured divisions'. Fortunately, the extent to which Nazi broadcasts had influenced British opinion was never put to the test.

The radio Blitzkrieg was a technique that could only be used to reinforce parallel military action. For the most part, Nazi propaganda directed at foreign audiences followed the well-tried techniques, based on well-tried principles, which were already controlling the thoughts and actions of the Germans themselves.

Beneath all the Nazi theorizing on the subject lay an instinctive belief in the primitive (some critics have said feminine) appeal to emotions. Even when the leaders themselves were cynical, they believed that the masses must be instilled with faith. Hitler, convinced of his own mission, declared that 'only he who harbours passion in himself can arouse passion'. Goebbels was prepared to manufacture passion where the real thing was lacking. In either case, the audience was to receive the impression of unity, strength, and unquestionable victory at the end of the struggle.

This was, as I said, an appeal directed primarily at the masses. The people were seen as the disciples of the Führer, where necessary his slaves, who could be manipulated into serving their leader and the Nazi Party. They were malleable, even corruptible.

From this follow all the other principles on which Nazi propaganda was based. The manufacture and manipulation of passion was a higher truth than 'bloodless objectivity' because it promoted the Nazi, and therefore the German, cause. Lies could be told in its name, because not only are the masses gullible enough to believe them, but, if the lies are exposed, they can be attributed to the enemies of Nazism, the Jews or communists. Positive propaganda is always preferable to negative. There must be permanent attack. The Party is always strong, the army invincible. The best tense is the future tense: what is predicted *will* happen. This worked well until

1943, when Goebbels had to reverse the theme. He then began a
paign of positive pessimism to ensure resistance to the last br
so ghastly would be the consequences of defeat. The masses must have
a concrete identifiable enemy, a hate object on to which to direct their
natural aggressiveness. The Jews are therefore 'filthy', the Bolsheviks
are 'Untermenschen', ruthless, lustful, 'swampmen'. The British are
hypocritical, cruel, dominated by plutocrats. The Americans are
boastful, uncultured, money-mad. But there must also be simple
positive concepts to hold on to and identify with—like 'fortress
Europe' and Aryan blood.

As a vehicle for passionate, positive propaganda, the Nazis preferred the spoken to the written word. It was more immediate, more
vibrant, more personal. The ideal occasion for creating emotion
through the human voice was the mass rally, but radio was the next
best thing. Hitler was aware of the power of his own voice. He would
deliberately keep his audience waiting, then satisfy their pent-up im-
patience by bringing them emotional release. This device worked best
when he appeared in the flesh. He was never happy with his radio
performances. But the build-up technique was applied to his radio
speeches, even though people were not kept waiting and hungry in a
stadium but could meanwhile carry on with their normal life. The
opposite technique was Roosevelt's 'Fireside Chat'. But that was not
Hitler's style, he wanted to arouse, not calm, his audience, inspire
them, not reason with them. For that, even a small build-up of
artificial tension was helpful.

Another principle of Nazi propaganda was that it should lead to
action, to a change of behaviour, not just to a temporary mood.
Goebbels realized that it was relatively easy to influence people's
Stimmung, their mood, but it was more difficult to change their
Haltung, or behaviour. This explains why Nazi propaganda was so
closely linked with the apparatus of civil and military coercion. Not
only were people compelled to act according to the blueprints publicized by the propaganda organs, but policy was co-ordinated with
the propaganda. Pogroms and death camps went hand in hand with
the spreading of anti-Semitism.

It is hard to know what in Nazi propaganda is a principle and what
a technique. Anti-Semitism, for example, was a corner-stone of the
Nazi credo, but it was also a tactic to attract an audience and persuade them to follow the rest of the message. As Goebbels wrote in
his diary on 10 May 1943: 'The anti-Semitic bacilli naturally exist
everywhere in all Europe; we must merely make them virulent.'[7]
Hitler believed that anti-Semitism was the most potent of all Nazi
propaganda weapons. In many areas of Europe, particularly in the
east, he was correct. But because the Nazis were unable to make a
clear distinction between their audiences, their propaganda also

alienated listeners in foreign countries where the 'bacillus' was less common. In America, particularly, the anti-Semitic campaign was counter-productive.

The creation of stereotypes was both a principle and a technique. On the one hand, it was a part of Nazi mythology and ritual-building. But it also had tactical uses. Enemy could be turned against enemy, the Poles and the French against the British, the Americans against the British, the western Allies against the Russians, and so on. It was a device, too, for turning the people against their leaders—Churchill and the City plutocrats were, for example, natural targets for British socialists who, indeed, showed the strength of their feelings immediately the war was over. On the other hand, blind belief in national and ethnic stereotypes influenced the Nazis themselves to the extent that the German army in the Ukraine failed to take full advantage of the antipathy there towards the Russians. The harsh treatment of the Ukrainian people, because all Slavs were *Untermenschen*, harmed Rosenberg's attempt to set up a puppet state. It was impossible to think of an alien people as sub-human and deal reasonably with them at the same time. Propaganda developed a momentum of its own.

To din the Nazi message into people's minds and, above all, hearts, the propagandists used a number of specific techniques which were more or less consciously based on psychological theory. One of the most important was repetition. The audience was bombarded, saturated with the same information, the same slogan, endlessly repeated phrases. This was done partly to reinforce the stereotypes, partly to lay the propaganda on so thick that no other voice could compete. People would start to believe things they initially, and reasonably, rejected because it would become too much of a strain to resist the concentrated bombardment.

However low their estimate of the masses' intelligence, the propagandists took no chances. Broadcasting in Germany contained 'hardly anything except, on the one hand, concentrated propaganda hammering home the daily directive of the Propaganda Ministry, and, on the other, distraction which releases the mind from thought'.[8] The only danger was that the most resistant and discriminating elements would be encouraged to disbelieve everything they heard and, despite all attempts to prevent them, turn to outside sources for their information. There were some non-conformists who took this course, and it was mainly to these that the BBC and others directed their German-language propaganda. But the Nazis were less concerned about losing a few dissenters among the intellectuals than they were about keeping their grip on the masses.

The slogan was an important element of the repetition/ritual technique. Some of the crudest methods of early Madison Avenue were seized on by the Nazis. Hitler always referred to the '*Diktat* of Versailles'. Other slogans varied from the most punchy—'Sieg Heil!' —to the most arch—Austria was before *Anschluss* a mere 'hallucination'.

The concept of propaganda by bludgeoning extended also to the use of obscenity and atrocity propaganda. Jews were described in terms reminiscent of the caricatured faces and sewer rats of the film *Jüd Süss*. Russians were alleged to have committed crimes that could only reinforce the idea that they were sub-human. Sometimes the crudity was such that it made nonsense of the professionalism of the rest of Nazi propaganda. Before the war, for example, on the German Radio's *Here Speaks Moscow* programme—which presented the least savoury extracts from Soviet newspapers—any Jewish name would be pronounced in sarcastic terms and followed by a loud 'ha! ha!'.

Psychological manipulation was frequently quite blatant, as the language in this extract from a talk broadcast in English on 26 February 1941 demonstrates:

We all know that fear will transform even the timidest creature into a dangerous and uncertain animal. Dogs will often snap from fear and from no other cause. And the cornered rat is an example known to us all . . . the warmongering clique in Britain is in fact a cornered rat in our present period of unremitting strife. The British people, having been prepared for and led into war by the appeal of fear, is now being systematically trained and educated by those with the mentality of the cornered rat who are making even louder and more urgent appeals to the human being's basest and most dangerous instinct, fear, stark fear.

This did not prevent the Nazis from using techniques which were in total contrast, even contradiction. Suddenly the tone would become sweet and friendly. There is the story of the announcer who proved how relaxed he was with his listeners by getting up to shut the window because the noise of a barking dog outside could be picked up by the microphone. International broadcasts in German, those to America especially, tried to create a camp-fire all-Germans-together spirit. Soft music—not too schmalzy, not too jazzy—put the audience in a receptive mood. Before the war, seventy per cent of Zeesen's output was music, and other entertainment dominated the rest. Over the years radio simulated the tried and tested technique of interrogators the world over: first the man with the cigarette and the friendly smile, then the threatening bully, and so on until the victim is confused and demoralized. Only in the last desperate years of the war did the friendly variant disappear.

It would seem that, given the variety of tones, individuals should have been able to develop their own styles at the microphone. But this was not so. Apart from such high-ranking personalities as Hans Fritsche, all speakers were trained to use the appropriate tone for the 'role' they were playing. When the script called for derision, the broadcaster would adopt the standard Nazi 'derision' tone, when it called for respect, the announcer would be correspondingly 'respectful'. There was an approved way of rendering all emotions and all styles. This had the added advantage of allowing propaganda messages to be more easily inserted into otherwise anodyne and straightforward programmes. Goebbels was aware of the 'subliminal' effect, a technique that was to become more notorious with the spread of television.

As the years went by, and particularly when victories began to turn into defeats, Goebbels grew more and more impatient with direct attempts to persuade his audience. Either they should be stampeded into believing him, or they should be tricked. This is reflected in his emphasis on the slanted news bulletin. As he wrote in his diary on 15 April 1942:

> I am particularly stressing news in our foreign-language broadcasting services, but am seeing to it that news items are properly slanted.

And on 10 May in the same year:

> News is a weapon of war. Its purpose is to wage war and not to give out information.

In its most obvious form this can be illustrated by a comparison of news items put out by the BBC on the one hand and German Radio in the other. This one concerns the appointment of Sir Stafford Cripps to the War Cabinet:

> The formation of a new War Cabinet was announced this morning. Sir Stafford Cripps joins the Government as Lord Privy Seal and Leader of the House of Commons. [*BBC*]

> At last Stalin's agent, the Kerensky of Britain, has received a job assigned to him by his lord and master. Reuter announces that the drawing-room communist, the earner of record sums, Sir Stafford Cripps, has been appointed Lord Privy Seal. [*Deutschlandsender*][9]

Note especially the attribution of the information about Cripps's political and financial infamy to 'Reuter'.

In the same way, false opinions were put into the mouths of the enemy. Sometimes there was a grain of truth in the attribution, as when an American Nazi's opinion would be transferred into: 'it is being said in America . . .' At other times it was simpler to lie or invent.

Just as the Nazi propagandists were prepared to lie, twist, invent and add colour without reference to truth, so were they prepared to doctor reports and programmes which purported to be real. One of the most powerful, and admired, of their techniques was the *Front-berichte*, the front-line reports which recounted the feats of the armed forces in battle. In fact they were montages, sound pictures put together in the studio. Although the correspondents' reports came from the front, and some of the sound effects were recorded on the same occasion, the programme was produced—concocted—with an eye to the maximum dramatic effect. When the BBC came to cover the Normandy landings in 1944, they were tempted to adopt the same technique, so brilliantly evocative of the heat of battle had been the *Frontberichte*. In the end, however, they decided to do no more than edit the material recorded on the spot.[10]

Nazi war reporting was a mixture of fact, drama, and psychological manipulation. To give a flavour of this kind of output in English, here is a short extract from a reporter's despatch describing the sinking of a British freighter by a U-boat:

We approach a pile of wreckage . . . our gun crew gets busy, and a rain of shells . . . starts fires throughout the ship . . . (? coloured) sailors raise their arms in horror . . . while waiting for the blazing ship to take her final plunge, we hail one of the boats filled with frightened niggers to come alongside. After a few questions, they realize they're not going to be (? hurt), and laugh and chatter like monkeys . . . life in the British Merchant Navy must have come to a sorry stage . . . what's the use of modern defence weapons when gun crews stampede into the boats when they should be in action? Will these niggers be content to return to the jungle after this war, or will they form part of the (? floating) population of British (? peoples), to the horror of every white woman living there?

The high spot of Nazi radio propaganda—and the one technique that no radio has rivalled ever since—was the *Sondermeldung*. A perverted atmosphere of revivalist religion pervaded much of Nazi broadcasting, but this was its apotheosis. News from each front was often prefaced by its own fanfares, drum-rolls and songs; the *Sondermeldung* itself was a pre-packaged montage of bombastic classical tunes and warrior songs interspersed with dramatic silences. They accompanied only the most important announcements of Nazi

achievements. They would be well trailed, but used sparingly to ensure that the audience was expecting something truly out of the
ordinary. On 29 June 1941, no less than twelve *Sondermeldungen*
announced the success of the first days of the Russian campaign.

This technique was aimed first and foremost at the internal
audience. But, for the most part, the techniques we have been discussing were also applicable to the Zeesen programmes for listeners
abroad, particularly when they were also German-speaking. On the
other hand, there were some types of programme suited only to the
External Service. For example, the Nazis were pioneers in the use of
the 'Mail Box' programme, in which listeners' letters, or questions
purporting to come from listeners, were answered over the air. Every
External Service now has some variant on this programme.

The Zeesen broadcasters also had certain functions to perform that
did not apply in the same way at home. They devoted a great deal of
time to discrediting the local information sources in the areas to
which they were beaming their own signal. This was accompanied by
attempts to create and aggravate fifth column scares, and to recruit
small numbers of people to propagate the Nazi message to a far
wider audience than the original signal could hope to reach.

The formation of sympathetic groups and clubs was a primary aim
of Nazi foreign propaganda. One of the reasons it made so little impact in the United States was because no more than a very few such
organizations were set up there. The same was all the more true in
the Soviet Union. On the other hand, in Latin America there was
ample opportunity for members of the large German communities to
get together and help the Nazi cause (there were 600,000 Germans
in Brazil alone at the outbreak of war, and 150,000 in Argentina).
South Africa too was fertile ground for Nazi propaganda and many
listening 'cells' were established there.

Some attempts were made in America during the war to analyse
the impact of Nazi radio propaganda. But these attempts amounted
to little more than picking out the themes of propaganda itself,
virtually nothing was discovered about the effects of it on American
listeners, or about the extent of the listenership.[11] After America's
entry into the war, and especially after Hitler's defeat, it was all the
more difficult to assess its effectiveness. No-one would admit to having been persuaded of the rightness of what, with the knowledge of
hindsight, turned out to be a losing cause.

There is some evidence for believing that German propaganda to
the British in 1939–40 was shaking morale more than the government would have liked. But in the Soviet Union, despite the evidence
of collaboration particularly in the Ukraine, there is no way of
finding out the impact of Nazi propaganda. The same is true, for
different reasons, in America.

So we are left with the techniques, and with the principle that 'total' propaganda must be accompanied by political and military success in order to succeed in the long run. No country went so far as Germany did towards the logical conclusion of this concept. Goebbels was the only exponent of total propaganda. Mussolini tried to imitate the master, but the model he tried to copy was not adapted to the haphazard quality of Italian organization, nor proof against Italian cynicism. Rome Radio had no 'master plan'. Instead, it followed the fascist line as the rest of the bureaucracy did, at once mechanically and arbitrarily. Having got off to a good start in North Africa before the world war—programmes were put out in eighteen foreign languages as early as 1936—the service deteriorated as the fortunes of the war swung away from Italy.

Radio Paris and the other captured and appropriated stations in German-occupied Europe were toned-down versions of the domestic German service. Unlike the German programmes, however, their intention was to keep the temperature cool and to avoid provoking hostile actions against the occupiers. Radio Paris was the best of them all, partly due to the sophistication of its director, Friedrich Sieburg, the former correspondent of the *Frankfurter Zeitung* in Paris and lover of the high life and French culture. It satisfied the majority of the French listening public, at least until liberation became a reality.

The Japanese never developed their international radio propaganda to the extent that the Germans did, but they did make effective use of racial themes.[12] The unequal treatment of negroes in the United States—for example, the colour bar in the armed forces, the Detroit race riots in June 1943—was exploited to the full and used as a means of splitting the Americans from their Pacific and Asian friends. Broadcasts to the Philippines harped on the theme that the Americans treated the Filipinos as racially inferior, and those to India emphasized the racial tension between Indians and British. The Japanese faced a dilemma, however, with their propaganda to China. On the one hand, the Chinese were their racial brothers; on the other, Japan was an occupying power.

But the main dilemma was caused by the paradox that the Japanese thought of themselves as racially superior to all others, while at the same time they insisted on the slogan: 'Asia for the Asiatics'. In all their appeals for Asian solidarity against the white Americans it was difficult to hide their underlying intention to make the Far East their own.

The Japanese foreign-language broadcasts lacked the professionalism, and the intelligibility, of their Nazi counterparts. In particular they misjudged the mood of the United States. The programmes were based on the assumption that the American people had been dragged

B

into the war unwillingly by their leaders, and stressed American weakness and decadence in the face of Japanese strength. This led to too much gloating, and to some excessively naive interpretation of what was normal dissension within the United States. Their most telling attacks were on the theme of Allied disunity.[13] Yet Thomas Grandin reported that the Japanese-language programmes gained considerable influence in Hawaii before the war among the large (almost forty per cent) Japanese population of the islands.[14]

For post-war radio propagandists, the content of the Nazi, fascist and related radios grows less relevant with the passing of time. But the tone and the techniques are still influential. We shall see, for example, how the strident and emotional appeal to the masses of Goebbels' *Deutschlandsender* reappears in the early days of the Voice of the Arabs. The opportunism and racism of Nazi radio are echoed today in South Africa's propaganda both to home and to foreign audiences. The Israeli radio may be said to have learnt at least partly from Zeesen the value of creating and reinforcing small groups of listeners who preserve an ethnic bond with the motherland while living abroad. In many a war situation radio propagandists consult textbooks of psychological warfare, to which Nazi radio contributed as much of value as its enemies did. It is natural to compare any propaganda coup to the techniques pioneered by the master himself, Joseph Goebbels. Indeed, the stronger anyone's faith in 'propaganda' as such—as opposed to persuasion, education, agitation or other variants—the closer he is to Goebbels' thinking. It is a mark of Goebbels' success that he made propaganda a science which, although nor respectable, is nevertheless worth studying.

Goebbels pushed to the extreme the idea that propaganda could change not just hearts and minds, but behaviour. It is the very opposite of this concept that underlies the BBC's philosophy of radio propaganda: that, far from being a subject worthy of study and analysis, it should be ignored, and any tendency to incorporate 'scientific' principles of propaganda into broadcasting should be actively resisted.

It is the prevailing wisdom that the BBC's suspicions are well-founded. At its most successful, under the leadership of Ed Murrow, the VOA too went far in this direction. And it is undeniable that in the long haul of peacetime a reputation for attempting to tell the truth consistently is more valuable than the ability to arouse temporary passion. Yet the 'hard sell' of Nazi propaganda was the only plausible adjunct to a political system which was based on what Mussolini described as 'power first, principles afterwards'.

Goebbels may, as Professor Briggs suggests, have exaggerated the value of radio. But was he not, on his own terms, successful? Briggs says no:

The machine which he created was far less efficient than it appeared to be and the weaknesses behind his whole approach to propaganda itself were ultimately exposed.[15]

But this is a harsh judgment, assuming as it does that its efficiency is the standard against which its effectiveness should be compared. It is true that the propaganda machine was in constant conflict with the Foreign Ministry, and that propaganda was by no means an exact science like physics which could be applied in the real world according to laboratory models. Indeed, under Dr Goebbels, there was as much quackery as real science. But he was enough of a politician to know that propaganda also depends on the art of compromise. The point is that he set out to create an organization which would complement Hitler's grand political and military designs. He knew he could not capture his Argentinian audience in the same way as the *Wehrmacht* could capture the Austrians. Nevertheless, where the propaganda was conducted in close conjunction with military operations, he could claim to have succeeded in his limited objectives: in Poland, Austria, Czechoslovakia, France. And, of course, he achieved his first and most important goal almost completely: the subjugation of the German people themselves.

Goebbels' biggest failures coincide with the military failures. Total propaganda demanded that he taunt the British with the fear of imminent invasion. When it did not come, his propaganda was that much more damaging to himself. Similarly, the BBC scored a notable propaganda victory by recording Hitler's pronouncements about the timing of the total collapse of the Soviet Union. When Moscow and Stalingrad survived, and the tide of war turned, those recordings were played back.

It is difficult to separate criticisms of the effectiveness of Nazi propaganda, and radio in particular, from the broader moral criticism of Nazi tactics and methods. It is generally accepted that Nazism was evil. But value judgments tell us little about the effectiveness, within the context of an evil system, of one part of that system.

In retrospect, propaganda was one of Nazism's most successful elements. The fact that even the *Propagandaministerium* could not measure its effectiveness despite intensive attempts to do so—Goebbels desperately wanted to test his propaganda in a scientific way—only proves that propaganda is inherently immeasurable. Radio as a vehicle for propaganda is no less elusive a subject for scientific analysis. Even so, Goebbels was proud of his organization and the role it played. In the light of such evidence as there is on its techniques and its impact, it was a crude, ugly instrument, but no less frightening and dangerous for that.

The international effect of German radio propaganda had, by the end of the war, shrunk almost to nothing. Defeat cannot be explained away. But what might have happened if the fortunes of war had been reversed? If German military expansion had spread out as far as its radio signals reached, a great many more people would surely have been hanging on to Goebbels' every word than there were in April 1945 among the battered but still hopeful citizens of Berlin.

2 *The Communist Appeal*

The system developed by Goebbels to exercise totalitarian control over all the media has some parallels in the communist world. The Leninist principles of agitation have, at least superficially, a great deal in common with the Nazi persuasion techniques. But there are crucial differences. In the first place, Hitler and Goebbels were only interested in maintaining their power at all costs and by all means; the Russians and the Chinese believe in a set of fundamental truths, and that history is inexorably on their side. One consequence has been that there have come into their propaganda broadcasts, for each other as well as for the 'enemy', an all-pervading note of worthiness, a predictable tone of sermonizing, which appeal to the converted but have a blunt quality as a weapon compared with the Nazi arsenal of pikes and broadswords.

Of course Soviet propaganda preceded the Nazi era. Indeed, Soviet revolutionary messages were the first to be recorded in the history of wireless propaganda. Under the call-sign 'To all . . . to all . . . to all . . .', the Council of the People's Commissars' Radio put out Lenin's historic message announcing the start of a new age on 30 October (12 November in the new calendar) 1917:

> The All-Russian Congress of Soviets has formed a new Soviet Government. The Government of Kerensky has been overthrown and arrested. Kerensky himself has fled. All official institutions are in the hands of the Soviet Government . . .[1]

The message was an international one. It was intended to reach potential revolutionaries in Europe as well as actual ones in Russia.

Later messages were directed specifically at foreign workers, containing calls to 'be on the watch and not to relax the pressure on your rulers'. On rare occasions they were put out in a foreign language. From 1929, reports, information and instructions were broadcast regularly on the All-Union Radio in German and French, and, from 1930, in Dutch and English also.

At the same time, Soviet radio was brought under strict central control. For Lenin, radio was a 'newspaper without paper . . . and without boundaries', one of the most important means at his disposal to communicate communist ideas to the scattered, ill-informed, and often illiterate people of Russia, and to the outside world. He encouraged the rapid development of wireless telegraph techniques and established a radio broadcasting station in Moscow as early as 1922. At the time it was the most powerful station in the world. In August 1925, the world's first short-wave station went into operation in the Russian capital.

For four years radio was under the control of a joint-stock company; it was handed over to the People's Commissariat for Posts and Telegraphs in 1928 and then became the responsibility of special radio committees. In 1953, overall responsibility was transferred to the Ministry of Culture and finally, in 1957, radio and television were placed under the control of a special department, the USSR Council of Ministers' State Committee for Radio and Television Broadcasting.

On the radio side, Moscow Radio is the largest and most important element, but both domestic and foreign programmes originate from a large number of regional stations as well. As for international broadcasting, Moscow Radio is responsible for three-quarters of the output. But the central network was joined in July 1964 by an important newcomer, 'Radio Station Peace and Progress', the voice of the People as opposed to Officialdom. Its director, Lev Talanov, said in an interview with *The Times of India* that 'we definitely have a point of view. It is the point of view of our public, contained in declarations of Soviet public organizations.' The 'voice of public opinion' amounts in practice to little more than a device to vary the international radio diet. It is claimed by some in the west that the station is controlled by the KGB. The fact that it is channelled through 'public organizations' indicates that it is hardly a forum of free and spontaneous expression. But Peace and Progress does put out programmes more outspoken and often more bitter than Moscow Radio. If other countries take offence, the Communist Party and the government can hide behind the shield of 'public opinion', over which they have 'no control'.

As a result of all these outlets, the Soviet Union is the world's second largest international broadcaster, and from 1969 to 1972 in fact put out *more* programme hours than the United States.* In 1948, the Soviet Union broadcast 380 hours per week; in 1973, about 1,950 hours. There are at present programmes in eighty-four languages, far more than any other national service can muster. Soviet and eastern European broadcasts directed to North America and western Europe amount to about 1,350 hours per week. Beamed back at the east there are a weekly 1,100 hours of Radio Free Europe and Radio Liberty and about 820 hours of Voice of America, BBC, and the official radios of France, West Germany, Italy, the Vatican, Israel, and the American-run Radio in the American Sector of Berlin (RIAS). The propaganda Cold War is far from over.

In 1970, the budget of Moscow Radio External Services was estimated at 63 million roubles—which represents approximately the same sum in dollars. This must make the Soviet operations (with the addition of regional services and Peace and Progress) at least as expensive as the official American voices. What do the Russians hope to get out of it? We shall see that they have a number of objectives specific to their own operations, including the function of arbiter of the Moscow line to all non-Russian communists and, with regard to their broadcasts to the west, the spearhead of a diplomatic effort to put an end to the radio propaganda emanating from the opposing camp. But the Soviet External Services also play a national role like those of any other sovereign state. Ever since Stalin declared 'socialism in one country', the concept of a truly international service which happened to have its headquarters in Moscow was forgotten. It gets only a passing mention in the statement of goals spelled out in the 1962 Central Committee resolution on improving broadcasting in the Soviet Union. These goals are to:

> . . . skilfully consider the particular features of individual countries and sections of the population, and provide broad coverage of the life and foreign and domestic policies of the Soviet Union; publicize the achievements of the world system of socialism; comprehensively illustrate the international importance of the USSR's experience of communist construction; reveal the anti-popular politics of the imperialist states; and show that in the Soviet Union friendship and mutual brotherly assistance between the peoples have secured remarkable progress in the political and cultural development of the population of all the republics, autonomous regions and national areas of the country.

In other words, stress what is positive and wholesome about the Soviet Union.

An American Presidential Study Commission, set up to investigate and reorganize the funding of Radios Liberty and Free Europe, said

* for details see Appendix B

the same thing in a slightly different way.[2] The motivating forces of Soviet international broadcasts are, according to the report: a 'two-pronged ideological struggle' to 'counter the spread of "imperialist" ideology and to rebuff challenges from within the world communist configuration'; to 'portray the USSR as a world military and industrial power whose developmental model is to be emulated'; and to provide the 'support and advancement of foreign policy goals' and the 'dissemination of the "correct" line to cadres abroad'. As we shall see, this last point is an important one, determining the high priority put on broadcasts to other communists, and particularly those who have 'deviated'.

What handicaps all communist broadcasting to the west—Russian, Chinese, eastern European—is the lack of an audience beyond the faithful few. By these I mean, for the most part, active Communist Party members and sympathizers, and active opponents of capitalism. As far as the pro-Moscow faction is concerned, Maoists are a target for different reasons; the same is true of 'revisionists' for the Chinese. For the rest there are the amateur enthusiasts and chance listeners, not to be ignored as potential candidates for persuasion. But despite large communist parties in Italy and France, the total number of regular listeners to the Soviet External Services in non-communist countries is small compared to the number in Russia and eastern Europe who tune in to western broadcasts.

The Russians do not release estimated figures for their total audience. They did announce, however, that in 1967 they received about 120,000 letters from abroad. The BBC received just over 300,000 letters in 1973. Their ratio of, very approximately, 150 listeners for every letter-writer may or may not apply to Moscow Radio as well, but it is the only guide I can suggest. In any case, it is safe to say that there are less people around the world who tune in regularly to Radio Moscow than tune in to the BBC or the Voice of America.

It is a characteristic of 'open' societies that people are disdainful of information coming out of 'closed' societies. This is not so much a question of ideological aversion as of the apparent inability or unwillingness of centrally controlled media to adapt their presentation to the appetites of audiences both conditioned and sated by their own media.

Soviet international broadcasts have adapted slowly since around 1960, but not fast enough to keep up with western tastes. Long diatribes, ideological nit picking, slogan-mongering, blatant one-sidedness, my-country-right-or-wrong, all this may have been toned down on Moscow Radio and Peace and Progress. (The same cannot be said of Radio Peking or the Albanian External Services.) But still the tone is too ponderous for most western listeners.

Partly the problem is one of unevenness. On the one hand, there are question-and-answer programmes which can be relaxed and open—those presented by Joe Adamov, for example, in his programmes to the United States. Even a hard-liner like Professor Barghoorn has admitted that there is less dodging of questions now on Moscow Radio than there used to be. Russian and eastern European broadcasts all make extensive use of the listeners' questions technique (so skilfully manipulated earlier by the Nazis). A former national manager of CBS TV News, Chester Burger, is on record as praising the Moscow Mailbag programme.

On the other hand, political commentaries still tend to be monotonous, predictable and too obviously concocted from guidelines. Extracts from Party leaders' speeches are read out in ten-minute gobbets or more. Some individual commentators, like Anatoli Gan in English, stand out from the general run, but they are few. News is too Soviet-oriented for all except those who listen in simply to fill the gaps in their knowledge of the Soviet scene left by the inadequate coverage of their own media. How many people want to know whether the meeting between President Podgorny and some distinguished visitor—almost invariably such meetings head the bulletin—was held in 'an atmosphere of friendship and cordiality' or any of the other clichés of diplomacy and protocol? But, above all, the ravages caused by censorship are infuriating to listeners used to instant information about disastrous trade figures, government wrangles, defence debates, and so on. (Air crashes are now reported in the Soviet Union only because the news was consistently broadcast by foreign stations.)

The Russian External Services used to be caught out saying one thing to one audience and another to a different audience, but the directive system has in recent years been tightened up. The lack of confidence implicit in this type of deliberate deception has disappeared. A Radio Free Europe research paper commented on one way things have improved:

The introduction of a program in Hebrew and Yiddish may be another example of the growing sophistication of Soviet external broadcasting, which now seems to regard itself as competent to handle convincingly a program monitored by both Arabs and Jews.

Without being patronizing, it is fair to say that the Russians have improved their radio techniques considerably since the Stalinist period. But their broadcasts to international audiences still suffer from ponderousness, parochialism and partiality. In addition, they are, and sound, defensive. One of the lessons of wartime broadcasting, learnt by both the *Propagandaministerium* and the BBC, was that it does not pay to answer back. Yet the Russians cannot resist reacting to criticism. Even when extolling their own virtues, they do so in a way which stresses their feeling of being surrounded by unbelievers and sceptics. When confident, they are likely to bluster.

Western and Chinese broadcasters know that there are some particularly sore spots which provoke an angry Russian response: the Katyn story, for example, or the threat of a pre-emptive strike against China, anti-Semitism, concealed unemployment, national dissensions, the Nazi-Soviet Pact. In return, the Russians pick on Ulster, the Suez fiasco, colonialism, Greville Wynne, Vietnam, racism, and, for China, the excesses of the Cultural Revolution, or the fall of Lin Piao, Mao's trusted comrade-in-arms. But when there is a direct polemic with the west, it is usually a case of a Russian reply to a foreign broadcast, not the other way round.

In general, Soviet external broadcasting operates on an uncertain middle ground. It is neither positive, attacking the opposition without deigning to notice criticisms, as Goebbels advocated, nor is it sweetly reasonable. It has never tried to build up a faithful audience through achieving high standards of credibility like the BBC has. Soviet propaganda does not aspire to be 'objective' in this sense. The Russians openly condemn the use of this term. It is a consequence of their attempt to identify and propagate truth of a particular, socialist kind that people will believe it or not according to their pre-conceptions, not according to the facts of the case. Moscow Radio and Radio Vatican share the same problem.

The Russians are therefore caught between the two poles of effective broadcasting. At either end of the spectrum—whether total propaganda as a weapon of naked power, or the search for truth in the 'balanced' presentation of all sides of the question—propaganda can reach even those who are initially sceptical. In between, there is a grey area of ideological finger-wagging which may avoid controversy at the point of origin and satisfy the already converted, but leaves no mark on the outside world. The Americans have oscillated between this middle ground and attempts to rely on objectivity, with unhappy results. The communists, for all the changes of detail in their presentation techniques, remain stuck with their backs to the ideological wall. On the other hand, their defensiveness has a positive side: the constant mood of optimism. 'Fraternal greetings' are always being expressed, achievements listed, everybody congratulates everybody else. For sceptics it can be irritating. For many people, fed up with the depressing quality of their own news, it is a welcome relief. At least somebody thinks that '*tout est pour le mieux dans le meilleur des mondes possibles*'.

But optimism by itself is not enough to attract to the communist External Services a large following in the developed countries of the west. It is as obvious to the Russians as it is to their ideological opponents that long-distance propaganda aimed at an audience not predisposed to listen, in bad reception conditions, and not reinforced by action of any sort, is bound to have a very limited effect. Jacques Ellul writes:

> The Soviet Union . . . does not seek to reach western peoples by its radio. It confines its propaganda to organizations in the form of national Communist parties inside the national boundaries of the people to be propagandized.[3]

While this is in a literal sense untrue, it is fair to say that as far as radio propaganda is concerned, audiences other than those in the west have a far greater priority. Outside the socialist camp, the principal target is the Third World.

The impact that communism has had on the Third World, after a period in the fifties and sixties when the retreat from colonialism left it apparently receptive to the message, has been quite small however. The propaganda failure has followed the political failure. For all its inherent weaknesses, non-alignment has seemed a preferable option to many poor countries. Moscow's own methods of neo-colonialist exploitation, for example in Egypt, scared off many potential friends, while at the same time lending support to the line put out by other foreign radio stations. Above all, the Sino-Soviet split provided the Third World with a far superior choice to becoming the client state of one or other of the communist powers (in preference to the west): to play the communists off against each other.

Despite some reputed success in gaining a substantial audience in India,[4] and a large investment in staff and transmitters for broadcasting in minority languages, no audience survey that I have seen provides any evidence of widespread listening in the Third World to Moscow Radio, Radio Peking, or any of the eastern European stations. On the other hand, it is premature to suggest that the failure is permanent or endemic. If the Soviet broadcasters, for example, were to take more literally their stated goal of 'skilfully considering the particular features of individual countries and sections of the population', they could surely build up Third-World audiences at least on the scale of the major western stations. The communist dialectic is not unsuited to the direct, black-and-white presentation of Russian ideological propaganda. It can be simplified without being deformed. What is lacking is the understanding that different audiences need different treatment. The potential for greater flexibility exists now that the vernacular services have been expanded.

But the problem is still to vary the output according to the variety of audience.

If a failure to understand, and so appeal to, the Third World has so far hampered communist radio propaganda in this direction, the same is not true of broadcasting within the communist camp. Here broadcasters and audience understand each other well. On the purely theoretical plane, radio helps keep intact the body of Marxist thought, Marxism being, as Karl Mannheim says, a rationalized conception of history which 'serves as a socially unifying factor for groups dispersed in space'. Propaganda is required to explain at what stage of development on the Marxist scale they find themselves, when to act, what is the correct response to this or that problem. The same medium can also be used, of course, as a link in the chain of command in matters more practical than theoretical. For the Soviet Union, the prime target of its External Services since the war has been its satellite states in eastern Europe, and, in more recent years, China. For China, the Soviet Union is top priority.

In eastern Europe, Soviet propaganda has been the adjunct of military and political pressure. It has always paid the people living there to know what the Russians are thinking, or at least saying. But this does not mean that the Soviet Union has a large and sympathetic audience in eastern Europe for Moscow Radio. Direct radio propaganda has been only a small part of the total Soviet strategy. More important has been their indirect influence on the domestic media in each of the countries except Albania and Yugoslavia. Even compulsory inserts like the *Moscow Speaks* programmes have been dropped in favour of less crude methods of 'co-operation'.

Among the eastern European states themselves, there is no 'first country of socialism' and therefore more open competition for listeners. But here radio propaganda is more important as a political gesture from government to government, or party to party, than as a means of popular persuasion. The Bulgarian 'Radio Rodina' ('Homeland') was a gesture of defiance towards Yugoslavia over the Macedonian question, not just, as it purported to be, a link with Bulgarians abroad. Although it was taken off the air in December 1971 after almost four years of operation, it was replaced by Radio Blagovgrad—a town in the centre of Pirin Macedonia—which could be heard clearly across the border in Yugoslavia. Similarly, the Albanian External Services, partly the proxy voice of China in Europe, carry on an endless polemical battle with the External Services of the Soviet Union and other eastern European states— without any real intention of influencing public opinion on either side.

But there have been moments of crisis in eastern Europe when international broadcasting has played a far more active role. Radio was one of the few ways in which Stalin could hope to undermine Yugoslav solidarity after 1948. Before the split, Soviet broadcasting to Yugoslavia amounted to a mere twenty-four hours per week. In 1949 this had risen to seventy-seven hours, in 1951 to 193. But after the partial reconciliation the output began to decrease, falling to sixty hours in 1958 and less than thirty today. In an even more dramatic way, the Russian broadcasts to Czechoslovakia jumped from seventeen hours per week just before the August 1968 invasion to 168 at the height of the crisis, falling back to eighty-four by September.

The biggest test of Soviet propaganda in eastern Europe came in Hungary in 1956. The Russians were fortunate in having the Suez crisis, which just preceded the first intervention in Hungary, to point to as an even more flagrant example of foreign interference. They were able, for example, to make propaganda capital out of an appeal to the Americans, who also opposed the Suez venture, for joint Soviet-American action 'to crush the aggressors by force'. Later, communist propaganda was also to seize on the 'provocative' role of Radio Free Europe in inciting Hungarians to revolt, undermining the confidence of the remaining opposition which began to feel both misled and let down.

On the first question, Prague Radio summed up the Soviet view in a reply to the BBC commentator, Maurice Latey, who had compared the Hungarian 'intervention' unfavourably with the Suez 'campaign':

Can he claim that the Israeli, British and French troops were invited into Egypt by the Government of that country, as was the case in Hungary? Can he maintain that the Soviet troops entered Hungary to capture a Suez Canal for a bunch of shareholders, as was the case in Egypt? And, lastly, is it not clear that the Soviet troops are in Hungary to put an end to murder and terror, whereas the western forces entered Egypt to start a war and to establish a reign of terror?[5]

These were powerful points. The left-wing opposition in Britain agreed at least with the first two. On the same day, Bucharest Radio, in an English-language broadcast, was repeating the line of all the communist stations, that the 'atrocities' against the security forces in Hungary and others had been committed by 'those who were encouraged, instigated and supported by the Voice of America and Free Europe'.

A similar line was put out by the Soviet Union to eastern European countries themselves. Moscow's short-wave broadcasts, for example, were resumed to Bulgaria after stopping in April 1956, and to

Czechoslovakia after a gap of more than two years. Broadcasts to Hungary were also stepped up, one of the main themes here being the support for the Soviet action expressed in the media of the other east European states.

Moscow Radio continued to mount a bitter campaign against Radio Free Europe long after the fighting had stopped. A broadcast in Slovak on 23 November said:

There were detailed instructions on how to provoke riots and pogroms and how to transform peaceable demonstrations into a bloodbath.

But a generally milder and more defensive tone became apparent in all the Russian External Services broadcasts as the hostility of world reaction was brought home. In an English broadcast on 28 November, a Moscow Radio commentator admitted that there were 'departures from affection for the USSR'. Parallel to this mood was a rather jolly attitude towards the British-French withdrawal from Egypt—now we know, said one commentator, 'why the Sphinx is smiling!' An enemy defeat is the very best condition for international propaganda. But the events of October 1956, in Egypt and Hungary, showed that both in easy and in difficult circumstances, Russian radio propaganda had become a sharp and penetrating weapon of international diplomacy.

It is the very lack of any identifiable defeat or failure within the target area that so handicaps Soviet propaganda to China. Yet today China is the number one target of Soviet radio propaganda. Chinese-language broadcasts increased from seventy-seven hours a week in 1967 to two hundred hours in 1972. Programmes in Mongolian have doubled since 1967 to nearly thirty-five hours a week.[6] But while the Sino-Soviet quarrel has forced the Russians to adopt a more reasonable tone over both ideology and Soviet achievements in broadcasts to the west and to eastern Europe, to the Chinese the tone of Russian radio propaganda is still sharply polemical and self-righteous. There is a great deal of pointing out of Chinese errors and refutation of 'revisionist' charges. In addition, the Russians display a bitterness that must, at least in part, derive from fear.

Most of the Soviet attacks relate to political and ideological differences, the details of which need not concern us here. One interesting line of attack does, however, involve radio itself. In his English-language commentary on Moscow Radio recently, Geliy Shakhov said:

In this connection just let me quote something the BBC said in a broadcast at 11 p.m. Moscow time on Saturday. The programme quoted an unnamed Labour Member of Parliament who said that in his opinion the BBC was playing a 'truly unique role'. For one thing, this is a Peking-style of radio journalism: 'One West European said', 'One Asian added', 'One Latin American supported', and so on . . .[7]

Shakhov is here criticizing the BBC on the grounds that it uses the underhand methods of Peking! It is a similar case to the more substantial criticism of the Voice of America: the Voice, claimed Moscow Radio, had picked up and rebroadcast Radio Peking allegations that the Soviet Union was making exorbitant profits out of arms sales to the Arabs. Another Russian broadcast, in January 1974, accused a New China News Agency correspondent of contacting Radio Free Europe and Radio Liberty to obtain information hostile to the Soviet Union.

This kind of polemic is only symptomatic of much more important areas of mutual hostility. But what role does radio propaganda play in the dispute? What the Soviet Union would like to do is get its message through to the Chinese people—both the Russians and the Chinese make a clear distinction between the people and their leaders—but the two countries have political and security systems similar enough to know that even reaching the broad masses, let alone influencing them or causing them to act in any way against their governments, is at best a very long-term hope. Broadcasting from the Soviet Union into the sealed-off world of China is even less promising than the reverse. The Chinese look further into the future than the Russians, and are prepared to let time work for them. Their broadcasts are also intended to stimulate and take advantage of the current of opinion sympathetic towards China and Maoist thought which, though existing more strongly in the west than in east Europe, could nevertheless grow over the years to provide the strongest challenge so far to the stability of the Soviet and ancillary regimes.

Like Russian broadcasts, the Chinese ones too reflect a consistent truth and logic, which to non-believers is partial and misleading, but which is nevertheless not opportunistic or dishonest in the way that Nazi propaganda could be. And so each side keeps on trying to export its own special truth, knowing that at least for the time being the opposing authorities are listening in and taking notice.

The Chinese started broadcasting to the Soviet Union in 1962. The fact that this was the year of the Cuba crisis, which the Chinese still regard as a major political and propaganda failure on the part of the Russians and of communism in general, is not a coincidence. It was also the year of the Sino-Indian war, which embarrassed the Russians and angered the Chinese since it put the spotlight on Russian diplomatic and economic links with India. But the main reason for inaugurating the service was the deterioration of relations between China and the Soviet Union.

The Chinese People's Republic is now the third largest international broadcaster in the world. While Asia is the principal target, a high proportion of the output is aimed at other communist countries. The biggest foreign section by far is the Russian—output in that language is a third more again than the English-language output to audiences in all five continents, and even slightly larger than the entire Chinese-language (Kuoyou, Cantonese, Chaochow) output.

Late in 1968, after the invasion of Czechoslovakia, the Chinese began to broadcast in Czech, Polish and Romanian direct from Peking. Previously, they had relied on Albanian broadcasts to put their point of view. Albania, indeed, still broadcasts more to these countries than China does, and also sends out programmes in Bulgarian and Hungarian, contributing to its status as the world's seventh largest international broadcaster. But recent differences with the Chinese over Sino-American rapprochement have shed doubt on the idea that Albanian broadcasts are a simple reflection of Radio Peking.

Maoists take the long view. They have no illusions about instant persuasion, particularly when it cannot be more tangibly reinforced. Nevertheless, they have considerable faith in the power of radio as a medium. Inside China, radio is an important, though by no means separate part of a network of propaganda systems, from wall newspapers to dancing groups to films and exhibitions. Its unique importance is held to be its power to hold the ear of every single Chinese citizen at the same time. Mao Tse-tung's wife, Chiang Ching, took a special interest in the use of radio at the time of rapid changes during the Cultural Revolution. The medium is strengthened by the widespread use of wired radio whereby a single programme is relayed through loudspeakers into all the places where people live and work. Radio has been the best way to spread the new political vocabulary which, as every visitor to China knows, now comes readily to the lips of the humblest Chinese peasant; and as an implement of mass mobilization, literally and figuratively, radio has been the key medium.

These remarks relate only to the use of radio inside China. In a country where, as Mao said, 'each must be a propagandist for all', the means of instant communication have a special role to play. But this also has the effect of making outside sources of information difficult to absorb and, as a corollary, making Chinese news and propaganda difficult to export.

The first of these consequences is something that the authorities welcome. The second, with the possible exception of their attempts to reach the Russian people, is something to which they are almost indifferent. The historical Chinese aloofness towards the outside world is reflected in their radio output as much as in other aspects of Chinese diplomacy. Only recently, along with China's entry into the United Nations, has some effort been made to play a more positive and active international role. To quote the Radio Free Europe Research Department again:

> What has been observed in reference to the Soviet Union also applies to Chinese international broadcasting: its tremendous expansion in the 1960s has now been followed by a period of consolidation and program refinement.

But 'program refinement' is still an optimistic way of looking at Chinese international broadcasts. There is indeed some improvement over the crude techniques and monotony of the earlier period, but listening to Radio Peking still requires a degree of devotion rare even among the most committed to the Maoist cause. No attempt is made to distinguish between audiences. In fact, foreign programmes are little more than translations of domestic output. The same jargon reappears, the same long homilies. There is no Russian who is not at the same time 'revisionist', no American who is not 'imperialist'. Even the programme which answers listeners' letters deals preponderantly with esoteric points of doctrine. A lead item in a news bulletin is likely to be: 'The workers in the capitalist world are continuing the class struggle.' To casual western listeners, stories of the productivity feats of some heroic human bean-farmer, related at length and in infinite detail, the role of Mao Tse-tung's thought duly stressed and restressed, sound like parodies or clumsy CIA spoofs.

It would seem that some of the broadcasters themselves in Radio Peking are anxious to improve their presentation techniques. But two factors have so far inhibited them. One is their fear of authority. Who will dare suggest that reading out the entire speech of some respected functionary is boring? Who is going to say that the slogans and ideological polemics are virtually meaningless outside China? Who is going to insist that radio demands a language and a style that are different from formal political texts? The other factor is money. Technical resources—in terms of staff, studios and transmitters—are inadequate for the scale of Radio Peking's worldwide operation, and every radio station knows how inhibiting lack of money can be.

The same inhibition affects Radio Tirana. Since the mid-sixties, Albanian foreign broadcasting has expanded at a rate hardly exceeded anywhere in the world. In the early sixties, considerable Soviet help was provided for transmitters and other facilities, and later the Chinese financed new and more powerful transmitters.

Nevertheless, the scale of the radio propaganda operation, a third of which is beamed to other communist countries, puts a heavy burden on the national budget. Certainly quantity of output is the primary object of this expenditure, not quality. If the monotony of the message may be put down to ideological causes, the often comically unprofessional quality of the speakers is as much a consequence of financial embarrassment as of the problem of persuading foreigners to sample the austere life of the Albanian capital.

The professionalism of many of the other eastern European services is in strong contrast to the Chinese and Albanian programmes. Hungary's 'Homeland' service addressed to Hungarians living abroad is a successful example of a subtle and professional approach, both in terms of its message—'let bygones be bygones'—and its variety of programming. One reason for its success is that Hungary has the smallest External Service of all the eastern European states, and can devote more resources and attention to each of the component parts.

The Czechoslovak foreign-language services, on the other hand, reflect the overall drop in quality of the national media since 1968. A harder, safer line is the rule, both internationally and domestically. Elsewhere, even in Bulgaria, the trend has been in the other direction. Domestic services have been livened up, partly in response to the challenge of western and other foreign stations.

In Romania, a hard-line cultural campaign in July 1971 reversed a slow trend towards greater cultural and political freedom in the media that dated from the mid-sixties. But by 1973 signs that the pendulum was slowly swinging back the other way were becoming visible. Romanian foreign broadcasting as such is a harmless mixture of tourist-attracting features and bland ideological and economic optimism. A more sensitive question is domestic broadcasting in Hungarian, designed not just to cover Transylvania but also to pick up listeners in Hungary itself and so counter the residual feeling there that Transylvania properly belongs under Magyar rule. Similarly, a powerful (1,000 kilowatt) transmitter was installed in 1971 in Iasi, the capital of Romanian Moldavia. Its message is clearly audible across the border in the Moldavian SSR, or, as Romanians think of it, Bessarabia.

As for Poland, her foreign broadcasting lacks the professionalism that is more and more apparent on the domestic channels, although success is claimed for its service to Poles living abroad. East Germany's External Services have contracted since the mid-sixties. It now devotes special attention to the developing countries, far more than any other eastern European service, but there is no evidence that any special qualities are exhibited by this arm of the DDR's diplomacy.

In general, it is difficult to avoid the conclusion that a great deal of communist external broadcasting is just for the record. Having listened to their output over a long period, I cannot see that any serious attempt is being made to appeal to westerners who are not communist, and only half-hearted attempts are being made to get through to a Third-World audience. The only international broadcasting with serious political intent is that among the members of the socialist camp, and especially between the Moscow and the Peking factions.

As far as the non-communist world is concerned, the Russians and east Europeans would certainly prefer to have a complete embargo on radio propaganda, in both directions. I shall come back to this question in the chapter on 'Interference', but some points need to be made here. The basic Soviet position—the Chinese stay aloof from the debate—is that the west is interfering in the internal affairs of sovereign states, and that communist broadcasts are simply intended to counter this hostile propaganda. While the legality of this argument is dubious, clearly the communist states, as closed societies, have more to fear from outside sources of information and opinion than the open societies of the west. But, as we shall see in the following chapters, the west is not simply providing information for deprived peoples. In the east-west ideological and political struggle, radio propaganda is a weapon wielded by the west with great effect. For the communists, propaganda directed at the west is very much a rubber sword. It becomes a real weapon only when used in the internecine war.

This helps explain the defensive tone of Russian and eastern European broadcasting to the west. The first aim is to discredit the west's own services, to point out that cross-frontier broadcasting only exacerbates international relations. Their worst enemies in this respect are Radio Liberty and Radio Free Europe. But the Russians want to build up a lobby, particularly in America, Britain and West Germany, to persuade those who provide the money and the facilities for all the major western services that it is money not just wasted but misapplied. When the East Germans complain about the BBC's *Lügenküche* (the lies-kitchen where Austin Harrison concocts scurrilous replies to mythical letters), when Moscow Radio accuses the BBC of carrying spy messages, or the Voice of America of sabotage, the object is to sow doubt in the west as to whether their External Services really do contribute to détente, or whether the communists would not be better off left to their own devices.

This is substantially the only message that the Russians and east Europeans want to put across to their western audience. The small circles of devoted listeners to the recitals of positive achievements are all to the good, and radio is the ideal medium to keep them informed and up-to-date on the correct line as new problems crop up. But they could readily be dispensed with if, in return, all western broadcasting to the east were to cease. Radio attacks are not the only way of bringing pressure to bear to this end. Diplomatic representation and other means are just as important. But the frequency and intensity of the attacks on the media as such, and not on the views they put forward or even always on the governments that back them (the Russians alternately ignore and mock the 'independence of the BBC') are clear evidence of the Soviet wish to see all western stations off the air.

3 Voices of America

Criticism of America's official radio station can be harsh:

The Voice of America, the biggest gun in America's propaganda arsenal, sounds pontifical at worst, distant at best, and not because of the static. The bulk of Voice programming is world news and analysis, plus commentary that reflects American policy, music and features on American life. The music is fine: Willis Conover's venerable 'Voice of America Jazz Hour' offers better jazz than most stations inside the United States. In the news department though, America's biggest gun turns into a small bore. Since the mid-'60s, when the Voice was strident and dogmatic in its defense of President Johnson's Vietnam policies, the station has rehabilitated itself into a bland, inoffensive, steadily dull mouthpiece for official Washington.

VOA doesn't propagandize its 50 million or so listeners so much as sedates them with snippets of speeches, news conferences and handouts. It plays the news reasonably straight from Vietnam, reports dutifully Lord Carrington's belief that peace has prevailed in Europe largely because of NATO and answers a letter in which Mr. Trevor Whatsisface of Chittagong, Bangladesh, asks why May Day is known as May Day. But the Voice is Olympian, removed, inhuman.[1]

In terms of techniques, and programming and objectives, American radio propaganda in general has more in common with the communist model than with either the Nazi or the BBC alternatives. The Voice of America, Radio Liberty, Radio Free Europe, the American Forces Network, Radio in the American Sector (RIAS), are all state-funded, though through different channels. Policy is laid down by a system of directives. The VOA particularly suffers from dullness. There is a strong ideological commitment. The 'truth' to be transmitted is a consciously American-democratic anti-communist truth.

Newsweek's description of the 'Voice' picked on some of its glaring defects. In a way, they all derive from a single cause. The VOA is indeed an official mouthpiece, the largest single element of the United States Information Agency, but whose mouthpiece is it? America's? The Administration's? The President's—since the USIA is directly responsible to the White House? The USIA's? Some Voice broadcasters and officials even argue that the confusion of responsibility allows them to choose their own line independently. In any event, the VOA has always existed in an atmosphere of controversy over this question.

The Voice began in an emergency, seventy-nine days after the Japanese attack on Pearl Harbour. In February 1942, only about a dozen suitable short-wave transmitters were available in the United States. These had to be requisitioned from the commercial companies that had used them for some fitful and half-hearted attempts at foreign-language broadcasting, and pressed into war service.

Equipment was not the only thing lacking. Attitudes towards international propaganda had to be reversed, isolationist feelings put aside. Radio itself was obliged to forego its role as merely a profitable vehicle for advertisements. New techniques had to be learnt. Although radio as a medium of rapid and far-ranging communication had been developed as rapidly in America as anywhere (KDKA had broadcast the results of President Harding's election in 1920), it was caught in the all-American cycle of isolationism and commercialism. A world war was needed for the state to take on something more than the most general controlling interest over frequency allocation.

As soon as the VOA came on the air, the question of its role, and who was in control, began to cause trouble. The Office of War Information, with overall responsibility for American war propaganda, and the 'Overseas Branch'—successor to the Foreign Information Service and predecessor of the CIA—plunged into the same struggle that the European allies were waging over the relative importance of 'black' (clandestine) and white radio. The VOA often found itself caught between the Administration, the military and the commercial media.

In the end it came out of the war with some credit. It was General

Stilwell's announcement, carried by the Voice, that he had taken 'a hell of a beating' in Burma, that first gained it a reputation for credibility. But the VOA never created the kind of reliability myth that was to surround the BBC. Asa Briggs is uncompromisingly critical:

> In general, American propaganda to Europe throughout the war was both too distant and yet too brash, too unsophisticated and yet too contrived to challenge the propaganda forces already at work on the Continent.[2]

But it was in the first decade after the war that the real problems began. In the first place, there was a widespread horror in the United States about propaganda, both the word and the operation itself. It was felt to be something German, or Russian, certainly undemocratic and unnecessary. America had done her bit. There was no need to blow trumpets. Certainly no need to spend dollars on pulling the wool over foreigners' eyes. Despite some fears that the British would be left with a virtual monopoly in presenting the western view to the world, Congress cut the appropriations for all surviving elements of the US propaganda effort until almost nothing was left.

Then came the Cold War, the Russian atom bomb, Korea. In 1948 the Smith-Mundt Act was passed by Congress, guaranteeing funds for the Voice of America, and inspiring William L. Shirer to write in the *New York Herald Tribune* on 8 February:

> It is not very often that either house votes unanimously on anything, and when both do it—as they did the other day in giving legal authority to a permanent State Department international information and cultural program—one can only describe it as a unique performance indeed.
>
> What is even more unusual is the remarkable change of mind manifested by the members of Congress. For it was only a year or so ago that the same gentlemen decided to still the 'Voice of America' and leave the war of words to the Russians and the British...
>
> It is supremely ironic that the Congress should have completely reversed its stand on the whole matter because of a belated misunderstanding of what the Russians were up to. It could be said, of course, that the Russians were up to the same thing two years ago, but the news had not at that time reached Capitol Hill.

This was the news brought back, after a twenty-two-country visit, by Senators Smith and Mundt.

So the Voice was saved, and at once put to work to broadcast abroad President Truman's 'Campaign for Truth'. The campaign was a deliberate counter to Russian success in associating the word 'Peace' with their own policies. Edward W. Barrett, a VOA man himself, claims credit for bringing 'Truth' into the American camp, heading off, by means of this slogan for the President's keynote speech, such otherwise unavoidable headlines as 'Truman Declares Propaganda War'.[3]

$121 million was appropriated by Congress for the 'Campaign for Truth' against communism. In the following year, 1951, the President set up a Psychological Strategy Board, responsible to the National Security Council, to advise on the broad lines of American propaganda. In 1953, President Eisenhower appointed a personal adviser on psychological warfare. Although this appointment lapsed after only one year, propaganda had now established itself as a top priority in the Cold War strategy. The stridently anti-communist tone of the Voice reflected this priority.

This was not enough for Senator Joe McCarthy. The USIA, created in 1953, and the Voice in particular, came before his committee. The Hickenlooper Report, criticizing the VOA for its 'woolliness', gave McCarthy some official ammunition. Some heads were required to roll, morale fell apart, the budget was cut; but the basic structure of the USIA and the VOA remained, and indeed has stayed unchanged to this day. Although there have been bad times since, none has come close to the brief but traumatic period of the McCarthy hearings.

In 1950 the Voice was putting out around 500 hours a week. Five years later this total had risen to almost 850, but subsequent cuts over the next ten years, and then increases to some particularly important audiences, such as the Vietnamese, meant that this level declined and then was reached again by the late sixties and early seventies. Today, thirty-six languages are regularly scheduled, others are used in special situations. In addition to direct broadcasts, the VOA and USIA posts overseas place ready-prepared programmes in 4,000 local radio stations, notably in Latin America.

The Voice's operating budget for the fiscal year 1974 was almost exactly $50 million. This compares with $39 million in 1970 and a mere $11 million in those tentative days in 1948. The present figure means that the Voice gets the same as Radio Liberty and Radio Free Europe combined, and a quarter as much again as the BBC.

The VOA complains that with worldwide overheads far more onerous than the Munich operations, 114 transmitters of which seventy-three are overseas, and a staff of 2,300, it is the poor cousin in the American radio propaganda field. It can afford only a small and irregular Audience Research Department and is constantly struggling to keep such facilities as a tape library operating efficiently.

Above all, salaries are uncompetitive, from the highest to the lowest grades. This means that top journalists and administrators particularly are reluctant to take up posts. In 1953 Barrett wrote:

> America's information-program budgets have gone up and down like a yo-yo. When Congress is frightened, personnel is hastily recruited, screened for loyalty and security, and laboriously trained. Then a lull descends, funds are cut, and much of the trained personnel returns to private industry. A few months later, the Kremlin growls again—and up goes the yo-yo.[4]

The money supply is more assured today, but it still has to be fought for and still does not permit the payment of salaries remotely comparable to those received by leading figures in the private communications field.

There is a residual suspicion in Congress about financing propaganda organizations, however they are dressed up. The one man who actually made the Voice popular with Congressmen, and with Americans generally, was Ed Murrow. Murrow was a Kennedy appointee and friend, a brilliant reporter whose wartime despatches from London made him a household name, and who later became a top TV reporter and executive. Under his directorship, the USIA was upgraded and accepted by the Administration as a genuine arm of American diplomacy. But this was not to last.

After ill-health had forced Murrow out of office, President Johnson appointed first Carl Rowan, a black journalist, and then Leonard Marks. During these years in the late sixties there was a series of clashes, of both personality and policy, between the USIA directors and a succession of VOA directors—Henry Loomis, a public-spirited technocrat who clashed with Rowan, John Chancellor, who introduced a more swinging image and promptly left for richer pastures, and then John Daley, who left after a fight with Marks. Under Frank Shakespeare, a pro-Nixon campaigner and ideological hard-liner, and his successor James Keogh, the USIA continued to enjoy a fluctuating but, in general, declining prestige, marked by an unimaginative conservatism. At the Voice this line has been eagerly supported by the latest director, Kenneth Giddens, an ultra-conservative southerner whose money from housebuilding bought him influence with Nixon, though not enough to prevent such policies as rapprochement with China or SALT, of which Giddens disapproves.

The mixture of political appointments at the top levels, Congressional wariness and an uncertain chain of command has led to what one VOA correspondent described to me hopefully as 'creative tension', but which can also be described as plain muddle.

At the Voice itself there is a further level of confusion—that between 'administrators' and 'journalists'. One of the advantages of Murrow's reign at the Agency was that he was supremely a journalist. Keogh is sufficiently a journalist to see things in this light, but also enough of a conservative to object, for example, to a mention by the Voice of a 'soft' story from a newspaper source before official White House reaction is known. But, at the very least, the directors and the 'Policy Office', which issues daily guidance notes for all section heads, are likely to be more conscious of their accountability to Congress, the State Department, the President, and indeed the taxpayer, than those who report, prepare news bulletins, or write commentaries.

The broadcasters claim special reasons for being granted more independence within the USIA than the other component parts: radio is a fast medium; there is a tradition of no government interference in all the American media; the staff is multi-national and independent-minded; memories of the McCarthy era persist; and the VOA preceded the Agency by eleven years. In fact, a daily compromise is reached. Staff read the fairly broad guidelines from the Policy Office. Foreign correspondents, who usually work inside their embassy building, have all the opportunity they need to discuss policy with State Department officials.

There is also a 'Charter' in existence—in fact a directive by VOA director George Allen, dating from 1960. It makes general points about the output being 'reliable', 'authoritative' and 'accurate'; that the Voice should 'represent America and not any single segment of American society' and that it should 'present policies of the United States clearly and effectively . . . and also responsible discussion and opinion on these policies'. The broadcasters believe this gives them sufficient freedom to interpret the news as they see it; the Charter has no legal authority anyway.

The restriction on the range of opinions expressed in Voice commentaries does not derive so much from excessive guidance from above, as from the fact that all commentaries are written by staff members. Whereas the BBC, in its English-language World Service, relies almost exclusively on outsiders (though chosen and balanced by the BBC), the VOA carries nothing but its own, and hence ultimately official, comment. This not only restricts the range of opinion but also poses problems of credibility. It is natural to expect that under these circumstances opposition views are given insufficient weight.

Even the use of stringers (journalists hired on a story-by-story basis) to send back reports from overseas is being curtailed, both for financial reasons and because the lines of communication with Washington tend to become overstretched; in other words, the stringers fail to receive their instructions on time. The African Service does, however, enjoy more autonomy than most, and the separate location on the island of Rhodes of part of the Arabic Service permits the staff there to operate more freely than in Washington. Also, there is a sufficiently large network of foreign correspondents to avoid the output being overloaded with summaries prepared in Washington or New York.

As for the orientation of news and comment, what happens in practice is that output concerning matters of foreign policy follows the State Department line with only minor divergences. Generally, a single telephone call is enough. A rare case of open disagreement occurred when the State Department tried to suppress the news of the execution of former Prime Minister Menderes on a request from the Turkish government, but the Voice carried the news nevertheless, as did other media. During the Cuba crisis, when Allen himself was critical of the overkill barrage against Castro, a State Department official was attached directly to the VOA. The protests by the Voice were more the result of hurt feelings than of any wish to oppose the official line or assert their independence. On internal questions, however, the comments are more free. Partly this reflects the lack of a single source to provide guidelines. But the VOA is also anxious to avoid either representing any 'segment' of America, as the Charter puts it, or of losing credibility when American domestic dissensions are so well publicized by the non-government media.

Very little is known about the audience itself, estimated by the VOA to be in the order of 50 million a week. Congress has on occasions vainly tried to establish the cost-effectiveness of the station, but the impact of the VOA is even more elusive than the total numbers listening. Like all radio propaganda stations, the VOA operates in the dark.

The station's own priorities are reflected in the number of hours broadcast each week to the various nationalities. The USSR is the number one target area (168 hours)—this includes broadcasts to the Baltic States and the Georgian, Ukrainian, Uzbek and Armenian Republics in their own languages. Broadcasts in Mandarin rank second (70), in Vietnamese third (56), and those in Arabic and Spanish to Latin America next (49 each). The countries of eastern Europe, excluding the USSR, receive 87 hours 30 minutes per week. The biggest output, although dispersed to all parts of the globe, is in English (222 hours per week), part of which is audible in the Soviet Union and eastern Europe, though it is not planned with this audince exclusively in mind.

These figures, which apply as of 30 September 1973, show that the communist audience is still very prominent in VOA thinking. At one point, after the North Vietnamese had crossed the demilitarized zone in the spring of 1972, programmes in Vietnamese were put out for eighteen hours a day, but were later reduced to their present level of less than half that figure. Every few years, the USIA reviews the numbers of languages used and the airtime allotted to each. But dramatic increases or reductions on the Vietnamese scale are rare. At present, according to the VOA, the overall picture is unlikely to change substantially for some time to come unless there are major and unforeseen political changes in the world.

When I asked whether the recent spirit of détente had influenced Voice policy in broadcasts to the Soviet Union, Serban Vallimarescu, Deputy Director of the VOA, replied:

> While there has been no change in Voice *policy*, there have been certain changes made in broadcasting *techniques* designed to take advantage of the absence of constant artificial interference. A slightly increased use of music for greater audio 'texture', an ability to treat many subjects at somewhat greater length, the chance to humanize broadcasts more by talking with ordinary Americans . . . There have been accusations from some quarters to the effect that VOA has 'mellowed' its tone in its broadcasts to the USSR in keeping with developments towards détente, but those charges have been shown to be a matter of subjective judgment.

Clearly Mr Vallimarescu is not anxious to accept charges of 'mellowing'.

Unlike the BBC, the Voice pays far more attention to ideological enemies than to friends. The Italian and Japanese Services have been eliminated altogether; no English broadcasts are specifically directed at the United Kingdom. Even the African 'phase' is over, as a Voice correspondent put it. And the Latin American Service, while regarded as politically important, is given only a moderate time on the air (forty-nine hours a week in Spanish, twenty-one in Portuguese).

On the other hand, the Chinese Service, especially now that official visitors have confirmed that the signal is audible there, is seen as of key importance. The only trouble is that despite audibility, there is no positive evidence of any listeners. In Russia and east Europe, however, there is plenty of evidence of a substantial audience, estimated at a weekly 13 million. To this figure must, however, be added a substantial number of East Germans who listen to the Radio in the American Sector which came into operation early in 1946, and also the millions who tune in to Radio Free Europe and Radio Liberty.

There has been talk of a merger between the Voice and these two stations. It has been suggested, for example, by Arthur Goldberg, former American ambassador to the United Nations. But the idea was ruled out by the Presidential Study Commission on International Radio Broadcasting, which published its report in 1973.

The purposes and functions of VOA are quite different from those of RFE and RL. There is no conflict between them. The VOA is recognized as the official radio voice of the United States Government. Like all other USIA activities, it gives preponderant emphasis to American developments. VOA programming contains relatively little information about internal developments in its audience countries.

RFE and RL programming . . . gives citizens of the communist countries information on conditions, attitudes, and trends within their own countries and on international developments as they relate to the special interests of the listeners . . .

It would be neither proper nor consistent with its basic mission as the official United States Government Station for VOA to concentrate on this type of programming.[5]

Certainly the staff of neither organization would have welcomed a merger.

Not only are the functions of the VOA and of RFE and RL quite different, their respective histories are too. The Voice was the product of the world war. Radio Free Europe and Radio Liberty are what former Senator Fulbright, speaking in the Senate on 17 February 1972, called 'relics of the Cold War'.

RFE was set up in December 1949 as a private, non-profit organization incorporated under the laws of the State of New York. Its first broadcast was made on the Fourth of July, 1950, from a small ($7\frac{1}{2}$ kilowatt) mobile transmitter near Mannheim. Regular broadcasting services to its target countries went into operation between May 1951 and May 1952.

'Radio Liberation' was established in 1951 as a similar corporation under the laws of the State of Delaware, but broadcasts did not begin until a few days before Stalin's death in March 1953. The name 'Radio Liberty' was adopted in December 1963.

Both stations broadcast from studios in Munich, RFE using transmitters in Germany and Portugal for its programmes in Polish, Czech and Slovak, Romanian, Hungarian and Bulgarian; RL from transmitters in Germany, Spain and Taiwan for its programmes in Russian (over half the output) and seventeen other languages spoken in the Soviet Union. Plans are afoot to introduce programmes in the three Baltic languages—Lithuanian, Latvian and Estonian. Other functions include monitoring communist broadcasts and operating a large Research and Analysis Department.

RFE claims that, in early 1974, 60 per cent of the population in Romania were listening to their broadcasts, 57 per cent in Poland, 55 per cent in Hungary, 43 per cent in Bulgaria and 39 per cent in Czechoslovakia—after a peak of 65 per cent in the aftermath of the 1968 invasion. Of these listeners, two-thirds tune in regularly, which in RFE terms means twice a week or more. RL estimates 40 million listeners throughout the Soviet Union—a fifth of the population.

The broadcasting staff of both stations is overwhelmingly émigré, although these exile broadcasters account for only a quarter of the total RFE personnel (an average of 1,273 in 1974). But the fact that the stations are fundamentally American propaganda organs has never been in doubt. Guidance from New York, though given now less frequently than in the past, is the basis of all policy. As the Presidential Study Commission says:

> From their inception, the moving force behind Radio Liberty and Radio Free Europe broadcasts has been American. Both stations were privately incorporated in the United States largely at the instigation of the United States Government. Basic broadcasting and operational policies have always been established by Americans occupying senior management positions, although former citizens from Eastern Europe (many of them today naturalized Americans) as well as citizens of a number of other European countries play important roles in the two stations. All direct financing of the stations has been American.[6]

Not only 'direct' financing, but also covert financing. For twenty years the CIA channelled undercover funds to the two stations, deceiving not only the audiences but also the American Congress. The cover, however, grew progressively thinner, and now the Presidential Commission has brought what it calls 'the episode of covert financing' to an end. While hoping for assistance from western European countries in financing the stations, the report recommended that the President appropriate the first half of the capital needed to run them and that private citizens and the business community match that grant over a three-year period. In fact, the US government has been landed with the entire $50 million annual bill.

The body that administers both RFE and RL, and which was set up on the Commission's recommendation, is called the Board for International Broadcasting. The Board represents the stations before the Congress, one of its tasks being to guarantee regular and sufficient funds. The possibilities of fund-raising in western Europe are only at the investigation stage; so too is a merger of the two stations at an administrative level.

The CIA connection was symptomatic of the Cold War mood. It is not, however, the most important issue in the almost continuous debate as to whether RFE and RL should continue to exist. The key questions are the effects of the broadcasts on the listeners and on the communist governments. In other words, do they incite the people to revolt, and do they damage détente?

The first thing to be said about incitement is that the crude and insensitive propaganda that led to accusations of stirring up the 1956 revolt is a thing of the past. Despite the lack of documentary evidence that there was any direct call to take to the streets, even RFE officials now admit that the total effect of the broadcasts was such that an excited and frightened audience might have been expected to over-react. For example, talk of a 'UN delegation' was taken by many Hungarians to mean that the Korean formula for American intervention would be repeated. RFE was, in fact, guilty of doing just what John Foster Dulles hoped to avoid when he said in 1950: 'We do not want to do to the captive peoples [of eastern Europe] what the Soviet Union did to the Polish patriots in Warsaw' —in other words, deceive them over the imminence of 'liberation'. The *Boston Herald* said after the uprising: 'This is the equivalent to the legendary boxer's manager who savagely yelled from the ringside: "Fight him, Butch. He can't hurt us".'

In contrast, during a lull in the fighting, Budapest Radio put out a statement praising the moderation of the BBC:

We express our appreciation of the London radio station, the BBC, for the objective information given to the world about our people's struggle. We were particularly pleased to note that there was no incitement to extremism, and that the tone of the broadcasts expressed solidarity in our joy over victories, and in our sorrow for our dead.

Hungarians on both sides saw outside incitement as the main threat to their cause.

Since 1956, there has been in Munich a deliberate retreat from the hard-line position, although present-day guidelines are a model of double talk and disingenuousness, both about tactics and the nature of propaganda.* A Hungarian newspaper acknowledged the softer approach, while at the same time raising the question of whether the change simply amounts to deception under another name:

Today Radio Free Europe no longer openly incites its listeners against the Soviet Union and the socialist countries, but tries to

* see Appendix C

remain 'objective' and 'unbiassed', and to broadcast the facts impartially. But it is a fraud since these 'objective statements' are usually taken out of context, and cause and effect are not analysed. An uninformed person inevitably believes that what he hears is true.[7]

But what *is* true in the first place? For a communist, a great deal of the facts and interpretations selected by RFE and RL are 'untrue', or at least not the whole truth, while the same facts and interpretations to an anti-communist are by definition 'true'. What is clear is that RFE and RL are anti-communist. Fighting communism is their raison d'être.

It is this rationale which gives the stations an activist, subversive function which other propaganda radios do not share, or at least share only in part. Programmes from Munich are deliberately provocative to the communist governments. They make a habit of broadcasting émigré petitions and extracts from banned books. They take more literally than other stations the 'right to know'. Radio Liberty says of its output:

> Readings from and discussions of [samizdat] documents account for approximately 25 per cent of RL's Russian feature programming and still larger percentages of the feature programming in other languages. RL helps the Soviet people surmount the all-pervading censorship system by broadcasting and backgrounding the contents of writings by novelists like Solzhenitsyn and Pasternak, and scientists like Sakharov and Medvedev; by airing the views of various nationalities within the Soviet Union such as the Ukrainians, Crimean Tatars and Lithuanians; and by broadcasting the appeals of Soviet citizens struggling for religious freedom.

RFE and RL also attempt, unlike other stations, to provide an alternative 'Home Service'. In this they largely succeed. Poles call their programme 'Warsaw Four' (the other three channels carry domestic programmes) or 'Warsaw West'. Other countries have their popular equivalents. This role is intended to undermine the state monopoly over the media in the target countries.

The problem is not whether such a monopoly is right or wrong, but whether another country has any right to break it. The main defence of the outside propagandists is that the people inside want an alternative source of information and opinion. The Presidential Commission Report quotes Alexander Solzhenitsyn's Nobel Prize lecture ('which the peoples of Eastern Europe could hear only when it was transmitted on the airwaves of RFE and RL') in support of this contention:

We are threatened by destruction in the fact that the physically compressed, strained world is not allowed to blend spiritually; the molecules of knowledge and sympathy are not allowed to jump over from one half to the other. This presents a rampant danger: *the suppression of information* between the parts of the planet . . . A muffled zone is, as it were, populated not by inhabitants of the earth, but by an expeditionary corps from Mars; the people know nothing intelligent about the rest of the Earth and are prepared to go and trample it down in the holy conviction that they come as 'liberators'.

Solzhenitsyn and other Russian dissidents have also given specific testimonials as to the value of the Munich broadcasts.

On the other hand, not all dissidents see the support given by RFE and RL to their cause as an unmixed blessing. Many are communist reformers. Support from right-wingers in Munich discredits them with the communist authorities. It also prevents the reformers from building up a mass base—their efforts are all too easily shown to be 'anti-Soviet'. In a very general way, too, it can be argued that the activities of RFE and RL make all reformers less energetic. Their work is being done for them. Besides, as Fulbright says, if China can get by without an American-sponsored alternative Home Service, why cannot Russia and the rest of eastern Europe?

Another claim made to justify RFE and RL is that they are often first with the news, and sometimes the only source, when items are suppressed or delayed in the target countries. *The Right to Know* cites a number of such instances, but almost all concern cases where other western stations did carry the news in question. In particular, it was quite false to assert that Solzhenitsyn's lecture was 'only' heard on the Munich programmes: Solzhenitsyn made special arrangements for the original Russian text to be made available to the BBC. The Munich stations do, however, put out and develop news of purely internal interest, and they can react more quickly and in more detail to some situations than less closely observant stations. Fifty-seven per cent of Poles questioned by RFE, for example, said they first heard of the Gdansk riots through RFE, which picked up the news by tuning into the local radio station. This news was not put out in full detail on the Polish national channels.

But the case for an alternative Home Service sponsored from outside, as opposed to the sort of broad informational services provided by the main national stations in the west, remains open to question. One suggestion was put forward by Robert Kaiser, who follows the debate as a Moscow correspondent of the *International Herald Tribune*:

The benefits of shortwave broadcasts to the Communist countries can be preserved without maintaining Radio Liberty and Radio Free Europe in their traditional form. Indeed, a fundamental re-organization of the stations, giving them new names, new personnel and new outlooks, could increase their audiences. Their old reputations obviously detract from their appeal now.

Despite the correctness of the final statement, it is hard to see how a new name on the package would change the product fundamentally. What is needed is for the stations to be run down in return for greater access to communist countries in other ways: more visits, a wider distribution of western newspapers, books, films, and, above all, more freedom for the people in the east to travel, and even live, outside their present over-protective motherlands. During the brief Dubcek period in Czechoslovakia, when it seemed that 'socialism with a human face' might have come to stay, serious consideration was given to closing down RFE's Czechoslovak Service.

Meanwhile, the stations are seen by western negotiators as too important to be devalued by promises that they will be discarded at some future date. At the Geneva Conference on European Security, what the Russians see as a network of 'radio saboteurs' and spies in Munich is a sensitive issue. West Germany, the host country, is under constant pressure to chase RFE and RL off its soil. Jamming is still directed at these two stations, though it stopped against other western stations just before the Conference opened. To cut off funds, as Fulbright had advocated, would be in diplomatic terms what the London *Times* called a 'gratuitous act of appeasement'. If the Russians want the broadcasts stopped as badly as they appear to do, say the western negotiators, then a high price must be exacted in return.

The Presidential Commission even asserted, rather ominously, that cutting off the stations carries a financial price above and beyond the liquidation costs:

The cost of the radios cannot be considered separately from our nation's total cost of working for peace and deterring aggression. Over a long period of years, this contribution can obviate military expenditures many times greater than the broadcasting costs. Contrariwise, elimination of the radios could lead over time to increased military costs.[8]

On the other hand, it is perfectly possible to foresee that ending the stations would reduce American costs if, by contributing to détente, a more genuine co-existence grew up, leading to mutual reduction in armed forces and disarmament.

In any event, RFE and RL, although they play a unique role, are by no means the only weapons in the American propaganda arsenal. There are not only the VOA and RIAS, but also other radio stations—in particular the Armed Forces Network, which dates back to 1943. (Like RFE, its birthday is also on the Fourth of July.) Of the American Forces Radio and Television Service, Fulbright wrote that 'the potential danger of its misuse is more than a little disturbing'.[9] And he described AFRTS as the 'world's largest television and radio network under single control'. It attracts a considerable local audience outside the US forces and their families, particularly in Asia. In addition, there are a few small-scale commercial radio stations which broadcast internationally—WRUL from New York, for example. But more important than any single element is the very immensity of what the Russians have called America's 'electronic imperialism' and what other critics, like Herbert I. Schiller, have called 'communications diplomacy'.

Direct radio propaganda is the crudest and most obvious part of America's communications empire. The iceberg itself consists of television shows, Hollywood films, satellites, wire services (which are dominated by American news), advertising, and investments in foreign radio and TV stations. As Schiller says, electronics and economics are together the equivalent of the 'blood and iron' of the 'primitive empire-builders'.

Marshall MacLuhan has written:

Propaganda does not consist in the conveying of messages by press or other media, but consists in the action of the total culture (language, food, ads, entertainment, etc.) upon its participants. The idea that propaganda consists of packaged concepts peddled to unsuspecting citizens is no longer tenable.[10]

Most of the American impact derives indirectly from the sheer pervasiveness of things American. Sixty per cent of Canadians are in range of US television. Countries at the other end of the world find that American programmes and products affect every part of their lives. American infiltration of other national communications systems is on such a huge scale that it is the subject of a projected study at Sussex University by a large international team of academics, and already a great deal of investigative work has been done in American universities. But we are principally concerned here with overt, direct propaganda. It is not separate from all the other 'actions of the total culture', but it is more easily identifiable as propaganda. And it does have a particular target: socialism in all its forms. The explosive force in the warhead is the Good Life as lived in the United States. The battlefield is foreign public opinion.

c

In 1964, the Committee on Foreign Affairs stressed that 'the recent increase in influence of the masses of the people over governments . . . has created a new dimension for foreign policy operation'.[11] And a 1966 government report declared that 'telecommunications has progressed from being an essential support to our international activities to being also an instrument of foreign policy'. The days are over when Dean Acheson could pour scorn on foreign reaction to the US and the tendency of the American 'to stare like Narcissus at his image in the pool of what he believes to be world opinion'.[12] Or, as J. F. Dulles once said when refusing to accept the USIA as an integral part of the State Department: 'If I so much as took into account what people in other countries are thinking or feeling, I would be derelict in my duty.'

Dulles later changed his mind. Today, Americans are acutely sensitive of their image in the world. Vietnam, racial riots, Watergate and other national traumas have hurt that image in ways which no propaganda can put right. Nevertheless, both officials and people agree that some attempt to present another, better side of America is desirable. While it has become more and more apparent that the American way of life has an enormous influence on the world, whether Americans like it or not, and regardless of how consciously they are spreading the message, it is also apparent that this influence is uncontrollable by government.

So, despite MacLuhan, 'packaged concepts' are regarded in US government circles as the basis of direct American radio propaganda, even if they are not what the entire propaganda machine 'consists of'. It is, however, the contrast between the subtle pervasiveness of American advertising, entertainment programmes and all the rest, and the transparent ideological insistence of the VOA especially, that makes the official voice so crude. In particular, the VOA sounds old-fashioned. The reporters have deep, slow, serious voices. The pace is measured, responsible. Debates are conducted in the utmost earnestness. Rebellious youth is given its controlled, allotted say—Schiller accuses the VOA of 'tokenism' in this respect.

In his spell as Director of the VOA in the late sixties, John Chancellor tried to give the Voice a more swinging image. But there is no way, it seems, that an official voice can sound less than official, no way that the crudeness of the ideological message can be disguised. The further American radio gets away from an official role, the livelier its sounds. RFE and RL are already lighter in tone; the forces network begins to sound like the domestic commercial channels, indeed it takes a great deal of their output. It would be wrong for the VOA to copy the abbreviated news-and-jingle format. On the other hand, its very opposite sounds too evidently un-American and therefore suspect.

But adapting the sound of the Voice is not the real answer. The problem is more fundamental. Should the VOA project America positively, present the good sides which the other media neglect? Or should it tell all? Different directors stress each in turn. The result has often been something in the middle which is, and sounds, a compromise. Ronald I. Rubin wrote the following about the USIA in general, but it applies to the Voice in particular:

> The USIA has failed to determine conclusively whether its purpose is to serve as an information—or propaganda—disseminating organization, or both of these simultaneously . . . The American information program has oscillated between a strident preoccupation with Communism, on one hand, and the casual dissemination of material about American life, on the other.[13]

There are some conservatives in America who deplore what they see as the soft-sell of the Voice, accusing it of doing too much 'balancing', reporting, for example, lurid details of race riots to Russian citizens who had much better be left in ignorance. Liberal opinion agrees with Galbraith's strictures on the Voice's parent organization:

> The Washington USIA is horrible. Day after day it belches out dreary and boring attacks on the USSR and China in the most repulsive and stinking prose. Nothing could do more to promote neutralism, or anyhow total inattention.[14]

Yet this too is exaggerated. The Voice may be, as Morgenstern said, 'Olympian' and 'inhuman'. Today, especially since it is reflecting a new emphasis on détente, it is seldom blatantly one-sided and propagandistic.

Under Frank Shakespeare, a more insistent hard line was evident in all parts of the USIA. Shakespeare was indeed once criticized by Secretary of State Rogers for embarking on an unauthorized campaign to attack the role of the Soviet Union in the Middle East. But on the whole, at the VOA today, the journalists themselves ensure that a continued commitment to anti-communism nevertheless avoids the obvious crusading approach of the fifties and sixties. At present, if only temporarily, information has the upper hand.

The trouble is that when this happens the Voice tries too hard to be fair. It spells out all the details of what the Secretary of Defense said *and* the conflicting views of American editorialists *and* worldwide reactions. The message is too obviously: 'see how open and free is the debate on this channel'. The soft line is given the hard sell. The ideology of freedom is audible beneath *all* reporting and comment. As a result, whether information or propaganda is in the ascendant, the overall effect still sounds similar to the constant optimism and Soviet-achievements-are-best of Moscow Radio.

We come back again to the ambivalent attitude in America to 'propaganda' and 'professional persuaders'. The ethic of free enterprise is such that many Americans, Congressmen very much included, prefer the operation of market forces, whether through multinational companies, sales campaigns or any other way, to state intervention in the selling of America. If propaganda can be sold as 'education', that is all right. If there is a defence aspect (the US Department of Defense has a world network of thirty-eight TV and over two hundred radio transmitters[15]), again there are extenuating circumstances. But an official government voice sounds to them too like communism. Indeed, in a literal sense, they are right.

4 The BBC

The BBC's objectivity may or may not be a carefully cultivated myth. What is not a myth is its reputation for telling the truth. People all over the world believe what the BBC says. They use it to check up on news they have heard from other sources.

When I was in Bucharest just after the invasion of Czechoslovakia, everyone was frightened that the Russians were about to turn south into Romania. Romanians all over the country were listening avidly to Radio Free Europe. But everyone told me that if the worst happened they would switch quickly to the BBC—just to make sure. A former Managing Director of the BBC External Services, Oliver Whitley, declared in *The Times*: 'It has been said in Saigon that if the BBC were to announce the death of the Prime Minister of South Vietnam, and he were to appear next day in the streets of Saigon, no one would recognize him.' One of the thousand letters received weekly by the Bengali Service in the wake of the Indo-Pakistani war was from a Dacca student whose radio was the focal point of village life: 'Uneducated old people approach me in the streets and ask, "What did the BBC say?"'

It is the experience of BBC staff travelling round the world that the reputation for credibility is as dangerous as it is flattering. When a BBC news item specifies: 'Agence France Presse reports that . . .', many listeners will think: 'the BBC said that . . .'. People ask when their local situation is confused or frightening: 'What does the BBC think will happen?'

Such listeners may fairly be said to represent the less sophisticated part of the regular audience of 60 million. The British are far from having a monopoly of the truth. Their sources are no different from those of any other news-gathering organization. Other listeners are more inclined to suspect 'perfidious Albion' of deep duplicity in fostering the idea that the BBC tells the truth. But the fact remains, and it is well documented in places far removed from Bush House, the London headquarters of the External Services.

This reputation is a uniquely British product. As Chile exports copper, and Australia wool, so Britain exports honest information. The decline in Britain's political and economic strength does not affect the quality of the product; in fact it adds the extra guarantee of disinterestedness. Whether the reputation is justified, not just as far as news bulletins are concerned, but also in current affairs programmes and commentaries, is a question to which we shall return. Meanwhile, how did it start?

It would be an exaggeration to trace its origin back to the pre-war Empire Service. Started in December 1932, the Empire Service was the brainchild of Sir John Reith, who fostered it with the same stern but scrupulous attention that he applied to the domestic services, with the aim of bringing the scattered dominions closer to the mother country and of seeing that British expatriates were not deprived of the benefits derived from listening in to the Home Service. But the imperialist function, the upper-class bias and tone of the Empire Service narrowed down its appeal to those who shared that same patriotic confidence in Britain's role. It was an honest reflection of a point of view honestly held, but limited nonetheless.

The government of the day kept aloof from the Empire Service, firstly in order to avoid having to pay the bills and secondly because it felt that 'the suitability of the broadcasting medium for the purposes of controversy on subjects not primarily matters of purely domestic concern is open to question'. The Foreign Office had a 'gentlemen's agreement' with the BBC that there would not be too much 'controversy'. To start with, all programmes were lifted from the thoroughly non-controversial domestic services.

In June 1937, Sir Walter Citrine, the leading trades union figure, wrote that 'the BBC has a mission to tell the world what this country stands for', voicing an opinion that was becoming more and more widely accepted, that the Empire Service should be developing away from homely chats about sentimental ties to a positive attempt to project the national and international policies of Britain. Felix Greene, the BBC's representative in New York, was another of those critical of the Service's patronizing and remote attitudes. On the other hand, even while the world was evidently moving closer to war, the editorial policy remained firmly committed to the principle of impartiality. Reith's concern for accuracy and truth within the framework of independence from government ensured that, as he wrote, 'the BBC would be trusted where the government might not be'.

But the real testing period began with the creation of foreign-language services in 1938. The Arabic, Spanish and Portuguese (for Latin America), and then the French, German and Italian Services were set up as counters to foreign propaganda. It was at this point that the decision had to be made whether to continue the policy, so easily defensible in times of world peace and harmony, of low-key emphasis on facts both pleasant and unpleasant.

The European Services got off to a poor propaganda start. Their first function was to translate and broadcast Chamberlain's post-Munich speech in which he declared: 'How horrible, fantastic, incredible it is that we should be digging trenches and trying on gas-masks here because of a quarrel in a far-away country of whom we know nothing.' The German translator, Robert Lucas, could find no typist and copied down his version in longhand which the announcer, an artist named Goetz who had never been in a studio before, was hardly able to read. He had to stop at the end of one page and wait several minutes before the next was ready.

Gradually, the BBC's Empire and European Services began to learn the techniques of international radio. Units were set up to study the target audiences, instead of disseminating programmes conceived with a British audience in mind to anyone 'abroad' who cared to tune in. Then came war. The pressure was on for the BBC, as the guardian of all British white propaganda, to prove its effectiveness or lay itself open to takeover from harder-line government or armed forces propagandists. As the editor of the *New Statesman*, Kingsley Martin, wrote of the BBC staff:

> In the long run their assurance, their comparative scrupulousness and their old-school-tie methods have undoubtedly some long-run advantages. But in this war there may be no long run.[1]

There now began six years of wrangling, crises of confidence, and persistent struggle between the Political Warfare Executive, the Ministry of Information, the Foreign Office, and the BBC's many services and sections, out of which eventually emerged an unequalled reputation for truth-telling, honesty and reliability. As the American academic, Dr Burton Paulu, wrote years later:

> The BBC probably gained more prestige from its victory in this context than has any other broadcasting organization from any single project in which it ever engaged.[2]

But this reputation was by no means a foregone conclusion. Bruce Lockhart, Chairman of the Political Warfare Executive, declared in his memoirs:

> Whitehall's ignorance of the techniques and possibilities of propaganda and, more particularly, of broadcasting was unnecessarily prolonged . . . On the other hand the initial attitude of the propagandists was ostrich-like.[3]

Harold Graves criticized the early attempts to sway American opinion—the *Britain Speaks* slot was inaugurated on 28 May 1940 and a special transmission to the United States came on the air from 7 July—as giving the impression of 'unpreparedness and complacency'.[4]

The story of how the BBC evolved to gain its wartime reputation is long, detailed and complex. It has been related authoritatively in the third volume of Asa Briggs's history of the BBC, and picked over in numerous memoirs and articles. All the more honest accounts stress how fragile was the foundation on which the reputation is based. Once it had become history, only then did it become secure.

That the BBC's reputation has lasted so long is due first of all to the Allied military victory, no less surely than it was the defeat of the Nazis which destroyed the effectiveness of their propaganda. The propaganda war in Europe was itself evenly fought. Even the famous V campaign—in which the V symbol for *Victoire* and *Vrijheid*, dreamt up by the BBC's Belgian Programme Organizer, Victor de Laveleye, was dunned into the enemy through slogans, signature tunes and the famous Churchillian gesture—was only a qualified success. The Germans appropriated it, proclaiming the V as their own victory symbol, and so weakened its impact that the BBC had to scale down plans to exploit it all over Europe.

Nor was the BBC's propaganda sufficient in itself to resist defeat or ensure victory, any more than the German propaganda was. Even the brilliant BBC French Service was dangerously close to losing its audience in the early part of 1944, and was saved only by the invasion of Normandy and the establishment of the Second Front.[5] Besides, European resistance, the promotion and encouragement of which was the BBC's special task, was itself only a small contribution towards Allied victory: the Russian war, as Briggs puts it, 'forces the V campaign into the margins of history'.

The BBC's Far East broadcasting policy was characterized by confusion and procrastination. The Japanese Service was a mixture of direct broadcasting and relays from the United States and India, only picking up a significant number of listeners in the last part of the war. Broadcasting to India had not been an unqualified success, mainly owing to the nationalist feelings in India against Britain's imperial role. As for programmes to the United States, reporting of a standard as high as that of Ed Murrow, plus, of course, the entry of the US into the war, made the BBC's message virtually redundant. Critics in America complained of the BBC's highbrow, abstract tone, its 'non-energizing' references to the past (sea power, Empire) and its narrow concern to prove the Nazis guilty under international law.[6] There was no broadcasting to the Soviet Union for fear of upsetting the delicate relations between Britain and her essential but difficult ally.

So one comes back in the end to the European Services. They were the key element in British radio propaganda, and its success in overcoming the early strains during the period of Nazi victories and in exploiting the final Nazi defeat was due ultimately to three factors: strict adherence to certain principles, the quality and motivation of the staff, and the large scale of the European operation.

Sir Hugh Greene, who organized the wartime programmes to Germany and later became Director-General, said that the basic principle on which the German Service operated was:

> To tell the truth within the limits of the information at our disposal and to tell it consistently and frankly. This involved a determination never to play down a disaster . . . Then our audience in Germany and in the German forces, having heard us talking frankly about our defeats, would believe us when we talked about our victories, and the will to resist in a hopeless situation would, one hoped, be effectively undermined.[7]

It is doubtful whether the broadcasts did weaken the German will to resist, but the approach at least commanded respect. The BBC *was* believed when it began to talk about Allied victories. Its reputation was not based on what its programmes did but on the acceptance that what they said was true.

Sticking to this principle meant that the BBC had to reflect national policies which, from a propagandist's point of view, were harmful: insistence on 'unconditional surrender', for example. Had the BBC either been part of a propaganda 'master plan', or willing to select its material opportunistically according to its propaganda value, it would never have publicized such obviously harmful material as Vansittart's *Black Record*, detailing German heinousness throughout the ages, and so identifying Nazi crimes with German culture.

The German Service was the only one not to use as broadcasters nationals of the target country. This was to avoid the service being labelled as the voice of traitors. It turned out to be the nursery of considerable broadcasting and administrative talent. In the other services, however, there was a great deal more scope for listeners to identify with the broadcasters, either as personalities or, particularly where the microphone was made available to governments in exile, as future political leaders, an aspect of broadcasting which I look into more fully in the chapter on Broadcasters. The specific function of combining the voice of London with those of foreign governments gave British propaganda an extra degree of prestige, but at the same time it was a source of constant friction. The governments who were given airtime wanted more. Those who were not were jealous and resentful.

At the outbreak of war, the BBC was broadcasting in more languages (thirty-nine) than any of the other twenty-six countries with international services. Germany was putting out programmes in thirty-six languages, the Soviet Union in twenty-two and the United States in twenty-one. By the spring of 1945, the Nazi international service boasted fifty-two language sections, compared with the BBC's forty-five. Both these totals resulted from a constant buildup throughout the war. But in the first days of peace, when the *Propagandaministerium* and Zeesen were no more, the BBC was transmitting more hours of international programme time each week (over 500) than any other two states combined. It was not until six years later that the BBC lost its position at the head of the league, later sinking to the fifth place it occupies today.

During the war, the BBC provided a virtually complete coverage of Europe. Although some of the smaller sections were on the air only a few minutes a day, there was almost no one who, circumstances permitting, could not listen in to London. Since then, the ideal of comprehensive coverage has been deemed too expensive. For example, the Dutch and Scandinavian (except Finnish) sections were axed, the Portuguese section disappeared between 1958 and 1963, and the Italian section was drastically reduced.

Today, the BBC External Services broadcast in English and in thirty-nine other languages. Some of the excised sections have, in effect, been replaced by quite different ones: notably in African and Asian languages. But, reflecting wartime priorities rather than present-day reality, there are still extensive German and French Services. The fact that the Arabic Service is the largest single vernacular service is more clearly related to the political importance of the target area. (The BBC claims that seventy-seven per cent of the adult population of Abu Dhabi are regular listeners—possibly their most responsive target audience.)

The argument for broadcasting at all in 'neutral' languages like French and Italian is a double one: in the first place, eliminating them would make the BBC a broadcaster only to hostile and sensitive areas, which would cut the ground from under the fundamental principle that the BBC is a worldwide service, available indiscriminately to everyone, rather than a propaganda operation to further specific political aims. Secondly, in May and June 1968, Frenchmen suddenly became aware again of 'la BBC'. There is evidence of massive listening in those troubled days when the government-controlled services of the ORTF were even more suspect than usual. And no-one can claim that the Italian political system is so stable that, one day, wartime listening habits may not be revived. Even so, the scale of the French and German Services is disproportionate to the Italian. What is needed, and appears likely, is a multilingual western European service, both to reflect the political realities and to amalgamate the unnecessarily disparate units which exist at present.

The Soviet and eastern European audiences are a high post-war priority of the BBC, but, in terms of cost, broadcasting to them is a small item compared with the services to more distant audiences which, apart from the ordinary running expenses, demand costly relay systems such as those in Ascension Island and Cyprus. Political troubles plagued the siting of the Middle East relay which moved from Somalia to Perim in the Bab-el-Mandeb strait, and from there to Ma'alla in Aden before settling finally on the island of Masirah off the coast of Muscat. A joint station with Deutsche Welle on Antigua, to serve Central America, the Caribbean and the United States, is hanging fire for lack of money, and the BBC is still searching for a politically and geographically suitable site for a new relay station for Asia after the Malaysian government ended its role as host of the Tebrau station. But rather than claim that any one target audience is more important than another, the BBC believes that comprehensive coverage of the entire globe is the top priority. The five minutes per day in Maltese are as important in relation to consumption of BBC resources as the round-the-clock World Service in English.

Most relay stations and overseas transmitters are negotiated and owned by the Diplomatic Wireless Service. This is one of the three ways in which indirect control is exercised over the BBC by government. The Foreign and Colonial Office also has the last say in what languages are used for programmes and for how long they are broadcast to each audience ('prescription'). And the Treasury, through an FCO grant-in-aid, controls the budget of the External Service.

This compromise, whereby the broadest financial and political control is exercised by government, and editorial control is exercised by the BBC, is the result of the compromises of the pre-war and wartime days of the BBC overseas programmes. It works now, as then, on the basis of a 'gentlemen's agreement'. The BBC accepts that it is its duty to find out the government's policy towards the various countries of the broadcasters' target areas. The Foreign Office has a duty to inform the BBC of that policy.

In practice, the Foreign Office interferes very little beyond ensuring that its views are known at the relevant level of the BBC. On the whole, what the BBC does with that knowledge is its own affair. But the FCO checks, through transcripts, that there is no continuous conspiracy afoot to oppose the government line. It accepts that its line may not necessarily be the only viewpoint put forward in the programmes, but it would not stand for alternative views to be the only ones aired.

Although the job of Liaison Officer at the FCO is something of a sinecure, there have been minor brushes with the BBC and at least one occasion when the delicate relationship was put to the test.

This relationship, as it existed in wartime, was described by the Controller of the European Services, Eric Newsome, in a memo of June 1940:

> The principle has been accepted in the highest quarters that the European Service shall act as an entity, as an army attacking clearly defined objects, and using a strategy laid down broadly by the Commanding Officer, and not as a series of guerrilla bands or group of partisans, with no cohesion and entirely self-ordained plans and aims.

But, comments Professor Briggs, 'such arguments were always resisted within Bush House, a house with many mansions, not to speak of the corridors'.[8] And once the war was over, the importance of the editorial function, actually preparing and broadcasting the programmes, grew steadily greater than the remote and retroactive control function. Contact between BBC service heads and chiefs of the regional desks at the FCO has been close or distant largely depending on the personal relations of the opposite numbers, but complaints of interference in the BBC's affairs are rare. Periodically, the Foreign Office likes to give tangible proof of its prescription powers, or display its majesty by despatching a junior official to tell off a senior BBC mogul. This game is played in reverse by the BBC. But there was one critical moment in the relationship between the two hierarchies as a whole—Suez.

In late October 1956, the Conservative government sent in British troops as part of an Anglo-French-Israeli force to prevent Colonel Nasser from nationalizing the Suez Canal. This last attempt at British gunboat diplomacy was opposed bitterly by non-Conservatives. The BBC, including its External Services, felt bound to reflect that opposition in proportion to its strength in the country.

The government resented the effect this had on international opinion
in general and on the enemy in particular. It sent in Duncan Wilson
as liaison officer *in situ*, but he, an anti-Suez rebel, lasted only a few
days. There then arrived a straight-laced official, Langham Tichener,
to lay down the FO line.

In Bush House, J. B. Clark, the Director of External Broadcasting,
whose experience of fighting battles with government dated back to
the Empire Service, allocated Tichener a small, undistinguished
office, without a carpet, shared by the Bush House defence correspondent, Rear-Admiral Nichol. While direct confrontation was
avoided, Tichener was in effect frozen out. The government's only
other option was to take over the BBC's External Services altogether, which was impractical. But the end of the fighting intervened,
and the crisis died down.

In a sense, by reaching the threshold of open confrontation, and
pulling back, the air was now cleared of mutual paranoia. Both sides
had tested how far they could go. Compromise was seen to be a work-
able formula, not just a holding operation until something better
could be dreamed up. On the other hand, the FO, essentially the
loser, was determined to exact its revenge, if only in a number of
small but humiliating ways. The Suez crisis explains why the
government-controlled Central Office of Information was awarded
the right to export television programmes to foreign countries. The
BBC would dearly like to capture this lucrative and influential
business. It explains, in part, the axing of the Albanian Service in
1968, when cuts in government expenditure gave critics of Bush
House a case for demanding at least a token cut in the External
Services.

Memories of Suez are still being recalled, by both critics and supporters of the BBC, in a debate over potentially massive cuts which
would reduce the BBC's annual budget of around £15 million by
about ten per cent. This would involve the closing down of between
a quarter and a third of programme output.

Yet, when an important editorial decision has to be taken, even in
a politically sensitive situation where the Foreign Office might be expected to counsel caution, the BBC, after Suez, has felt strong
enough to go it alone. A good illustration is what happened in April
1967 when the Colonels conducted their coup in Greece. The country
remained a NATO member, and therefore 'friendly', but the coup
had clearly introduced dictatorship. The broadcasters had to decide
on their reaction quicker than government. They made up their mind
to criticize the Colonels. The effect on the audience was instantaneous.
The numbers listening to the BBC rose hugely and rapidly. Had
President Makarios permitted a medium-wave signal to be relayed
from the Cyprus station, which, from the BBC's point of view is

regrettably just outside British sovereign base territory, the impact of London's voice would certainly have been greater.

Within the BBC, disapproval of dictatorship, of left- and right-wing persuasion, is something which is taken for granted. That this is a positive point of view, not an absence of one, is the subject not only of some self-congratulation, but also of some cogent criticism which raises fundamental questions about the political role of the External Services above and beyond whether it is or is not the mouthpiece of government.

The first point is that there is such a thing as a centrist bias. It has been made, for example, by the Indochina Solidarity Conference, which complained in a pamphlet:

> The BBC has no reason to fear intervention [from the Foreign Office] most of the time since it operates within the spectrum of consensus politics as do its ultimate bosses in the FO . . . The rule of the game is self-censorship.[9]

The pamphlet cites as evidence the choice of actively pro-American contributors to present 'objective' evidence about Vietnam, with only sparse reference to opposing views, and a deliberate avoidance of obviously controversial topics such as the CIA involvement with the opium traffic, the torture of communist prisoners, and so on.

While the BBC cannot help being limited, as the pamphlet admits, in the choice of speakers and commentators who are both accessible and literate, when it comes to Vietnam or any other topic, the underlying argument is a persuasive one. If President Thieu is on the right, and the Hanoi government even further on the left, it does not necessarily follow that President Johnson is in the middle and therefore to be given the tacit support of cancelling out all other views on the grounds of extremism. It may be a reasonable reflection of British liberal centrism to aim in general at supporting the middle position, but in particular cases the centrist bias may prove to have given undue emphasis to the status quo, to the currently accepted wisdom of uncommitted, and possibly uninformed and prejudiced opinion, or to self-seeking policies which have the veneer of liberal respectability. The British middle-of-the-road consensus view may always be safe but it is not always either in the real centre or correct.

There is a parallel here with the middle-class assumptions on which the BBC is frequently accused of basing its editorial decisions. Again, it is true that Britain is a society in which the middle class is the ruling class, and the BBC has to reflect that society. It is obliged by its Charter to be the voice of social orthodoxy and to criticize only within the accepted limits of debate. On the other hand, as the author of a bitter article in *Time Out* declared, there is a sameness about the various voices of Bush House which can be attributed only to an identity of views among 'Establishment-OK'd BBC chaps' who watch over and prepare the output.

In this one week [in October 1973], the BBC thought it worthwhile to issue scripts on: 'The Centenary of Landseer', 'Horse Brasses', the 'Stately Homes Boom'; 'Memorial Gala for John Cranko'; reviews of several London art exhibitions; and 'The Cecils of Hatfield House' . . . Rail strikes are met by the British public with 'good humour', bombings with 'calm'; even the Middle East conflict will end 'soon'. Everything has a happy ending.

'Left-wing' staff members with 'disruptive sentiments', the article claims, are cajoled into conforming with the accepted ethos, and even end by accepting it as the truth. They will find themselves, like the others, giving 'full credit to the Prime Minister', missing 'no opportunity to glorify Britain and make the most of every "British achievement" '; they will say that 'militants are "hotheads", revolutionaries are "self-styled" ', and use phrases like 'what the Chile junta is up to' making it sound like a group of 'mischievous children'.[10]

As far as feature programmes are concerned, this makes the BBC External Services no better and no worse than the British Tourist Authority, with its thatched cottages, or Radio 4, with the Archers. The danger is the extent to which these limited social attitudes colour political comment. But, with no system of direct policy guidance, it is difficult to identify causes and effects within Bush House. There is a broad identity of views among producers, editors and controllers, indeed among the entire 1,000 members of programmes staff. But this is not so much a conspiracy as a consequence of the BBC's indeterminate aims and the type of person who applies to join the 'team'. On the whole, the younger and more vigorous staff members protest against the lack of excitement in the output more than against its bias.

A few interested people argue that the World Service Pop Club, Victor Sylvester, the Science and Industry output or the arts programmes, or, with more reason, English by Radio, do more than anything else to attract listeners to Britain and to things British, but the really big guns are the news and current affairs programmes. *Radio Newsreel* (reports from correspondents), *Commentary*, *The World Today* (background and interviews on one topic) and *Twenty-Four Hours* (a recently introduced mixture of interviews and a press review) are the basis of current affairs output.

The *Newsreel* is under the editorial control of the newsroom and is essentially back-up to the bulletins. The other three rely on outside contributors to a very large extent. Generally, a staff commentator or expert is brought in *faute de mieux* (he is also free). The selection of contributors, which determines, as it were, the 'BBC's' interpretation of an event, is nevertheless a somewhat random affair. These contributors may be journalists or academics or what are known in the BBC as 'people', in other words actors in the events discussed.

The Editor's view is: 'Isn't it about time we had X?' or 'Y has had too much exposure.' The producer's concern is to make contact with someone, on occasion anyone. The concept of balance is ideally built into the programme either by talking to a 'moderate' contributor, or by pitting left-wing against right-wing speakers, or, if the worst comes to the worst, building it into the narrator's script. In practice, balance often has to wait for another programme, or simply result from a general feeling among controllers, editors and producers that a particular viewpoint has been given too much or too little emphasis over a period.

If that sounds casual, it is. Any consistent 'line', say about Northern Ireland, is audible if at all only through constant listening. Arguably, there is too little consistency, but any way of interfering with the randomness of the process which, like water finding its own level, always seems in the end to reflect a 'sensible' view, would immediately involve a system of guidelines and directives which would change the entire character of the External Services.

But this does not mean that decisions about which topics are to be treated, and how, are left to chance. The editors are responsible for their programmes to their superiors in the hierarchy. At programme level, however, strong service heads influence particular sections, and single-minded producers can give their own programme an individual flavour. But if they become obsessive, fail to do the 'sensible thing', or 'see both sides of the question', they might find themselves assigned to some less sensitive area or to part of a more numerous group where their individuality is less conspicuous. There was once a post for a controller of output who reviewed the tapes and transcripts of each section in turn. This was felt to be a waste of time and the job disappeared.

In the newsroom, which is a central service independent of programmes, purely journalistic standards of newsworthiness apply and the compilers of bulletins do not have to make many of the awkward decisions about balance which face producers of current affairs programmes. But the news is the basis of the BBC's credibility reputation and the most liable to be criticized, misinterpreted and used in evidence in accusations of bias; and the selection of news does involve political decisions.

RFE and RL also have independent newsrooms. But the order of their bulletin items, and the items which are selected, conform to the particular function of filling the gaps in the audience's knowledge of their own countries, and of broadcasting otherwise unreported misdemeanours, crises and disasters. The BBC, as a national station broadcasting worldwide, is less oriented to the news which directly concern their audiences, and more towards world events and British news. Every section carries the same lead items, and no section can add to or subtract from the items about the particular region or country concerned. Direct relevance to any one audience is deliberately sacrificed to a British-eye-view of the world at large.

The most difficult dilemma facing the External Services' news team, and it affects the programme staff too, is how far the 'British' element should intrude. This is not just a matter of the proportion of news about, say, Northern Ireland, in bulletins for China. It also concerns the treatment and presentation of such news. Logically, there is a conflict between objectivity and the companion function of the BBC, 'projecting Britain'. One aims at information, the other at propaganda. Gerard Mansell, the Managing Director of the External Services, unravels the dilemma by saying that objectivity is a British tradition. 'To the extent that British society has a moral basis, and is fair, the BBC promotes it.' The BBC's Director-General, and former Managing Director of the External Services, Sir Charles Curran, has written:

We explain rather than proselytize . . . We do not seek to over-persuade, but rather to remind our listeners of those elements in the British case which it would be in their own interests to recognize.[11]

Vladimir Osipov, a Soviet journalist, while acknowledging the professionalism and accuracy of BBC world news bulletins and their usefulness to members of his profession throughout the world, sees objectivity not so much as a tradition, but as a purposeful device:

You can make people believe a fact if you express that fact 'without prejudice'. And facts can be selected in such a way that of themselves they will make the hearer reach the desired conclusion.[12]

Osipov detects a subtle formula to BBC news output: 60 per cent contains pro-British facts and 40 per cent anti. Like Curran, he sees the BBC as suggesting to the 'enlightened' that 'four' is the answer to the question as to what 'two plus two equals'. But, says Osipov, the BBC would never say so directly, and this is a mark of hypocrisy, not honesty.

Yet the fact is that the BBC has traditionally been committed to presenting a balanced view, and at the same time the principle of balance is consciously used (however imprecise its application) to sell a political message. The External Services put out information and propaganda at the same time because the very process of selection is part of that message. But, whereas the Voice of America hammers home the principle of free debate in a free country, the BBC merely intimates or implies. You, the audience, are assumed to be a reasonable person who shares that opinion; you are not the object of a conversion attempt by radio.

In news bulletins to communist audiences there is no deviation from this line. Comment and feature programmes tend, however, to be more overtly concerned here with democracy-versus-totalitarianism than in other services. The Russian Service was set up in 1946 in order that Britain should play her full part in the Cold War. Although the anti-communist ethic is now toned down, the BBC does not pretend to see both sides of the 'free flow of information' question. On the other hand, there is no substance in Soviet charges that the BBC is an arm of British Intelligence. If for no other reason, the BBC would never compromise its own independence of government in this way. Besides, since no programmes are prepared according to detailed plans laid down by the upper levels of management, any compulsory Intelligence inserts would be all too conspicuous.

In retrospect, some of the anti-communist polemics look a bit silly. The hundreds of scripts about how many East German workers can afford Wartburg cars ('regrettably few'), or whether creeping capitalism is undermining the strict application of Marxism (implying that because the Russians introduced the profit motive, 'we win'), have a dated sound. So do the opposition attacks, which have nevertheless continued in the same vein since the fifties. In January 1974, the BBC was accused in the *Literaturnaya Gazeta* of 'lacking elementary tact when it's a question of the Soviet Union, whether her present or her past', because the Russian Service had quoted a book about Chekhov which 'establishes the fact that Chekhov was far from a puritan in his relations with women'.

Moscow Radio is even more concerned to 'expose' the BBC's international role. As Geliy Shakhov declared:

The fact is that in recent years there have been quite a few scandals involving BBC correspondents abroad who, forgetting about their fig leaf of impartiality, produced several programmes that outraged the public in the countries where they were stationed. BBC representatives have been asked to leave India and several African countries because of their propaganda stunts . . . There has been particular resentment of broadcasts unceremoniously lecturing people in other countries as to how they should arrange their lives.[13]

Leaving aside the fact that most of the incidents were the result of reports criticizing high-handed abuse of power, and that avoiding outrage is *not* part of a correspondent's job, this criticism does point to a problem which the BBC, like any other global distributor of news and opinion, has to face: the fact that, however inoffensive it considers its own message to be, other people, at least part of the audience, find it actively offensive.

The BBC, like the VOA, is part of a wide network of international communications designed to increase and spread national influence. British 'communications diplomacy' is on a smaller scale than the American; nevertheless, the mixture of Forsyte Saga imperialism, export promotion, and training schemes for foreign technicians and producers, combined with the credibility reputation of the BBC, makes British 'communication diplomacy' by no means negligible.

The six radio stations of the British Forces Broadcasting Service, which put out programmes on military VHF frequencies to the forces and their families from Cologne, Gibraltar, Malta, Cyprus, Singapore and Hong Kong (a Gurkha service only), are small beer compared to the massive American equivalent. Their primary role is to perform the sort of information-and-command function at short notice that the Cyprus station was called upon to do during the 1974 troubles. They also have close links with the BBC domestic and international services, originating only a part of the entertainment programmes in London and locally. The Americans, too, overshadow the small British involvement in satellite communications. But in other ways, the BBC has the edge.

One of these is rebroadcasting. Outside Latin America, where American material dominates the foreign input to the mass of commercial stations, the External Services of the BBC are the most popular source of instant radio programmes. There are daily rebroadcasts of World Service news bulletins, sport and talks programmes in over forty countries, and over 160 daily relays of World News alone. In the United States, a daily selection of programmes is networked to 137 member stations. Taped programmes are mailed regularly to fifty-four countries. And English lessons, both on television and radio, which are produced by the External Services, are screened or heard throughout the world, including China and North Vietnam.

Since the British do not generally listen to foreign radio stations, very few people are aware of all this activity. But it is something that foreign governments have to react to. In some cases it is resisted as unwarranted interference, particularly in totalitarian societies, but also in some ex-colonial countries. Elsewhere, as in Iran, reaction varies from warm welcome to fury. In a few cases the reaction has been not to attack or praise, but to imitate and, as far as West Germany in particular is concerned, to rival.

In many ways, for instance because of the interchange of staff, the Canadian, Australian and New Zealand External Services echo the BBC. There are parallels also in political objectives and radio techniques between the BBC and the Dutch, Swedish, Japanese and some other smaller international services. But the most interesting comparison is that between the BBC and Deutsche Welle.

Since the mid-sixties, the West Germans have broadcast abroad slightly more hours per week than the BBC. Deutsche Welle, the biggest station, enjoys more freedom from government interference than the BBC. It is funded by the Interior Ministry which is largely indifferent to external broadcasting. The only contact between DW and the Foreign Ministry is a daily three-way telephone conversation (it includes a representative from the Deutschlandfunk, whose main function is to broadcast to the DDR), which is on an open line and generally perfunctory. DW is a member of the Association of West German Radio Stations (ARD) which makes sure that it is no Trojan horse of the government. This station has to interpret the 'national interest' itself; in this, it is its own judge and jury. This has led in the past to one or two diplomatic crises, as when DW was accused by Greece of trying to bring down a government with which the FRG had full and friendly relations.

DW operates under some technical handicaps. Audience research is minimal; there are too few transmitters despite a recent sweetener to Malta of £1 million for permission to erect a 600-kilowatt medium-wave relay there for its Arabic Service; and working conditions, because the station grew up piecemeal all over Cologne, are poor. On the other hand, the international respect in which Deutsche Welle is held has never been higher.

The reason is partly West Germany's financial and commercial influence, partly the lack of any imperial axe to grind, which might compromise its 'independence', and partly the audibly disinterested and well-informed quality of its programmes. In addition, no large international service, other than DW, can claim to speak for western Europe as a whole. That is why Gerard Mansell, while declaring that the BBC has 'non-imitable' political traditions and roots which make its voice unique in the world, fears the competition offered by Deutsche Welle more than any other rival.

Deutsche Welle's world role is important, therefore, precisely because it avoids a nationalist interpretation of other countries' affairs, while not ignoring political controversies. The BBC too plays this card, but nevertheless carries the burden as well as the advantages of a long history as the voice of a great imperial power.

But of all international broadcasting services, the BBC most abhors the 'maximum role' of radio propaganda: attempting to change the political course of the target country by stirring up popular resistance. As the leading expert on British wartime propaganda, Richard Crossman, said:

> In peace-time, the task [of psychological warfare] is extremely limited . . . It is limited to the job of building up credibility, studying the enemy, getting the organization set up so that, if the day comes for a more positive propaganda, it can be carried out immediately.[14]

That is what Sir Hugh Greene calls the 'fleet in being'. But the Russians especially have suspected Crossman and the BBC of harbouring more activist ambitions under the cloak of playing a long-term waiting game. They quote a lecture given by the BBC's chief commentator, Maurice Latey, who was once head of the East European Service:

> At present we are pushing at an opening door. The door may close again. In that case, we have our minimum objective. Broadcasting can still keep our foot in the door. It can guarantee that the Stalinist model of a completely isolated communist world can never again be attempted with any hope of success; and that is a great service to the cause of peace.[15]

Talk of feet in the door smacks of interference to the Russians, as does Latey's maximum objective of 'remaking Europe'. But in general, the BBC sees such objectives as very long-term indeed. Obviously, by broadcasting at all, some effect is hoped for. Merely informing people of what their censors do not want them to hear is a political act which is likely to influence at least a few individuals, if not an entire population.

Although the British, and hence the BBC, do not encourage social equality, particularly in the context of Marxism, and hold up liberal, Parliamentary democracy-cum-meritocracy as a model for others to copy, the lengths to which they are prepared to go to persuade others of these views is limited. Ultimately, the BBC says: 'This is what we think. Take it or leave it.' Over the years, that in itself can become an effective and influential message.

PART TWO

5 The Third World

On the face of it, the Third World should have become the principle target of international radio propaganda. The Third World is politically volatile, contains the majority of the world's population, is the object of economic imperialism which needs to be presented in other terms, and only recently became open to mass communication. But in fact the major international radio organizations, east and west, have been slow to afford the Third World the priority it apparently deserves or to adapt their techniques to attract the massive potential audiences.

There is no need to spell out how important politically the Third World has become since the general acceptance that colonialism is an evil word—even if it is still not universally agreed to be an evil practice. Neo-colonialism, economic imperialism, communization, non-alignment, Third-World solidarity, are all shorthand terms to describe the means by which the superpowers and other major or would-be major powers attempt to impose their ideologies. And there are still areas of open colonial conflict. Even within the Third World, countries like Brazil, Nigeria, Egypt, India, Indonesia, aim to spread their national influence and prestige among those colleagues which are smaller and further down the pecking order. So the political situation is ripe for propaganda battles.

And the audience is ready. Whatever the message, there is an unprecedented chance of being heard. The slow progress made in the elimination of illiteracy does not affect radio. It is the ideal medium for people whose cultural tradition is an oral one. In most areas of the Third World, radio has preceded a high level of literacy, making it, as W. Phillips Davison says, 'the greatest single instrument for involving people in emerging countries in political activity'.[1] The tight controls over domestic communications exercised throughout the Third World reinforce the impact of foreign radio. The lower the quality of the local media, the higher the credibility of foreign sources.

The equipment to hear the message is also there. Sales of short-wave receivers are increasing phenomenally in the Third World, although the number of radio sets per head is still below the figures for the developed world. In western Europe, North America and the white Commonwealth, there is one set for every two people; in Russia one for every five; in Spanish Latin America one for every six; in the Arab world one for every nine; in the Indian sub-continent one for every thirty, and in China one for every fifty. But the gap between rich and poor is closing, in this respect at least, all the time.

Yet the breakthrough has not happened. At different times and in different places, as we shall see in the following chapters, radio has indeed played a key role in forming political opinion and bringing about changes. The Middle East provides one of the most vivid examples. In parts of Africa, radio has intermittently shown its power, and there is every likelihood of it playing a far bigger role in the future. On the Indian sub-continent, it comes to the fore in times of conflict. But in Latin America, a commercialized radio network has remained on the margins of its turbulent history.

One reason is that international radio's limitations are, in fact, more marked in the process of broadcasting from outside to people whose level of education is on the whole low. It is difficult to cross the cultural gap when physical distance between broadcaster and listener provides a further dimension of remoteness. It is difficult not to sound patronizing. The outlook of the listener is likely to seem impossibly 'narrow' to the broad-minded internationalist broadcaster. Equally, the listener is likely to feel hostility towards the remote voice of privilege and affluence. As W. J. Cash said in *Mind of the South* of communication between Americans from the north with their fellow-citizens in the south:

> Contact with other peoples is often represented as making inevitably for tolerance. But that is true only for those who have already been greatly educated to tolerance. The simple man every-where is apt to see whatever differs from himself as an affront, a challenge, and a menace.

There is a real possibility that the common man in the Third World will be ignored by the international voices. On the one hand, the western democracies prefer to talk to the elite with whom the problem of an educational or cultural gap does not exist. On the other, the ideological stereotypes emitted from Moscow and Peking ignore the local conditions of the audiences, the differences among listeners, and their unwillingness to listen to long political diatribes about Marxist principles or steel output. Studies have shown that the mass audience in Africa and Asia demands more news of national or local interest than audiences elsewhere. International stations either have to resign themselves to getting through only to an elite, or face vastly increased costs involved in news-gathering on a local level. In no instance has any organization attempted to do what Radio Liberty and Radio Free Europe do, that is, provide an alternative domestic service in their target countries. Perhaps the nearest any Third-World operation has come to that is the Voice of the Arabs in its hey-day before the June war in 1967.

One aspect of the problem of the narrow consciousness of the Third-World audiences is the profusion of languages and dialects. English-language stations (American and British in particular) have an advantage in the fact that English is, after Chinese, the most widely-spoken language and is far more widely distributed over the globe than Chinese. It is the first language of international communication. 700 million people know some English at least. But again, those whose first language is not English but who understand it, are an elite, not the masses.

Neither the Voice of America nor the BBC, very largely for financial reasons in both cases, have been able to meet the challenge of providing services in any but a few of the African native languages. On the other hand, Moscow Radio and Cairo Radio have both made a strong pitch for audiences who speak in the vernacular. Moscow broadcasts in fourteen local languages to India and eleven to Africa; Cairo Radio's External Services include sections broadcasting in fifteen African vernaculars.

Diversity of language is of course paralleled by diversity of custom, tradition, and perception of the outside world. Radio, which comes from a single source and is designed to scatter its message over a large area, becomes increasingly ineffective the more fragmented the social structure of its broad target area. It cannot hope to make the same positive impact on people who regard radio as the agent of the devil as on others who see it as the voice of pure truth. It cannot overcome the resistance in all underdeveloped societies against news and information that has no immediate relevance.

By and large international radio stations cannot cope with the diversity and special needs of Third-World audiences. As Serban Vallimarescu said: 'Frankly, we [in the Voice of America] do not think in terms of broadcasting to the Third World as such.' The BBC, when faced with the prospect of having to decide where to make cuts in their international programmes, tends to choose, however reluctantly, those programmes which are aimed specifically at African and other Third-World listeners. On the communist side, despite the vernacular expansion by Radio Moscow and the intense political interest of the Chinese, the Sino-Soviet dispute has weakened the ideological credibility of both tendencies. Although the Russians have tried to improve on the dull, ideological approach of Chinese propaganda, they have failed to build up an audience that compares either in numbers or influence with their non-communist rivals. Their message is unalterably Moscow-centred. The memory of colonial links, and indeed the continuing presence of white Europeans all over the Third World, have given the ex-colonial powers an advantage when it comes to long-distance communication that no unfamiliar ideological appeal can begin to rival. The BBC still has a prestige value, even if this is meaningful only to the educated elite.

BBC broadcasters and engineers have also been responsible for advising many recently set up radio stations in the Third World, notably in Africa. This has contributed to the association in people's minds between the BBC model of broadcasting and radio as a medium. It also encourages an association between radio and the whole field of education. Raising the standards of education in the Third World is seen as an international concern, involving not just individual foreign countries (which are tainted with the suspicion of seeking political advantage for themselves) but also international organizations like UNESCO.

Rural adult education has been one of UNESCO's top priorities. The Radio Farm Forum was first developed in Canada and then applied in India, through All-India Radio, and in a number of African countries. The 1968 report of the Ghana experiment stressed that it was not possible to reflect the 'day-to-day activities of the people' while the programme content of Ghana Radio was still 'geared to the BBC'. Educational radio has to be very much a local affair. It is a case where practical help on a local scale should fit in with the capabilities of the medium.

Radio is an example of low technology. Already its high technology equivalent, television, installed in many countries in the Third World as a result of high-pressure salesmanship (usually American) on a prestige-conscious elite, is proving to be of no value at all to the people. The only kinds of programme that the stations can afford to put out are cut-price imported soap operas and documentaries of national folklore. Radio, on the other hand, is far more flexible and accessible, as well as being cheaper.

So although international radio has failed to make a big impact on the mass audiences of the Third World, radio as such has become popular everywhere. But the raising of the people's consciousness is a slow process, continually held back by economic and demographic pressures. So far, few national stations in the Third World have escaped the vices of American-style commercialism (as in Latin America, and some African countries), rigid government control (as in most of Africa, the Middle East and to some extent in the Indian sub-continent), or technical and editorial inadequacy. As providers of free and wide-ranging political communication, the domestic media of the Third World leave a great deal to be desired. In this sense, outside communicators have the field to themselves. But for the reasons which we have seen, and which we will examine in greater detail in the following chapters, they have not yet taken the opportunities open to them.

To begin with, communication was a one-way system from the rich, developed world to the poor, undeveloped world, and this is still largely the case. The voices of the Third World are heard not at all in the United States, Europe, the Soviet Union, or even China. The one-way monopoly has only broken down to the extent that the bigger Third-World powers have taken to propagandizing the smaller ones.

The External Services operated by countries within the Third World do not fall into easily identifiable categories. But the influence of one or more of the 'models'—the VOA, the BBC, the communist stations, and Zeesen—is apparent everywhere.

In no case, however, is the BBC line followed all the way. Some of the biggest external operations in the Third World claim to rival the BBC in 'objectivity'—the Japanese, for example. Brazil and India modelled the institutional structure of their foreign services on the BBC. But they all operate a tight system of directives, even if, in Japan's case, the control apparatus is contained within the broadcasting corporation itself. The Commonwealth legacy is also a strong factor. Canada, Australia and New Zealand all follow the BBC's example. And in Africa the foreign services of the Nigerian and other west and east African broadcasting companies pay lip-service to BBC principles.

In fact, shortage of qualified staff, of money and, most important, of political confidence, limit the extent to which Third-World radio services permit themselves to act as open forums for all kinds of political viewpoints. If one thing is evident in all their foreign broadcasting operations, it is a strong streak of nationalism. Just as the directors of the Voice of America are continually having to defend their station to suspicious Congressmen in terms of the national benefit it brings, so the staff of smaller national stations are accountable to their chauvinistic politicians. In countries where governments and individual leaders appoint themselves the sole interpreters of the national interest, chauvinism is compounded with a single, unquestionable political line.

The VOA system has been exported wholesale to many countries where the US interest predominates—the Philippines, for example. American influence is also detectable elsewhere: in Japan, Indonesia, Brazil, and Mexico for example. The tone of Havana Radio follows that of its political protégé, Moscow. Whenever a strong client-master relationship exists between two countries, the international broadcasting systems are among the first institutions to be harmonized.

Nazi broadcasting, because the political system it represented has been so discredited, is never acknowledged as a model today. But its influence cannot be ignored. Moscow Radio frequently refers to a foreign station that it dislikes for one reason or another as 'the heir of Goebbels'. But as this kind of description is applied indiscriminately, even to the BBC on occasions, it cannot be taken as anything but a ritual insult. It would be more accurate to cite, say, the Voice of the Arabs in its early years, the current Libyan and Palestine stations, Radio Biafra, or some of the virulent anti-communist stations, both clandestine and official. All of these have used, though not necessarily all the time, some of the techniques discussed earlier which characterized the Zeesen station. The tone has been strident, emotional, hysteria-provoking. Truth has been bent not for ideological consistency but as a planned exercise in distortion. In other words, they have descended to the crudest level of propaganda.

This is not to say that the propaganda of such stations copying Nazi techniques has not been effective. As we shall see, the Voice of the Arabs and Radio Biafra have both been described as highly influential propaganda organs. But both also oversold their message. The Egyptians realized this and changed their tone. Radio Biafra, like the Nazi Radio, represented a losing cause, and can only be judged by its reputation. It will be understood that the content of the message is a matter of indifference when talking of Nazi influence. The very point of this type of propaganda is that it can be made to fit any political line. It can be used by tyrants as well as freedom fighters, government as well as opposition.

Gradually, the lessons learnt from the long radio propaganda war between east and west and across the frontiers of the northern hemisphere are being applied throughout the Third World. The major broadcasters have been so busy abusing each other that they have not yet fully taken in the implications of the propaganda war in the Third World. But the shift in priorities will take place because it has to. The rich developed countries are going to have to rely on the raw material resources of the Third World to an ever greater extent. They can no longer assume favourable treatment through colonial connections or just plain old-fashioned force. And whether the struggles of the future will be about race, or about raw materials, or about living space, or about socialism, the focus of attention and the prize is the Third World. That is why the propaganda battle for and in the Third World is just beginning.

6 The Middle East

In the Middle East, hot wars, political hatreds, a public opinion lashed by propaganda to a raw sensitivity, and Third-World conditions of an educated elite and ignorant masses, all combine to enhance the power of international radio as nowhere else in the world. Radio is *the* medium here both for propagandists and propagandized.

The radio set is the accepted source of news and opinion. 'In the typical Egyptian village, the radio in the grocery store is played constantly, not only to entertain the proprietor, but as a service to his friends and customers.'[1] Nasser understood that the illiteracy counted for far less during the time he ruled Egypt than it had before. Radio meant that people in the most remote villages began to hear of what was happening everywhere and form their own opinion.

With a language more or less common to all Arab states, domestic services are planned with neighbours' ears in mind. Yet there is also in the Middle East an exceptionally high proportion of listeners who tune in to the Arabs' own international services, to clandestine programmes, and to foreign stations, particularly the BBC.

The Voice of the Arabs from Cairo has played the key role in familiarizing the Arab people with the power of radio. But Syria was the first country to introduce an External Service. In the fifties, Arab radio stations were of the most conservative, even primitive kind. The people regarded them with suspicion, although, as Frantz Fanon points out, they were important symbols of emerging nationalism. Writing of post-war Algeria, he remarks:

> The awakening of the colonial world and the progressive liberation of peoples long held in subjection involved Algeria in a process which reached beyond her and of which, at the same time, she became a part. The appearance of liberated Arab countries at this point is of exceptional importance. The first wholesale introduction of radio sets in Algeria coincided with the setting up of national broadcasting stations in Syria, Egypt and Lebanon.[2]

The Syrians were the first to popularize the medium, putting out pop music to lighten a diet made heavy by constant readings from the Koran. When relayed to audiences throughout the Arab world this had an electrifying effect.

It was not long, however, before the pan-Arab enthusiasm of

Colonel Nasser led him to set up an international service from
Cairo. Between the mid-fifties and the June war of 1967, the Voice
of the Arabs was, in Winston Burdett's words, the 'pulpit of the
revolution'. Amplified by four Czech-built 150-kilowatt transmitters,
watched over by German engineers, 'it created a public opinion where
none had existed before, among the illiterate and semiliterate masses
of the Arab world from its northern reaches in the Fertile Crescent
of Syria and Iraq to the bazaars of Aden and the desolate sands of
the Pirates' Coast. Neither illiteracy nor distance was a barrier to
the spoken word.'[3] The Arab writer Hazem Zaki Nuseibeh saw 'the
birth of a new folklore, the joining of the political diatribe to the
traditional song as both blare over the village radio'.[4] The nineteen-
fifties and sixties were a time of radical change in Arab society,
which can only be compared to Russia after 1917 or to China around
1949. As in the communist revolutions, it was a time for agitprop,
for direct, simple, emotional propaganda aimed at peasants and
workers. It was a time for revivalists.

Behind the Voice of the Arabs—and playing an important role at
the microphone too—was Nasser himself. He saw the station as a
personal mouthpiece and a key weapon in his revolution. The man
he chose to run it, and whom he kept as one of his closest confidants,
was Ahmed Said. Said was described to me by a disillusioned ex-
member of the Voice of the Arabs staff as a 'Goebbels-like figure
who refused to allow contradiction, who conceived every single
programme, even music, in political terms, and censored everything
himself. He would choose announcers for the emotional quality of
their voice, and would give regular broadcasts himself, haranguing
the people for about ten minutes a day at the top of his voice.' As
a director, Said was a tyrant, saved only from criticism from below
by his 'hot line to Nasser'. 'He was always shouting, cursing,
agitating.' But to his audience Said was the new voice of the Arab
people, both creating and relying upon a sense of identity and unity
that took an excited populace by surprise.

A few intellectuals worried that the pace was too fast and furious.
They criticized the Voice of the Arabs for stirring up feelings without a clear idea as to how they should be directed. And they resented
the immunity of the radio directors under Nasser's protection,
calling them 'the Untouchables'. But protests were ignored, if indeed
they were heard at all. The propaganda band wagon, once under
way, had a momentum of its own. Ronald Payne wrote in a recent
edition of the *Sunday Telegraph*:

Cairo Radio—and Arabic is a terrific language for invective—went
full go in the old days with a programme called *The Enemies of
God*, who almost invariably coincided with those of the late

Nasser. Getting at the British on one occasion they produced a very palpable insult by proclaiming, 'O British, your King is a woman'.[5]

That was what the Arabs wanted to hear.

In 1956, they also wanted to be reassured of the particular wickedness of the British, French and Israelis, who first threatened, and then carried out, a military invasion. Gordon Waterfield, at the time head of the BBC's Arabic Service, and personally a critic of the invasion, looked back ten years later at the effect he believed the Voice of the Arabs had had, not just on the Arabs themselves, but on the British government:

It was considered by many in this country that it was these broadcasts from Cairo which had interfered with British policy by preventing Jordan joining the Baghdad Pact in December 1955, and that in March 1956 the broadcasts had led to the summary dismissal of the Englishman Glubb Pasha from his command of the Arab Legion in Jordan . . . I think that the abuse and misrepresentation on Cairo Radio, which could be read next day in BBC monitoring reports, contributed a good deal to the angry mood which led the British Government down the road to Suez. The British and French Prime Ministers were reminded of Nazi propaganda under Goebbels and there were mutterings about Hitlerism and the dangers of a Munich.[6]

One of the troubles of putting out 'total' propaganda is that, ever since Goebbels, people will believe that it is bound to be a prelude to action. Goebbels knew that without political or military success to back it up, any propaganda of violence is self-defeating. It is assumed that anyone using similar techniques knows this too.

On the other hand, there have been attempts to deflate the role played by the Voice of the Arabs. Writing nearer the event, and possibly still smarting under the lash of official tongues and therefore anxious to defend the BBC's traditional moderation, Sir High Greene, the Director-General in 1956, wrote:

The power of Cairo Radio as a weapon in Colonel Nasser's hands has been very much exaggerated by many people. In so far as Cairo Radio achieves anything it is through the exploitation of feelings (pan-Arab, anti-British, anti-French) which are already there. It does not create them. Those who expect British, French or American broadcasts to compete with Cairo Radio are equally mistaken. Our policy is not one of lies and agitation and we should be false to ourselves, and do no good at all, if we descended to Colonel Nasser's level. The truth is an unexciting weapon and it

often works too slowly for those who, naturally enough, are eager
to see quick results.[7]

While this is an accurate reflection of BBC policy, Sir Hugh goes
against the more general view that the Voice of the Arabs did
indeed have a powerful short-term effect, using lies and agitation
certainly, though with a sufficient measure of truth not to lose all
contact with reality. Even 'exploiting feelings . . . already there' had
the effect of incitement. And it is probable that radio did contribute
towards creating them.

But, as always, hard evidence of mass enthusiasm stirred up by
radio does not, indeed cannot, exist. Eye-witness accounts of
clamorous groups around radio sets are not enough. Evidence of the
growing political awareness of the Arab people and its creation by,
and interaction with, government policy is too broad to attribute to
radio alone, or to any single factor. Radio's influence, once again,
can only be gauged by the number of people who claim that it has
been effective. In the case of the Voice of the Arabs, there is a
coincidence of views between Egyptians and outside observers that
makes particularly plausible the view that it did indeed have a very
powerful popular impact.

The fatal flaw did, however, prove in the end to be the habit of
lying. That was in 1967. But even before then, the Voice of the Arabs
displayed a disturbing quality that prepared the way for popular
disillusionment: its inveterate quarrelsomeness. Only Algeria—
because Nasser regarded Ben Bella as his 'adopted son'—escaped the
wrath of Cairo and the vicious radio attacks that this entailed.

The hate campaigns directed against every single other Arab
country in turn weakened the Voice's credibility as the unifier of all
the Arabs. Although it is sometimes said that Arab audiences were
able to believe the pan-Arab nationalist propaganda with one half
of their mind and reject the underlying Egyptian propaganda with
the other half, the distinction cannot be made with total clarity.
Waterfield takes the view that 'Arabs enjoy abusing each other as
part of the game of politics' but this, even allowing for charitable
interpretation, ignores the long-term effects of such abuse. The
threats against King Hussein's life, repeated with relish over Nasser's
radio station, could not but alienate those Jordanians whose whole
existence was bound up with loyalty to their sovereign. There was
similar bewilderment in Saudi Arabia, indeed all over the Arab
world. As for Iraq, the Voice of the Arabs was instrumental in
creating popular reaction against the 1958 elections, claiming that
they were 'falsified by the imperialists' and that the Iraqi Parliament
was a mockery. Premier Nuri as-Said once said that riots had been
caused by a Radio Cairo claim that he had murdered a number of

holy men in a mosque. Subsequent campaigns against the Ba'athists themselves created further bad blood.

Within Egypt, Said's downfall was the direct result of the role that the Voice of the Arabs played, or claimed to have played, in the disastrous June war. The Egyptian propaganda was already becoming dangerously erratic when, just before the war broke out, King Hussein was being described as 'the Hashemite harlot', a 'hyena [who] will not be saved by his open and exposed collusion with Israel, the USA and Britain from the punishment of death'; and then, after his reconciliation with Nasser on 30 May, as a potential saviour of the Arab world.

The final straw was the wildly optimistic reports of Egyptian victories in the first days of the war, at a time when Egypt was in fact undergoing the most humiliating defeat in her history. Claims of Israeli planes shot down by the Egyptians and Syrians reached preposterous proportions. After eleven-and-a-quarter hours of fighting the claim was that eighty-six Israeli planes had been shot down over Egypt alone. 'Victory is certain' was the theme; the Arabs are advancing.[8] As soon as the truth became known, Ahmed Said and the Voice of the Arabs were seen, not just as deceivers, but as the agents of Egyptian humiliation. Said was arrested, imprisoned and then kept under house arrest for some years before being released to lead a furtive existence in a still hostile Cairo.

While it is true that Said himself cannot be held responsible for all the mistakes of the war, his style had contributed to the myth-making that made Egyptian propaganda so vulnerable to events. When all was going well and Egypt was riding the crest of the nationalist wave, it mattered very little whether the Voice of the Arabs lied, or even whether it was found out. Lies were details. But telling lies had in fact undermined the Voice's credibility, and, what was worse, made those responsible for that policy blind to the dangers of lying.

This helps explain the mistakes of June 1967—not just the exaggerations, but also the disastrous policy errors. The worst of these was the agreement to build up as a key issue in its international propaganda the entirely spurious involvement in the fighting of American and British planes. It was a lie cooked up at the highest level and, although even Nasser appears to have been confused at the start about the truth of the matter, by the time it had been built up in the media, it was known to be a lie. And it was a lie that rebounded heavily on to the Egyptian and other Arab propagandists. As Goebbels learned in the last years of the war, defeat calls for a different approach to propaganda than victory. Above all, it calls for no self-deception at the top.

In the event, the lesson was learnt. The period of short-term propaganda successes came to an abrupt end with the June war. Broadcasting succeeded agitation. A more mature, realistic approach became policy. The Voice of the Arabs, it might be said, traded in a Nazi model for some kind of a cross between the BBC and Radio Peace and Progress. It is still an uncompromising ideological weapon, but it reflects an Egyptian point of view rather than an Arab one, and has broadened its appeal to the non-Arab world.

The Egyptian Deputy Prime Minister and Minister of Culture and Information, Dr Muhammad Abd al-Qadir Hatim, claimed in a broadcast in February 1973 that Egyptian foreign propaganda had had a big success in turning world opinion against Israel through the use of reasoned argument:

> Our goal regarding foreign information media is to win over supporters and the neutral states as well as neutralizing several other states. One of the results of the foreign information plan was that European public opinion began to shift against Israel. This was evident from Golda Meir's visit to France, Italy and the Vatican.

Hatim also claimed success in swaying African opinion. And indeed the Voice of the Arabs has been in the forefront of the Egyptian campaign to turn the black African states against Israel.

The events of the October war in 1973 confirmed the wisdom of the new sober approach. Arabs repeatedly refer to the 'maturity' that the war both induced and proved. The Voice of the Arabs was able to lay the ghost of the 1967 fiasco and point to the part it played in creating this maturity. Communiqués were to the point. War hysteria was avoided. Arab aims were clearly stated, with threats to 'drive Israelis into the sea' conspicuous only by their absence.

There is, however, a price that the Voice of the Arabs has had to pay. It is no longer the sole voice that claims to speak for all the Arabs. By its very moderation it has been overtaken as the voice of the masses by Tripoli Radio, by the Palestinian stations, and by the powerful (at least in terms of kilowatts) new voice of Saudi Arabia's Riyad Radio. Cairo's appeal, directed more and more to the Arab elite and to moderates, is in danger of being swamped, as far as the masses are concerned, by the more strident revolutionary voices which remember the pre-war success of Nasser's operation.

The threat comes from both right and left. The Saudis, whose king commands respect as 'keeper of the holy places', have since November 1973 been heard loud and clear throughout the Middle East. Riyad Radio could become, in time, as potent a weapon within the Arab world as the oil weapon has been against the non-Arab world. On the revolutionary side, Colonel Gaddafi encourages the spread of a propaganda line that makes all other national Arab radios seem pro-Zionist by comparison. Tripoli Radio's *Liberation Magazine* is a special programme designed to attack the 'feudal' state of Morocco and to persuade those who periodically try to overthrow the king to do the job more efficiently. The Moroccans, in turn, put out a special programme for Libya on the theme of Gaddafi's 'rule of terror, stupidity and ignorance'.

One potential weakness in the Libyans' propaganda campaign, however, is the danger of being accused of leading from behind. They were, for example, calling on the Jordanians at the time of the October war to overthrow the king and join the fight—but declined to send their own troops. What they did do after the war was to start up a new three-hour broadcast (expanded later to eight hours a day) called the *Voice of the Arab Homeland*. Ramadan Abdullah, the general controller, opened the service by declaring that:

> As is now noted in the Arab region, radios are now more clearly subjected to a will, one which may not express the will of the Arab masses. We hope, God willing, that this radio will truly be the only voice expressing the feelings of the Arab wherever he may be.

But the Libyan voice is not alone in making this claim, having powerful rivals in the Palestinians who are tireless radio propagandists. Many Arab capitals house groups of Palestinian broadcasters and give them airtime on their own services. The Palestine Liberation Organization also runs a station of its own. The contrast between the Palestinian line and that of Cairo is sometimes painfully apparent. For example, the Palestinians were notably virulent at the time of the fighting in Jordan in September 1970, stressing the massacres that the king and his bedouins were perpetrating and swearing revenge for the loss of Arab blood. The Voice of the Arabs was more sorrowful than angry, repeating appeals to Arab brothers to 'point their weapons at the enemies of Arabism'. Three years later, the Palestine radios were responsible for getting hold of, and then building up, the story of a mutiny in Amman, forcing strong action by King Hussein at a moment when they had focussed world attention on him.

They are proud of their independence, of their capacity to act as they see fit. The Voice of Palestine has specifically publicized the idea that the PLO broadcasts from Arab capitals owe no allegiance to their host states, declaring on 18 April 1973:

> Arab Radios and the rest of their information media do not present the truth to the masses. They are directed in accordance with the policy of the state. Since this policy is against and counter to the Palestine Revolution then it cannot possibly serve the Palestine

D

Revolution but rather helps to exhaust and strike it. This is in addition to the fact that there are other Arab information media which work to pacify the Arab masses to accept the Zionist presence . . . [Our] radios will remain a weapon interacting with the weapon of the fighter until the occupied homeland is liberated.

Cairo Radio is clearly one target of the Palestinian wrath.

It is not always clear, however, as to which group controls which outlet. In May 1973, the Voice of Palestine (Baghdad) put out a report that Muslim girls had been raped by the Lebanese 'crusader forces'. The next day they denied the report, saying that the message had been relayed to them by the clandestine radio equipment of 'foreign agents'.

Amid all this clamour other Arab voices are appealing for support and propagating the national line. Algeria, Tunisia, the Lebanon, Syria, and Iraq all have international radio services. In Iraq, a special reverence is accorded to the power of radio. As the official history of the 1958 revolution has it:

> If the Army and the Ministry of Defence were the mothers of the July 14 Revolution, then the Ministry of Guidance and the Iraq Republic Radio were the guardians of that blessed revolution . . . the Radio was the midwife by whose hands the republic came to life.[9]

Kol Israel (the Voice of Israel) is inevitably a lonely voice in this wilderness. But in the context of the whole of the Middle East, its Arabic Service is important. It is in fact a domestic service for the Arabs who live in Israel and the occupied territories. But its powerful signal gives it far more than the customary overspill, reaching well beyond the outer lines of Israeli occupation. The same is true, within a smaller orbit, of the Arabic-language service of Israeli television. A big non-Israeli audience is claimed for both radio and TV. People tune in not just to American soap operas, although these act as a potent bait, but also to news bulletins and comments. Not a small number of Arabs, especially at times of great tension or actual war, have a personal interest in what the other side is saying and thinking. Arab radios have not always provided them with accurate accounts.

At the founding of the Israeli state, there were two radio channels broadcasting with international audiences in mind: the Arabic Service funded by the Foreign Ministry in collaboration with Military Intelligence; and the Voice of Zion to the Diaspora (Kol Zion Lagolah) financed by the Jewish Agency. The domestic Israeli Broadcasting Service was directly under the control of the Prime Minister's office. Due to the exceptional security situation, liberalization from tight central control was slow in coming. But in the mid-sixties, internal broadcasting became part of the public domain with editorial responsibility in the hands of a public authority not unlike the BBC.

On the foreign front, pressure for a hard nationalist line was kept up for longer. One reason for the postponement of liberalization was the success of Israel's foreign radio propaganda. The June war gave it added prestige, and the only thing that held back plans for a massive expansion was lack of money. But the mood changed drastically with the October war of 1973. As Israelis began to realize that the Arabs were not so far beneath contempt as they had been led to believe, they understood that their media had oversold the Israeli line. Foreign listeners felt the same way. The military and political leaders were not disillusioned by radio, but its role is now being reappraised. They are preparing for a long haul, and pulling back from a position of hard, quick selling to produce instant results. That only worked when the military and political situation was itself overwhelmingly in the ascendant. Just as the Voice of the Arabs was condemned in 1967 for exaggerated optimism (to put it no stronger), so Kol Israel was seen to display the same fault in 1973, though to a lesser degree.

Another problem facing the liberal element in the Israeli External Services has been the pseudo-scientific advice of the official 'propagandists' in the Institute for National Security. In propaganda, a little science is almost always a dangerous thing. It leads to experiments in psychological warfare and to excessive preoccupation with precise ends and means.

In some cases this has led to a line being taken in the foreign programmes which was not taken in the domestic, with the inevitable confusion which that entailed, since the internal channels are also audible to a section of the foreign audience. For example, when Ben Gurion failed to reach an accommodation with Nasser at the start of the Egyptian revolution, he began to talk about the 'Egyptian tyrant'. This phrase was picked up and used exclusively by the media when referring to President Nasser. When a more liberal line was introduced internally in the mid-sixties, this deliberate mark of hostility was dropped, but the foreign services took another two years before they could bring themselves to drop the offensive phrase. More importantly, the foreign service can propagate a different political policy to the domestic media, as, for instance, when the government attacked the Jackson amendment making détente dependent on improved conditions for Jews in the Soviet Union. The External Services put out the government line exclusively. But the rest of Israel radio and TV argued the case hotly, giving all sides of the case and reflecting the division of opinion in the country.

With so many nationalities in Israel, and with political arguments raging while the country is in a permanent state of war, there are of course tensions between doves and hawks in the media as elsewhere. In the Arabic Service, the problem is compounded by the difficulty of mixing Jews from Arab states, Arabic-speaking Israeli Jews, and Arabs, all in one unit.

The other major international service, which is directed at the Soviet Union in a number of languages, faces its own special dilemma: how to get the maximum number of Jews out of Russia and yet not cause a backlash. So far the Voice of Zion for the Diaspora has done a sensitive job of raising Jewish consciousness—and keeping non-Russian Jews informed—without harmful negative consequences. It is probable that in this case, the directive system works better than total editorial freedom. Where the aim is so specific, it is hard to see how else a consistent campaign can be organized.

While a large number of Arabs, from Morocco to the Gulf, listen to Israeli Radio, they do so knowing that they are hearing the 'enemy' version of events. This still leaves room for other foreign voices to be heard. It is agreed even by its rivals that the BBC is ahead of the field here.

The BBC's Arabic Service was the first foreign-language section to be attached to the Empire Service. Created in 1938 as an antidote to the all too effective Italian and German propaganda, it was able to build on colonial links and capture a wide audience among the educated elite who were anxious to hear what their fate was to be in the impending world conflict. Just as the Foreign Office has traditionally had a special feeling for the Arab world, so did the BBC's Arabic Service become, and it remains so to this day, a priority second only to the English-language World Service. No expense has been spared to make the signal to the Middle East of 'Home Service' quality.

Nothing is permitted to impair that signal. The axing of the Hebrew Service in 1968 was a direct consequence of fears for the Arabic Service. When it became apparent that the only way for the Hebrew programmes to reach the target area was to set up a medium-wave relay from Cyprus, the plan was vetoed on the grounds that President Makarios would react strongly to this 'insult' to his friend Nasser and that he would ban the vital facilities for the Arabic relay. In fact Makarios hinted in private that he would not have minded a Hebrew Service relay on the island as long as he was not officially informed about it. Besides, he had much more cause to object to being the host of the 'hostile' anti-Nasser propaganda of the Arabic Service. Despite the flimsy excuse of blaming Makarios and despite the fact that the BBC's Hebrew Service was the only non-communist international broadcast to Israel, the Arabists had their way and the virtually inaudible Hebrew short-wave signal was abandoned in favour of establishing a small unit in London to supply reports for transmission on Israeli Radio.

While the BBC gives high priority to its Arabic Service, it is not, however, subject to the vacillations of policy that have character- ized the Foreign Office's own stance. Nothing could have illustrated this more clearly than the controversy stirred up by the Suez adven- ture. We have already seen how this affected the BBC's relations with the Foreign Office. Its effect on the Arab listeners was increased respect for the BBC. The Arab staff in London were under heavy pressure from Egypt to cease broadcasting. Partly in reaction to this threat they insisted—backing their demand by their own threat of resignation—on the strict maintenance by the BBC of its policy of impartiality and of representing all opinions within Britain. The BBC did indeed adhere meticulously to its traditional policy. Audience surveys later confirmed that this attitude prevented the otherwise inevitable loss of a large part of the audience. There was also the more cynical calculation by the BBC that they would certainly have lost a radio war with Cairo. Nothing could have been more sure to unite Arab opinion behind Nasser and boost the already enormous prestige of the Voice of the Arabs.

So the BBC kept its listeners, estimated today to be several million. The Egyptian government itself has not been indifferent to the potential threat of the BBC. From time to time campaigns have been launched against it, one of the most virulent occurring in the final weeks of 1972. Petitions were signed by intellectuals. A 'boycott' was called for. Both the medium-wave and two short-wave frequencies were jammed until almost the end of March the following year. And Radio Cairo's *Enemies and Agents* programme poured abuse on the BBC's head.

The reasons given for the hate campaign were numerous. They in- cluded the BBC's 'misreporting' of Soviet-Egyptian relations especially over the question of the ejection of Soviet representatives; describing as a 'coup' what turned out to be the escapade of a 'mad officer' who conducted a convoy to a Cairo mosque and called for war against Israel; and transmitting news of an Air Force plot against President Sadat. The British ambassador, Sir Richard Beaumont, was called in to explain the British position. Not coincidentally, when the BBC's misdemeanours were pointed out to Dom Mintoff the BBC's relay station in Malta was promptly closed. While the fury of this spate of attacks can partly be explained by the low state of Egyptian morale at the time—the redeeming war was still the best part of a year away—the very fact that the BBC does reach such a large and influential audience in the Arab world makes it peren- nially vulnerable to counter-measures from all Arab governments.

As David Hirst reported from Beirut on 23 November 1972 (at

the height of the attack, and the day when the Malta relay was closed):

> Although the Voice of America and, of course, Radio Israel, come in for attack, the BBC is the real target, for though the Arabs have their complaints about it—notably as regards Israel—it is about the only broadcasting service most of them take seriously.[10]

Maurice Latey, the BBC External Services' chief commentator who reported the October war from Cairo, describes London's voice as 'the radio they love to hate'. The Americans have not established anything like such an intimate connection between broadcaster and listener. Although VOA puts out the same amount of programme hours in Arabic as in Spanish to Latin America, and Dr Kissinger's activities have sharpened Arab interest in what Washington is thinking, the American radio impact has not been spectacular. Traditional links are still the strongest. But VOA officials are confident that the listening pattern will eventually change. They maintain a special service for the Arab world based on the island of Rhodes, backed up by a staff of two Americans and five or six Arabs in Beirut.

More than the British, the Americans are at the mercy of sweeping political upheavals in the Middle East. And the same is true of the communist propagandists, to the extent that what is bad for them is good for the Americans. At the time of writing, it is likely (though not measurable) that more attention is being paid in Egypt to the Voice of America than to the increasingly suspect voice of Moscow Radio. At all events, the Arabs are inveterate listeners to foreign radio programmes, from wherever they may come. Though to an outsider the airwaves in the Middle East may seem overcrowded already, radio propaganda has an apparently limitless market.

7 Africa

In a purely geographical sense, Africa is not the ideal continent for radio. Leonard Doob wrote in 1961:

> The frequency of electrical disturbance in Africa is only one of the reasons why the more satisfactory form of broadcasting, medium-wave, that is ordinarily used in Europe and America is 'economically out of the question' there. In addition, radio waves

along the ground are hampered by the African bush and by mountains. Then the population is so scattered that signals must travel a comparatively long distance . . . Every short-wave listener knows—especially in Africa—reception is 'never completely reliable'.[1]

Short-wave transmitters are more powerful now than they were then, but Africa is still notoriously the continent where radio reception is at its worst.

Bad reception has not, however, deterred the sale of radio sets. The number of sets in sub-Saharan Africa has risen fast: from 360,000 in 1955 to about 16 million in 1973. At the same time their cost has dropped, effectively ending the period of multiple listening to 'public address' type of systems.

Within non-Arab Africa, there are at present ten international stations which broadcast on a signal of 100 kilowatts or more. These are located in Angola, Brazzaville, Ethiopia, Ghana, Liberia, Mozambique, Nigeria, South Africa, Tanzania, and Zaire. In terms of hours per week, none of these rival the world's major international operations. Only Ghana (whose service has slowly declined since the mid-sixties) and South Africa put out more than 165 hours per week. Most non-local radio comes from outside Africa (the BBC, the Voice of America, Radios Moscow and Peking) and from Cairo. The French, the Dutch, the Germans, the Portuguese, and others, also beam in their message.

But the battle for the African audience has so far been fought in a surprisingly haphazard fashion. Up until quite recently the one thing that set Africa politically apart from the rest of the world was the isolation of the continent from outside contact. Now there is more international and internal communication than the people can cope with. Although the superpowers see Africa, even South Africa, as of peripheral strategic importance, and have every intention of avoiding a confrontation there, there is still a sense in which Africa is an ideological testing ground, where political systems can compete and point up the advantages and disadvantages of their rivals.

But Africans appear to have very little interest in being tested for the benefit of the competing ideologies of the superpowers. The independence movement, beginning in the early sixties with Ghana and spreading quickly out from the west across the continent, brought in its train a mass of political and economic problems which demanded solutions adapted to local conditions and traditions. The Organization for African Unity devotes itself to staying in existence. The last thing it or its members need is disrupting foreign propaganda.

The common factor among most black African governments is the desire to keep the political temperature down. This extends even to avoiding confrontation with the white-dominated areas of southern Africa. The OAU long ago gave up any hope that non-violent and constitutional agitation against the whites would lead to political change. But so far, few African statesmen argue that the time is yet ripe to draw the logical conclusion from this policy and go on the offensive.

A corollary is the neglect of the media by the black African states. URTNA (the Union of National Radio and TV Organisations of Africa) sets up endless conferences to discuss harmonization, a common approach, etc., but so far there is more talk than action. The divisions here follow those which plague the OAU itself. Only Tanzania maintains an uncompromising anti-colonialist, revolutionary line directed at a pan-African audience. In Nkrumah's Ghana, plans were laid for a huge international radio service which was to be the first stage in a concerted propaganda campaign by all the free and would-be free states of western, eastern and central Africa. But, like so many of Nkrumah's grand ideas, this one foundered on the rocks of indifference, lack of money and infighting.

Within west Africa, only Nigeria may be said to have attempted a comparable role. Its External Service still keeps up a flow of rhetoric. In November 1973 Lagos radio introduced into its transmissions abroad a programme called *African Crusade*, dedicated, an announcer said, 'to total victory in the struggle for decolonization, economic and cultural independence and the elimination of racism in Africa'. But this general goal is unlikely in itself to attract many listeners. Besides, technical and financial problems have prevented the creation of an efficient and professional External Service. It is even doubtful if General Gowon wants such a thing. The success of Radio Biafra in the civil war only increased his suspicion that radio could be a dangerously two-edged weapon. So Nigeria's emergence as the dominant power in west Africa owes little or nothing to propaganda.

A similar suspicion of radio exists in Zambian ruling circles. Even the domestic services are neglected financially. Zambia Radio puts out, four times a week, a programme entitled *Mirror of Zimbabwe*, presented by the Zimbabwe African National Union, but the External Service as such, which began in May 1973, carries as yet no international weight. It is indeed deliberately underplayed, so strong is the fear of counter-propaganda from Rhodesia and South Africa should the Zambian message find a powerful echo among the black victims of apartheid and racism. But at least the Zambians themselves, now that the Chinese-built transmitters for the External Service have been brought into play, can *claim* to be doing their bit. As Zambia Radio declared in May 1973:

[We will now be able] to beam newscasts to racist countries and other areas to tell them the truth about what is happening and counteract the horrible lies which are put on their radios and news bulletins. Until the commissioning of the new transmitters we were in such a bad situation that even Zambians in the rural areas were being fed only racist lies because they could not tune in to Radio Zambia because reception was so bad.

But the propagandizing of white listeners is a mere gesture. Neither side regards it as capable of upsetting the status quo.

If we discount the overspill from radio stations in neighbouring countries, we are left then with only one effective international service in black Africa, Tanzania's. The Liberian External Service, specializing in hot gospel, attracts some listeners, but with no significant effect. Zaire Radio consists mainly of music. The Voice of the Gospel, a Lutheran station transmitting from Addis Ababa, attracts a sizeable audience in east Africa especially, using carefully balanced news and music as a bait for its religious message. Kampala Radio's External Service has yet to be set up, although President Amin laid the foundation stone in January 1974. Though declaring that it was 'not for propaganda', the President will soon have a vehicle to propagate instantly the profusion of messages he despatches to his fellow leaders and 'brother' Presidents, but the value of the service itself is yet to be proven. In political terms, Radio Tanzania is up to now the only one that counts.

Radio Tanzania's External Service was inaugurated on the first day of 1968, in order, as the Information Minister said:

. . . to promote African liberation movements, report their activities and broadcast correct information to counteract the false and malicious propaganda broadcast by radios in Mozambique, South Africa and South-West Africa.

It is the first part of that statement that makes the station such an important one in Africa. African liberation movements use the facilities of Radio Tanzania as their international voice. It is the headquarters of their propaganda. In 1970, a special new department was created to promote the liberation struggles, uniting the programmes put out by the movements themselves with Tanzanian propaganda. This gave added weight to Tanzania's importance as the only socialist state in non-Arab Africa and to President Nyerere's line of self-help based on the village commune.

As usual, it is difficult to prove that the output of Radio Tanzania is directly effective, but as the one strong alternative voice, it has the advantage of being compulsory listening for left-wing activists all over Africa. On a tactical level, however, those involved in liberation struggles use Radio Tanzania as an outlet and a source of information which would not otherwise be available. In Mozambique, tribute has been paid to these broadcasts for contributing to the triumph of Frelimo.

Although Algeria, Zambia, and Congo Brazzaville give the liberation movements airtime, it is in Dar-es-Salaam that policy is made and the various factions compete for influence. There is also some evidence that the audience in South-West Africa (Namibia) takes note of the message from Tanzania. The boycott of the August 1973 elections in Ovamboland was, for example, partly due, in all probability, to the broadcasts put out by the SWAPO Party on Radio Tanzania's transmitters.

The transmitters themselves are a contribution from the People's Republic of China. They first went into action at the end of 1966, but they have not been trouble-free. As everywhere in Africa, the climate is more favourable to cockroaches and other insects than to transmitters, and the amplifiers and condensers frequently get clogged up with unwanted foreign bodies. Apparently, the design of the Chinese transmitters make them particularly attractive to these creatures. But the troubles have not all been due to natural causes. In 1973, a former BBC engineer was called in to make some improvements and modifications to the design.

The transmitters are in constant use. They are used, in addition to carrying the international programmes, for schools broadcasts and to carry a commercial programme. Despite this last function, which must astonish the donors, the transmitters remain under government control. The view expressed by the Tanzanian Minister of Information and Tourism, Mr Wakil, back in June 1964, still holds good:

> It is impossible to see a radio station working independently of the government . . . there must be some degree of control of government of a medium that is infinitely more powerful than printed words.

This is also the view held by the authorities in the white-dominated areas of Africa. Radio in Rhodesia and South Africa is a political weapon wielded by government. In 1961, the South African Broadcasting Corporation was brought under the control of two leading members of the Broederbond—the secret society that pulls the strings of the Nationalist Party—Dr Piet Meyer, Chairman of the Board of Governors, and Dr Albert Hertzog, the notoriously hard-line Minister of Posts and Telegraphs. This did not create state monopoly control, which existed before, but it reinforced the strictness of that control. The post-Sharpeville vigilance grew even more thorough.

In the summer of 1966, the new External Service of SABC, the Voice of South Africa, went on the air. The Director of Programmes announced:

> This service will be squarely based on facts, accuracy and responsibility. Every man engaged on the project has explicit instructions that these must be his guidelines . . . [It is an] effective means of overcoming barriers.

And indeed, given the fiercely racist tone of internal propaganda, the output of the Voice of South Africa has been remarkably moderate. This is, as the Director of Programmes said, the way to be effective. Internally, the racist line must not be allowed to flag. Externally, the best impression to give is one of sweet reasonableness. South Africa is not trying to convert outsiders, but to allay their fears and suspicions. Particularly in black Africa, she has every interest in not stirring up political passions, inviting polemics or, even worse, physical reprisal. In view of the slow progress of a concerted and effective international move to counter the grip of the white minority in southern Africa, neighbouring black African states have, on the contrary, been sucked into South Africa's orbit more and more. The effectiveness of South Africa's moderate propaganda line is evident. Since May 1974, the Voice of South Africa has cut back its broadcasts to countries outside the African continent in order to boost its output, and its impact, nearer home.

The South African External Service, therefore, is apparently close to the BBC's policy of soft-sell. But in fact its 'moderation' is a tactical, opportunistic policy which could change as soon as political circumstances demand it. The thinking behind it is closer to the Nazi model than to any other. South African propaganda to foreign countries has nothing to do with ideology, let alone with humanitarian feelings about the value of free information. If proof were needed, it is provided by the tight controls that the ruling whites exercise over the Bantu radio stations.

Under the guise of fostering Bantu culture, these large stations in fact stress tribal differences and act as a politically divisive factor. By their very existence, they also stress the separate development of black and white. They are an extension of the Corporation's original 'Bantu programme', set up in the early sixties after some of its African announcers were discovered broadcasting anti-government propaganda. This led at first to an internal reorganization, with white staff who had a knowledge of the African languages being appointed first to supervisory positions, and then to an entire network of stations for the pseudo-autonomous African territories under central government control. In 1973, South Africa rejected a proposal for a special radio station for Kwazulu on the grounds that SABC already had one in operation. SABC also runs separate programmes for Asians and coloureds.

Progressive Africans resent not just the fact that they have no independent system of radio communication for these territories, but also that the Nationalists have committed all domestic stations to conversion to VHF (or FM). Although this policy is partly due to the poor reception conditions which affect short-, medium- and long-wave signals, the primary reason, and the immediate effect, is to isolate all South Africans, white and black, from the long-distance short-wave signals from outside the country. Already FM dominates the South African airwaves. It is a serious problem to find in any shop a sensitive short-wave set. As the process of conversion continues, the problem will get worse. The only way round it for foreign broadcasters will be to join the VHF battle, but for that they will need a large number of transmitters stationed almost on the borders of South Africa. Already the BBC has one VHF transmitter in Lesotho. But even a whole string would not reach all of South Africa.

It is a moot point whether the arrival of television in South Africa in 1976 will help or hinder radio broadcasting, either internal or from outside. It has been resisted for so long, by Dr Hertzog in particular, on the grounds that TV watchers are 'inferior followers' and the whites must be leaders, that the attraction it will have over radio when it finally arrives will be all the greater for the time it has taken to come. Maybe many white South Africans will turn into passive viewers of soap operas and simplified news. On the other hand, so might the blacks. As a medium to impart mindlessness, which is after all one of the most important aims of some propaganda, particularly fascist propaganda, TV is far superior to radio. If, for the blacks, South African radio has now so little to offer them, and they are going to be effectively isolated from foreign stations, then there would seem to be a good chance that, on balance, the introduction of TV will help to weaken resistance to apartheid still further.

There is a final point to be made about the effectiveness of the Voice of South Africa. The station attaches great importance to broadcasts in the vernacular. By putting out programmes in Cicewa, for example, it has the edge over other foreign broadcasters in attracting audiences in Zambia and Malawi. Its only rivals on this score are Cairo Radio and Moscow Radio, neither of which can compete in the field of up-to-date news about local events in the southern, and more sensitive half of the African continent. Apart from these three, other international broadcasters limit themselves to English, French, Swahili, Hausa, and perhaps some Somali, Shona or Portuguese.

But broadcasting in even half of the numerous African languages and dialects is an impossible task for any international service. On the other hand, the more languages a station can muster, the better the chance it has of reaching a broadly based audience. The alternative is to aim unashamedly at the elite. This is, to a large extent, the BBC's solution.

In an article written in 1965, the London *Sunday Times* concluded that 'the radio war in East Africa today is between Cairo and Johannesburg, with the BBC fussing around at the edges. Peking and Moscow have still to make their mark.' Even in 1965 this was probably unfair to the BBC. Although bad reception in east Africa mars the impact of the British station, as far as the educated rich throughout Africa are concerned, it is *the* station to listen to. For some people the habit was formed when, in colonial days, the local radios would rebroadcast a great deal of BBC material. Kenya and Uganda still put out some of the BBC's English lessons and more harmless feature programmes, but straightforward relaying ended at the time of independence. This pattern has been repeated all over Africa.

But still the BBC can claim remarkable penetration in some areas. According to a recent survey in Nigeria, where listening to foreign stations is especially common, over half the adults in the main cities claimed to be regular listeners to the BBC. Among English-speaking Europeans living in Black Africa, it not surprisingly comes out top of the ratings in all surveys which examine the extent of listening to foreign broadcasting. These surveys also confirm the fact that it is the upper classes among the Africans that listen most to the BBC, particularly its English-language programmes.

Evidence for the BBC's impact also comes from criticisms levelled at it by, for example, Uganda Radio. Zambian Radio has on occasion warned of the 'snake in the grass'. The large Nigerian audience today remembers both the criticism and the praise for the BBC during the civil war. Frederick Forsyth wrote:

Throughout the whole war listeners were astounded by the number and variety of the misrepresentations of the situation presented by these [BBC] programmes . . . [People inside Biafra] became convinced there existed strong pro-Nigerian bias in the coverage of the story.[2]

But that is the kind of criticism that the BBC welcomes, because the partisan sympathies of the critic are so well known. It is as much a testimonial in their eyes as the more straightforward praise from an independent observer like John de St Jorre, who wrote that the BBC was accused of bias by both sides:

Nevertheless both sides listened to it avidly, if with a new scepticism and together with the Voice of America it remained the most reliable source of daily information throughout the war.[3]

It should perhaps be mentioned that reception conditions in west Africa for the BBC (from Ascension Island) and the Voice of America (from Monrovia) are excellent.

The Voice's eight transmitters located in Liberia argue more of an interest in Africa than is in fact the case. Up until the late 1950's, the only diplomatic interest that America had in Africa was as a dumping-ground for failed diplomats. President Kennedy, however, who had been chairman of the Senate Foreign Relations Committee's African subcommittee, promoted the continent to a higher priority level at the same time as Africa itself was moving towards independence. But the activity which this aroused in the USIA, and therefore in the VOA too, was half-hearted and temporary. The Voice broadcasts only in English, French and Swahili to Africa. Attempts to 'regionalize' output have amounted to little more than shows such as *African Safari*, the title of which only goes to prove the American-centred viewpoint of the broadcasters. Besides, the American voice is made no more credible by its attempts to underplay the racial problem in the United States.

But if the Americans seem unable to come to grips with the problem of communicating with the Africans, the communist radio stations are all the more remote. Despite investing in transmitters and training courses—the Chinese, for example, in Tanzania and Zambia, and the Russians in the Camerouns—the programming policy of Moscow and Peking is self-defeating.

The Russians may broadcast in a variety of African vernaculars, but they find it impossible to escape from stereotyped formulas when it comes to deciding what to say in them. Peking even more than Moscow merely translates Home Service news and reads out enormously long commentaries on matters which could never even strike a chord of recognition in their listeners. The standard faults of Russian and Chinese radio propaganda are particularly glaring when seen from the point of view of the remote communities of Africa. So despite the fact that no outsider devotes as much airtime to Africa as the Soviet Union, surveys show very low audience figures for the communist stations. Even among the few and devoted listeners, the infighting between the communist superpowers weakens the impact of their appeals.

As a result, the African masses are left very largely out in the cold. Despite poor-quality domestic services throughout Africa, the foreign alternatives have not filled the political and cultural gap. Perhaps only Cairo, with its new radio offensive to back up Egyptian wooing of black Africa, appears likely to win over audiences from the entire cross-section of the population. It is too early to tell how the campaign is progressing—whether, for instance, it will limit its appeal to mainly Muslims or mainly revolutionaries. Apart from Cairo, the only stations which make any serious attempt to fill the gap are the BBC, the Voice of the Gospel, the Voice of America and Radio South Africa's External Service. Ironically, it is the last which aims most consciously at a mass as well as an elite audience.

Africa is still a low priority for foreign broadcasters. All would do more if more money were available. But meanwhile, whites and 'wa-benzi' (Mercedes-Benz owners, hence the African ruling class) tune in to the detached, liberal coverage offered by the BBC and the VOA. Revolutionary activists search, probably in vain, for useful guidance from Moscow or Peking. Monitors pass their reports on to the appropriate authorities to interpret how the outside world is thinking. But no foreign propaganda service has yet got close to the African people.

8 East of Suez

In Asia, the influence of China and the Chinese looms larger than ever now that the world's most populous nation has emerged as an active superpower. Accordingly, Radio Peking makes a strong appeal to the Asian audience: ninety-eight hours out of its daily output of 190 are directed there. Some target audiences find all signs of Chinese nationalism offensive, as, for instance, the Malaysian communal riots demonstrated. The Indians, too, are deeply suspicious of Peking's motives. There is also a growing awareness in China of the Chinese communities throughout Asia.

Yet the Chinese cannot be said to have waged a propaganda war in Asia, except against Taiwan which is not seen as the object of an *international* campaign in the first place. Similarly, Radio Peking regards all Chinese outside the People's Republic as an extension of its domestic audience.

Although now playing an active role in the United Nations, and openly concerned about the political course of neighbouring countries, China's main barrage of propaganda has been reserved for the Soviet Union and, more importantly still, for the actual internal audience. Peking is more anxious to create a feeling of domestic racial solidarity against outsiders than antagonize other Asian governments. Besides, she is well aware of the potential anti-Chinese racism among many ordinary Asians who, for reasons of poverty, exploitation and persecution by the ruling classes, might otherwise be expected to provide a sympathetic audience for propaganda from Peking.

This has reinforced Radio Peking's lack of special effort to sharpen its programming policy for Asia or to alter the uniformly dull presentation of its broadcasts. Even towards countries on its doorstep it behaves more like the mouthpiece of a state religion than a force for political persuasion. Some of the obvious targets are attacked with both vigour and virulence, but there is no systematic attempt to subvert or overthrow a foreign power, or even to analyse consistently the political situation in neighbouring Asian states. Only in the case of Taiwan is there any parallel with, for example, the uncompromisingly bitter battles between North and South Korea and North and South Vietnam.

In both these last two areas, the propaganda war has never been so intense. The ending of the hot wars has even given a fillip to the word war. The terms of the peace settlements, allegations of infringements, and discussions about eventual reunification all provide the sort of material for a public political slanging match that the actual fighting drowned out. More and more, in both the Koreas and the Vietnams, the need to strike uncompromising attitudes and to weaken the convictions of the opposition has replaced reliance on outsiders to step in and settle the conflict. Clandestine radios back up official stations here in a double no-holds-barred contest.

All-India Radio has also played its part in all-out propaganda campaigns in recent years, both against China and against Pakistan. India broadcasts 320 hours of international programmes a week, but its main preoccupation is with the multilingual subcontinent itself. Its priority is not so much to persuade distant foreigners of the correctness of the Indian political line—although this is an inevitable function of All-India Radio—but to maintain a national Indian position against internal fragmentation and the threat posed by Pakistan. At the time of the 1962 Sino-Indian war, India was likewise more concerned to protect herself from the influence of Maoist propaganda than to undertake the futile task of undermining Chinese unity or morale. The tone of the Indian radio was distinctly hysterical during the short but disastrous war, partly because the Chinese were winning and no-one knew where their victories would lead, but also because the reasonable line the Chinese were striking, appealing to Indians for a quick peaceful settlement, was in danger of causing even deeper popular disillusionment than the military defeat. The very frangibility of the Indian state makes more than the minimum of foreign propaganda effort a dangerous luxury which the country cannot afford.

In India, towards the end of 1973, a number of opposition members of the Lok Sabha (Parliament) accused the ruling Congress Party of using All-India Radio for its own purposes, prompting a denial from the Minister of Information and a threat that he would deal firmly with any individual or party which set up a broadcasting station in defiance of the law. This is only one example of the way in which broadcasting authorities are obliged to oppose internal factionalism more than threats from outside India.

During the times when India has been at war with Pakistan, and particularly during the last war which ended in the secession of Bangladesh from West Pakistan, Indians were a great deal more united than usual. This conflict also served to highlight the split allegiance of Moscow and Peking, which defused the impact of communist propaganda directed at India. Nevertheless, many Indians are not convinced of the objectivity of their national media in times of crisis, even when events are moving in their favour. The same is true for the citizens of Pakistan and Bangladesh. The BBC claims vastly increased audiences in all these places whenever tensions heighten or there is open war. But the number of regular listeners to the British station also reflects the distrust arising out of the rigidity of government control over the national radios. A recent survey disclosed that the BBC's Hindi Service has an audience of fifteen per cent of the adult population of the main towns in northern India. At present, however, with the spirit of détente riding high in the subcontinent, the domestic media have a rare chance to re-establish their prestige.

All-India Radio is an amalgam of British thinking and American- or even Russian-style controls. It has a monopoly in India and was set up with the model of the BBC in mind, but it is not independent of the Ministry of Information or of the Ministry of Foreign Affairs. There is indeed a great deal of internal criticism about the 'heavy hand of officialdom'. The broadcasters themselves deplore the way the Prime Minister's speech will invariably lead the news bulletin. In recent years, however, there has been a move towards liberalization and freedom of discussion, at least in the English-language sections. A modern sound is being introduced. To counter Sri Lanka's much-acclaimed pop music in its English, Sinhala, Tamil and Hindi Services, the Indians now put out a lively stream of pop on their own networks. Ceylon Radio was also responsible in 1967 for the introduction of advertising on All-India Radio, such was the competition from across the Palk Strait. On the political plane, All-India Radio is professional enough to recognize that crude or aggressive nationalistic propaganda is counter-productive. It is said that many Indian officials and ambassadors, notably in sensitive border states, are still a great deal less aware of this truism than the present generation of broadcasters.

The External Services of All-India Radio broadcast two hours a day in Chinese and just over twice that in Pusto and Dari to Afghanistan. But the main thrust of the overseas effort is directed to Pakistan and to Indians living abroad. The Pakistani audience can of course eavesdrop in many cases on Indian domestic programmes as well. But the Indians in south-east Asia and in east Africa have to rely on special programmes entirely, in Hindi and Tamil in the first case, and in Hindi, Gujerati, Konkani, and Swahili in the second. These go out on an enormously powerful (1,000 kilowatt) transmitter.

The presence of Indians in the Middle East, and the political connection with Egypt as co-leaders of the non-aligned world, prompted All-India Radio to broadcast in Arabic from 1968. It can also reach Middle East audiences, as well as overseas nationals in the Caribbean and elsewhere, with a powerful world-wide English-language service. The Pakistanis put out an hour-and-a-half of Arabic programmes a day to their fellow Muslims, in addition to broadcasts by a large Urdu Service to the Indian subcontinent, the United Kingdom and the Middle East. In their different ways, India and Pakistan carry their rivalry outside the confines of their two states.

A similar situation is reflected in the international radio priorities of Indonesia and Malaysia. Although 'confrontation' is long over and done with, about half of the output of the Indonesian External Service is directed at Malaysia, and the Malaysian Service is likewise directed principally at Indonesia. Indonesia broadcasts in eight languages, and Malaysia in five in addition to Indonesian. Both sides seem prepared to face a new round of hostility, even if neither plans to begin it.

One of the more polyglot External Services in Asia belongs to the Philippines. As well as sending signals in a handful of major languages all round the world, its Asian programmes go out in, among others, five Chinese dialects apart from Mandarin, and in Tamil, Tibetan, Aonaga and Mongolian.

Probably the most important Asian voice of all is that of Japan. After the war, Japanese broadcasting was reconstituted, not along American lines, but with the BBC in mind. Nippon Hoso Kyokai (NHK) was made an independent corporation under government financial control, which before had been a monopoly. But over the following years NHK was flooded by a profusion of commercial stations.

The External Services, banned by General MacArthur in 1945 after ten years as the international mouthpiece of Japanese militarism, were given permission to start up again in mid-January 1952, in Japanese and English only. The Americans regarded this as a helpful move at a time when they were conducting the United Nations operation in Korea. Now Japan broadcasts in twenty-two languages, although the emphasis is still on the original two. The English and Japanese sections constitute the 'General Service'. All others are lumped together in the 'Regional Service'.

Not unexpectedly, the main aim of NHK's External Services has been to achieve influence through the promotion of business and trade rather than through political argument. They faithfully reflect Japan's economic diplomacy. Whereas the domestic services are forbidden (as is the BBC) to mention individual products or firms by name, the foreign services (again like the BBC) can freely plug brand names. Programmes describing visits to Japanese factories are a regular feature of their output. Despite the fact that only one per cent of NHK's budget is earmarked for the External Services as a whole, the proportion of that money spent on showing up the advantages of doing business with Japan and how beneficial to all Asia Japan's phenomenal post-war boom has been, is higher than the equivalent sums spent by other countries.

This line of approach may be both reasonable and convincing, but it has also attracted suspicion. Recently the Japanese have grown more sensitive to charges of economic imperialism, and this has in turn produced a softer sell in their international programmes. But NHK still faces difficulties. Any 'projection of Japan'—and that is the necessary aim of the Japanese External Services, like any other —is bound to arouse envy in at least equal proportion to admiration. It is possible that Japan's present difficulties have been as much of a propaganda advantage as any account of the economic miracle.

NHK has a legal duty, stipulated in its charter, to run an External Service 'to enhance international understanding and welfare'. But despite what the Managing Director of the BBC's External Services calls 'the Japanese desire to miniaturize the BBC formula and so turn out instant truth by radio', excessive caution and the lack of a tradition similar to the British one have prevented this feat of political engineering. Like the new Brazilian External Service, which plays a role of local superpower in Latin America similar to the Japanese role in Asia, NHK is as determinedly anodyne on political matters as it is aggressive in its economic strategy. So much so that NHK plays down in its foreign programmes anything that is 'shameful', anything which reflects badly on Japan. No 'extremist' is ever invited to the studio to argue his case. As one staff member described it to me, 'no unnecessary disturbances are aroused'.

Bad publicity would only be bad for business and might frighten the tourists away, and attracting tourists is an important function of NHK's foreign operations. All this explains why the Japanese recruiting policy is extremely tight. New staff members are generally recruited direct from university. If they have a suitable recommendation from their university president, they are then faced with special examinations, interviews and a three-month training-course. Nonconformists need not bother to apply. Again, the Japanese have taken over a BBC policy, but reduced it to near-absurdity.

Special care in the selection of staff is needed because, as in the Voice of America and indeed most international services, all political comments are prepared inside the Service. Sometimes journalists are hired for short-term contracts, but uncontrollable outsiders are kept at a distance. Although NHK prides itself on being modelled on the BBC, this is another fundamental difference.

As for their audience, the Japanese reckon to have most effect in Indonesia, India and the United States. But there is one area where a new and growing audience is detected: Australia and New Zealand. The signal here is good, and more and more letters are evidence of a growing interest in Japan.

In fact Australia herself increasingly rivals Japan, not only economically, but also as the source of international propaganda. Tenth in the world ratings, Australia's External Service has grown steadily since the war, putting out programmes today in Indonesian, Japanese, Mandarin, Cantonese, Vietnamese, and Thai, in addition to its English and French Services. It claims a regular audience of 10 million, and has ambitious plans to expand output. Whereas New Zealand concentrates its small international output towards the Pacific islands (broadcasting in Samoan, Rarotongan and Niuean) and hopes to catch the ear of the rare scientist in the Antarctic, Australia is bidding for an audience among the masses of Asia. Apart from the need to counteract the impression left by the 'white Australia' policy, the Australian authorities, like the Japanese, see the most important use of international radio as a commercial weapon.

It is not unreasonable to suppose that the impetus behind this commercial orientation has been provided by the American example. Indeed both Japan and Australia are in some sense trying to compete with the omnipresent American telecommunications network, having observed that intensive campaigns do deliver the goods if pressed hard over the years. International radio is only a small part of the competition for markets, but it is by no means a negligible part. Australia, like America, sees herself less as an outsider trying to penetrate foreign markets than as a physical presence in Asia, a presence that has to be brought to the people's notice not just through representatives on the ground, but through radio and television and all the other communications media.

One advantage which the British share with the Americans and Australians in their propaganda for Asia is the prevalence of the English language, for which the colonial legacy, since reinforced by the US presence, has been responsible. Despite military withdrawal from east of Suez, the British connection is not difficult to maintain at a distance. As in parts of Africa, large numbers still regard the BBC as a kind of alternative Home Service and follow its output with as much discrimination as the most blimpish expatriate.

At present, the BBC's headache is not attracting listeners but ensuring that the relay system which boosts the London signal remains intact. Since the Malaysian government gave notice that it would terminate the agreement to act as host, negotiations have begun with Singapore, probably the ideal site in Asia, but, while the government there is agreeable, the problem is to find enough open space to accommodate several miles of aerials. With Brunei acting as reserve, however, the real danger may turn out to be the threatened cuts in the BBC's budget.

In the end the BBC will make sure that it remains in the race for Asian listeners. Increasing competition will guarantee that. Already, the superpowers are heavily engaged. As for Moscow Radio, its pre-occupation with China prompted a new service, in addition to its regular programmes for Asia, directed at the Chinese communities living outside the People's Republic. Set up in 1970, this makes the competition for this audience a three-way one, with both Peking and Taiwan.

Competition from America is apparent throughout Asia. The American Forces Korea Network operates in seventeen South Korean cities. The forces radio and the VOA are active from Japan (five Army and one Air Force station, and one VOA station in Okinawa broadcasting in Chinese and Korean) to Thailand (where the Voice of Free Asia is part of a VOA operation) to Sri Lanka. And, of course, there are direct broadcasts from America.

In all parts of Asia except Japan, the communications battle is only just beginning. And radio, despite the long-term threat of TV, is the dominant medium.[1] India had only 35,000 television sets in 1972, but 16 million radio sets. In Asia generally, again excepting Japan, there are still thirteen times more radios than television sets. Clandestine stations flourish in an atmosphere of enthusiasm for the transistorized message.

9 Latin America

In 1973, there were 54 million radio sets in Latin America for a population of 285 million; not as low a proportion as in Africa or Asia (except for Japan), but not in the North American or European league either. Yet radio (and TV) *stations* proliferate as nowhere else. One estimate put the total at 3,600 radio stations in 1970.[1] There are thirty-one local ones in Guatemala City alone, one of which, Radio Mundial, can be heard deep into the United States, but most are small and low-powered. Brazil, the largest Latin American country, boasts 750 stations, of which 92 per cent are commercial.

Typically, governments throughout the central and southern part of the American continent own one or two stations themselves, or else demand time on specified commercial outlets at specified times. But the vast majority of radio stations are small-scale vehicles for jingles, pop songs, news, and local ads, fashioned on the North American model.

With Spanish as a *lingua franca* for most Latin Americans outside Brazil, international radio is to a large extent a question of overspill, most unintentional, some deliberate. In Central America and near the frontiers of the bigger nations to the south, people regularly pick up signals from neighbouring countries. But political propaganda is unlikely to be either a feature of the broadcasts or a subject which worries the ruling classes of the countries concerned. Generally, governments ignore the marginal effects of foreign radio stations on public opinion. But there have been exceptions. In January 1974, for example, the government of Uruguay shut down for ten days a radio station that was beaming news at Argentina, fearing repercussions on itself.

The number one international broadcaster in Latin America, and exception to all the above generalizations, is Cuba.

At present, Havana Radio provides only a faint discordant note in a symphony conducted and played by right-wing politicians and businessmen, and composed largely by interested parties in the United States. Their instruments are almost exclusively domestic radio and TV stations. International services have only recently been brought into the orchestra, and still their contribution is almost inaudible.

Since the military junta came to power in Chile in September 1973, the only left-wing voice which survives in the area is Havana's. Its force is not negligible. For one thing, Havana Radio's External

Service is the largest in Latin America, and eleventh largest in the world. It broadcasts over 350 hours a week, mostly in Spanish, but some programmes also in Creole for Haiti, in Guarani for Paraguay, and in Quechua for the Andes Indians in Bolivia, Peru and Ecuador. It has an English and Portuguese Service for the Latin American area; and English, French, Spanish and Arabic programmes are beamed across the Atlantic to Europe and the Middle East.

While Havana's broadcasts directed to audiences outside Latin America and the Caribbean can be safely ignored—like so many international services they are mostly for the record or for exiles— their impact as the lone alternative voice from Mexico to Tierra del Fuego is considerable. Havana Radio is the only evidence of Castro's revolution and the only daily witness of his prestige to most left-wing Latin Americans. It is not able to conduct long-distance subversion in any practical sense, but in an area where communications are the biggest problem for governments and rebels, those few who are actively engaged in resisting repressive regimes badly need their morale sustaining in struggles that all too often seem dangerously remote and unsupported.

Apart from Cuba, the only two countries with well-established External Services are Mexico and Argentina. Mexico's is minimal— a mere seven hours a week—and merits no discussion at all. Argentina's, on the other hand, is a story of wasted opportunity. It broadcasts in seven languages for over sixty hours a week, but makes only the barest attempt to come up to normal professional standards. It is under-funded by the government and bedevilled by nepotism and corruption. Yet Argentine culture is the most inter-national in Latin America and in so far as its roots and its continuing European connections are concerned, the opportunity was there to establish a reputation as at least the cultural, if no longer the political and economic, centre.

It is too late to rescue the situation now. Not only is Argentina held in suspense by a fragile Peronist revival, its stability and prosperity further threatened by the death of the President himself, but Brazil long ago seized the position of first country of the continent.

Brazil's burgeoning economic power and population have put it out of reach of any single Spanish-speaking country. But Brazil is on its own and aware of being the odd man out. Its cautious govern-ment is reluctant to be seen as a threat to the Spanish-speaking countries, when they can *only* unite in the face of such a threat. In a speech in Washington at the end of 1971, and in the presence of the Brazilian president, President Nixon once said out loud what every-one else knows but never says: 'Where Brazil goes, the rest of Latin America will follow.' The reaction was strong, creating an instant anti-Brazilian front. Countering other countries' fears of Brazil's power was a major reason why the Brazilian government decided to set up an international radio service, which first went on the air, after years of planning and postponements, in the autumn of 1972.

Radio Nacional de Brasilia's international service broadcasts in five European languages successively for one hour each daily. It is an exceedingly cautious operation, designed to soothe, not exacerbate. As with Radio Peking, central material is translated word for word from the original (Portuguese), without any effort being made to adapt it for different audiences. There is great stress on programming jolly music, anodyne chat and promotional features. The object is the maximum of prestige with the minimum of offence—at least so far. Once the organization exists, it is ready for any kind of propaganda purpose. At present it us unnecessary, in fact counterproductive, to strike a hard line. *Let's Listen to the Samba* is the soft-sell sound; or, as another daily programme title has it: *Music is also news*.

In President Allende's Chile, radio stations were allowed to reflect the different party lines, despite some curbs on the most extreme expressions of opposition. Politics was still fought out over the airwaves. Things changed dramatically with the 1973 coup. All Marxist stations were banned along with all the Marxist parties. And, early in 1974, the junta began to put out their own international propaganda to 'counter hostile communist propaganda'.

The output has been modest so far—a succession of twenty-minute programmes in seven languages—and the line has been quite predictable. Indeed the tone of this External Service is similar to the Armed Forces and Carabinieros Radio, which is the junta's internal voice operating from the commandeered Radio University in Concepcion. The keynote is one of hurt pride, a defensive reaction against the reports which have leaked out and been published all over the world of the brutal measures used to put down the opposition forces inside Chile.

More specifically, the 'hostile communist propaganda' referred to by the junta in their official justification of the new Chilean international service comes not just from Radio Havana but also from Moscow and Peking. Moscow in particular puts out a powerful signal to all Latin America, but its audience would appear, from western surveys at any rate, to be limited to those few whose concern is the correct Party line. In general, international broadcasters from outside Latin America attract very limited audiences in the target area. The BBC claims a much wider audience, although the weakness of its direct signal, which should be remedied when the joint BBC-Deutsche Welle relay station in Antigua comes into operation, probably in 1975, has held back its ambitions.

BBC planners regard a strong medium-wave signal into Latin America as essential, given the people's habit of tuning into this frequency range to pick up the numerous local stations. The BBC also reckons it has another strong card to play in the battle for the un-committed listener who is neither on the extreme left nor the extreme right: the widespread anti-Americanism which handicaps the Voice of America.

The United States has long been involved in the propaganda business directed at Latin America, an area that it regards as its own sphere of influence. Even before the last world war, some private American stations were beaming commercial programmes south of the border. But little attempt was made to counter either the signal strength or the political impact of the Nazi and fascist propaganda until August 1940, when Nelson Rockefeller became the Co-ordinator of Commercial and Cultural Affairs between the American Republics, later changed to the more manageable Co-ordinator of Inter-American Affairs.

Throughout the world war, Latin America was excluded from the mainstream psychological warfare operations. It remained a low priority until President Kennedy launched his *Alianza para el Progreso* at the start of the sixties. But this was little more than an instinctive anti-Castro drive and soon became bogged down. Robert Elder writes:

Because of domestic political pressures exerted by Cuban exiles through members of Congress, its [VOA's] Cuban broadcasts were probably less reasoned between 1963 and 1967 than its Soviet out-put (or that to Communist China).[2]

Even Chancellor's campaign to sound a sweeter note met stern resistance from rightist opposition. Former director George Allen claimed that, at the time of the 1962 Cuba crisis, the virulent line had been positively harmful. Castro, he said, was able to claim sympathy as 'the target for the largest concentration of propaganda effort un-leashed against an individual since Stalin tried to purge Tito in 1948'.

But this was not a conclusion which the VOA as a whole accepted. The hard line continued after 1962, yet it still appeared to fail in terms of impact on the audience. In 1969, Nelson Rockefeller returned to his old beat to report to President Nixon on US relations with Latin America. One of his recommendations was:

A major effort should be made to make the Voice of America (VOA) at least competitive with Radio Havana in the Central American-Caribbean area, including improved programming and standard radio band broadcasting by VOA.

Americans, USIA officials included, have never been sanguine about the effectiveness of long-distance persuasion by short waves in Latin America. They have preferred direct penetration, whether by businessmen or the CIA or any other means. In radio terms this means the sale or free distribution of ready-packaged programmes.

'Transcription' material and rebroadcasts are unquestionably the only way for outsiders to reach a substantial audience in Latin America. The USIA has for years had the policy of feeding free programmes, often the back half (i.e. after the news and comments) of VOA broadcasts, to the local stations, which are only too ready to accept them. Other original material is prepared in local 'field offices' tailored for local needs. This is taken by forty per cent of all the radio stations in the seventeen Spanish-speaking Latin American countries. Most university and classical music stations could hardly exist without American support by way of these free gifts.

The BBC tags on here to America's coat-tails. Although the total number of hours of British-made material rebroadcast in Latin America sounds impressive, the BBC suffers from a grave self-imposed handicap. It refuses to send out tapes for free. Given the cutthroat competition of the thousands of stations, desperately balancing income from advertising against programme expenses, free airtime is manna from heaven. The BBC is afraid of the precedent it would set by distributing programmes free to one area of the world, but the British are unlikely to make headway against the Americans unless they make an exception in Latin America.

The audience is there to be won. The elite audience is ready to be tempted with a good current affairs service and high-level cultural programmes, because the available fare is of such low quality. But it does not look to the United States to provide it. The Americans have too often attempted—and with success—to rape what they regard as virgin territory. They have built up a fund of resentment. Latin American intellectuals hanker after European culture and standards. The radical chic, as well as numbers of workers and peasants, react instinctively against US imperialism, but are also looking for something more sophisticated or entertaining than the predictable message from Havana or the more distant communist capitals. American material may constantly be available on every radio set, and many people therefore listen to it, but this does not mean that the propaganda purpose of making them like America is being achieved. The flooding of the airwaves with American radio hand-outs probably creates resentment even. Latin Americans may know that their anti-Americanism is still little more than exercise in the prisoners' yard, but being reminded so insistently of their imprisonment does not endear them to their gaolers.

PART THREE

10 Clandestine Radio

This is the Palestine Broadcast from Damascus to the destitute Arabs, instruments of the Revolution, to those marching on the morrow the plains of Galilee and hills of Negev, to those hoisting the Arab flag over Jaffa and Mount Carmel, for you, the Voice of Palestine from Damascus.

Every day this opening message of the *Palestine Hour* is broadcast in Arabic on powerful short-wave transmitters, courtesy of Radio Damascus. A similar service is offered to the PLO by Cairo, Algiers, Baghdad, Tripoli and Beirut. Omdurman Radio backed out when the Palestinians attacked the Saudi embassy in Khartoum at the beginning of March 1973.

Strictly speaking, these programmes are not clandestine at all. But no such thing as a precise definition exists. In the Middle East, as elsewhere, radio comes in a variety of shades from pristine white to hellish black—from, that is, the most open and above-board to the most devious, misleading and underground. While the major-league government stations are generally white enough, declaring their source and their policies openly, many others have at least a greyish tint about them. Pure black operations are rare outside local and/or temporary hot-war situations.

The word clandestine is used here, therefore, as a general term to cover all those stations which are not the mouthpieces of governments in power and which play some kind of subversive role by beaming propaganda at a particular localized area for tactical reasons, as opposed to disseminating an ideology or 'objective truth' to the world at large. I shall leave out of account 'pirate' stations, although they have been known to be linked with political protest. For example, there has recently been a rash of 'radio hooliganism' in the Soviet Union with overenthusiastic amateurs building low-power transmitters to broadcast pop songs and political barbs.

It is also a feature of many clandestine stations that for one reason or another they disguise their locations. This is true, for example, of the PLO's own clandestine station, probably at present operating from Damascus but formerly on a penetrating medium wave from

Deraa near the Golan Heights. The earlier location was detected only when the Israelis bombed the transmitter off the air. At that point the Syrians decided that the operation should be moved from their territory altogether, but Iraqi sources now say that they relented and that the station has started up again from Damascus. No monitoring service, however, can get an exact fix on its present location and, in the absence of any information from the source, it can only be guessed that the same broadcasters with the same policies moved from Deraa to the Syrian capital.

For all their virulence, the Palestine 'liberation radios' fill only a fraction of the turbulent airwaves in the Middle East today. Competing with them are the Voice of the Arabs, the Libyans broadcasting Gaddafi's revolution over the air from Tripoli and swiping viciously at Morocco en passant, the equally scurrilous replies from Rabat, the bitter attacks by Iraq on Iran and vice versa, the voices of Radio Free Yemeni South, of the Arabian Peninsular Peoples, of Radio Sorush with its Marxist message from Baghdad, and many many others from outside and inside the area. Radio is a weapon wielded as freely today as the scimitar was in the days of the Saracens.

But how effective is clandestine radio, as opposed to the overt stations, in the Middle East and elsewhere? What can it do that the straightforward mouthpieces of government cannot do? Or are the two types complementary rather than in conflict? One trouble when trying to answer these much-debated questions is that, in a sense, there are as many arguments as there are situations. As we observe who is conducting clandestine operations around the world, and where, and in what circumstances, it will become clearer how greatly those circumstances dictate the relative roles of the various kinds of radio station.

Clandestine broadcasts probably account for about five or six per cent of output in the worldwide communications battle. This represents a likely maximum, in terms of hours of transmission in any given week, of 1,000 hours, compared with the global total of around 17,000 hours of international radio.

Clandestine radio is prevalent not just in the Middle East but also on the continent of Europe and in the Far East. It is not, however, a uniformly international phenomenon. In Latin America, for example, it hardly exists. A rare report suggests that a Radio Libertade has occasionally and briefly surfaced in Brazil. There were no reports, however, of left-wing stations in Chile resisting the junta's coup in September 1973. The reason for the dearth of Latin American clandestine stations (although this does not explain their absence in Chile) is, generally speaking, the amazing number of commercial stations which not only swamp the airwaves, but also provide an irresistible target for guerrillas who take them over, use them for free, and get out. This was, for instance, the tactic of the Tupamaros in Uruguay.

In Africa, the appearance of clandestine radios has also been erratic. The Voice of Free Angola, and also Fighting Angola, are put out by Brazzaville and Kinshasa Radios on behalf of resistance groups. The Radio of the National Liberation Front of the Republic of Guinea used to be heard at one time or another emanating from an unidentified location. A more rare and elusive bird is the Voice of Free Zanzibar and Pemba, probably a South African- or Portuguese-inspired station which attacked President Nyerere and the late Dr Karume, ruler of Zanzibar. The BBC Monitoring Service can claim only one sighting.

African voices in the past included one station of high quality and unusual virulence, the Voice of Free Africa, operating from Cairo, and a fake Lumumbist radio which frequently succeeded in leading Lumumba's Congolese troops into ambushes. There was also a mystifying Freedom Radio which baffled South African investigators back in 1956. It came on the air with the familiar V-sign in morse, the announcer declaring:

This is your Freedom Radio station. This is the resistance. Calling all South Africans who love their country, their language and their culture, and are opposed to everything a Broederbond republic has to offer.

It was heard intermittently for some months expounding a wartime anti-Nazi theme. Some press reports suggested that it might be the work of a Natal separatist organization. Stanley Uys wrote in the *News Chronicle* in October 1956 that four young men had been arrested in Pretoria—after attempts to jam the broadcasts with 'Lies! Lies! Lies!' in morse and with 'rude noises' had failed to deter them. 'Special Branch detectives . . . even swooped on a scientist recording earth tremors out in the veldt. Valuable records and instruments were damaged,' reported Uys.

The seven blocks of airtime provided by Radio Tanzania for their protégés from African nationalist parties—including Frelimo, even after the political changes in Mozambique—are only clandestine in the sense that the sponsored PLO stations can be so described. Their source is clearly identified and they all claim to be the mouth-piece of governments-in-exile. But their role is of course subversive. Radio Biafra, to which we shall return later, was for a time an im-portant and successful station, though illegal and subversive in the sense that Biafra itself was illegal and subversive.

As for South Africa, it might well be suspected that the Secret

Service would regard 'black' radio as a natural choice of weapon to use against Africans inside and outside the Republic's borders. In fact the RSA's powerful international service has no need of such back-up, at least at present, and the Bantu radios do their work of fostering political and cultural separation effectively and openly. Neither do the various revolutionary groups opposing white domination make extensive use of clandestine radio. They mostly borrow the facilities of sympathetic countries—Tanzania, Algeria, Zambia, Congo Brazzaville. So far they do not have the urban bases in which to move large transmitters around; or else they have not reached the stage in their struggle, or simply do not have enough money, to acquire and run their own transmitters. The Organization for African Unity, what is more, does not encourage clandestine radio, preferring to be seen to have clean hands and fearing the divisive potential of sponsoring underground radio stations. The idea could all too easily catch on and be turned against countries fighting for the black African cause, or else lead to friction among member states.

Except in Latin America and, to a lesser extent, Africa, clandestine radio plays a key role as a political and psychological weapon to complement political and military action. Most of the techniques used today were first practised in the Second World War. It is this example which the clandestine broadcasters now follow.

There were instances of clandestine broadcasting before the war, however. The Russians began it all with their subversive calls to German workers to join them in the very early days of revolutionary struggle. In the inter-war years a number of ephemeral operations came on the scene, like Radio Corse Libre, or various anti-Nazi *Freiheitsender* in disguised mobile trucks. There was even an IRA pirate station in the thirties. The League of Nations made several attempts to ban all such stations. In 1938, the United Kingdom, New Zealand, Australia, India, Brazil, Denmark, Luxembourg and France all signed an International Convention concerning the Use of Broadcasting in the Cause of Peace. But like so many other worthy causes taken up by the League, this one too proved futile.

As soon as war broke out the radio war began too. Between 1939 and 1945 more than sixty black stations were established. The Germans had the early advantage of using transmitters captured during their advances, but the BBC was quick to expose the sham that, for example, Radio Paris still operated as it did before. 'Radio Paris ment, Radio Paris est allemand' sang their irrepressibly satirical exponents of the propaganda jingle. In the hot-war situation, all kinds of nefarious radio operations got under way, including such hopeful devices as a station covertly sponsored by the Nazis and purporting to be the voice of the 'Christian Peace Movement', whose message was to turn the enemy off 'ungodly' war and sue for peace. As the war went on, phoney Nazi freedom stations proliferated, from Subhar Chandra Bose's Free India Radio to Radio Mexican and an 'Iowan' station called Radio Debunk.

Towards the end of the war, the Germans brought into operation an unusual black station, Radio Arnhem, to confuse both the Dutch, soon to be liberated, and the advancing Allies. BBC programmes were broadcast on it from 6.25 a.m. to 11.00 p.m., but they were interspersed with bogus material including news and messages from prisoners. A Radio Arnhem statement in January 1945 praising General Montgomery and disparaging the Americans caused a stir in the highest Allied circles.

Europe was of course the supreme battleground of rival black stations, the details of which have been recounted in a number of memoirs, history books and treatises on psychological warfare. One of the raciest accounts is contained in the second volume of Sefton Delmer's autobiography, *Black Boomerang*.[1] Delmer, a former *Daily Express* correspondent who became chief of British wartime black operations, was a firm advocate of no-holds-barred propaganda, using deception, lies, bogus messages, guesswork, and sometimes obscenity to create a weapon as sharp as the BBC, 'with its inhibitions and passion for ideological debate,' was blunt. Though a partial witness to the role of black radio in the war, Delmer's motto that 'the simplest and most effective of all "black" operations is to spit in a man's soup and cry "Heil Hitler"!' is a terse and accurate description of how it is best done. But as Asa Briggs summed up the difference between black and white broadcasting:

> The 'black' broadcasters could set out to demoralize the Germans because they were geared to the war machine: the BBC gained in influence because it was always concerned with something more than demoralization.[2]

Goebbels himself admired the skill of the British black stations. The Americans had a measure of success, for example with Operation Annie, a primarily tactical station operating from the captured Luxembourg studios, and with other hard-hitting subversive stations. But in British eyes they were too crude and too easily identifiable as fakes. Radio Saipan broadcasting from San Francisco to Japan would even switch from white to black on the same wavelength.

On the eastern front, Moscow sponsored a radio station run by members of the Free Germany Committee, a group of high-ranking German defectors. But its success was limited to influencing other defectors and deserters at the front. It made little or no impact on Germany itself, partly because the Committee had ambivalent backing from the Russians and partly because the other Allies did not recognize the Committee. So its effect was divisive—there were Allied fears that it was a forerunner of a bid for a separate peace— and instead of causing the Nazis real concern, it gave them more ammunition to talk about the 'Disunited Nations'. Besides, the Germans countered with a black 'anti-Hitler' station which violently attacked Stalin as well for betraying true communism. Moscow's most brilliant coup was to be the first to superimpose comments, laughter and mimicry on the *Deutschlandsender* wavelengths. The first effects were stunning as listeners heard Hitler's tirades interrupted by noisy hecklers. But the German engineers learnt to synchronize wavelengths too, and the device was subsequently dropped by both sides.

On balance, Britain and Germany came out fairly even in the black radio war, with the Americans trailing behind. As the psychological warfare expert Paul Linebarger sums up the war on the western front in his PW textbook:

> No clear victor emerged from the Anglo-German radio war; the victory of the United Nations gave the British the last say. In the opinion of many, the British were one war ahead of the United States.[3]

The debate about the effectiveness of black radio still rages. It is generally accepted, however, that in some instances it does indeed provide a helpful back-up to physical action. This prompted governments and, particularly in later years, opposition groups, to study the lessons learnt in the war and carry on some of the techniques in the postwar years.

For the most part the propaganda Cold War has been fought out in the open, often with the participation of the same people who had staffed the anti-Nazi government stations whether in Moscow, London, Washington or elsewhere. The main American front-line weapons have been at most semi-clandestine. In the case of Radio Free Europe and Radio Liberty, there was never any secret about the fact that the émigré broadcasters were dependent on editorial guidelines from New York headquarters. The clandestine element consisted in the covert CIA financing of the stations, which went on until this became public in 1971. The Intelligence connection is also a well-known fact in the case of the Radio in the American Sector (RIAS), broadcasting in German from Berlin to the DDR. RIAS is part of the United States Information Agency (like the very official Voice of America) but it has also been involved in Len Deighton-style operations, particularly during the periods of crisis over Berlin.

An even less clear-cut cousin of RL, RFE and RIAS was Radio Free Russia, since 1950 the station of the militantly anti-communist Popular Labor Union (NTS), usually associated with the smuggling of bibles into the Soviet Union. Radio Free Russia transmitted from South Korea and Taiwan as well as from the Federal Republic of Germany. First of all, the former two sites were discontinued; and then the West German hosts closed down the Bavarian transmitter in 1974. This transmitter also carried religious propaganda in Russian and the Baltic languages put out by a parallel organization, Radio Omega.

At the time of the Hungarian uprising in October/November 1956, western propaganda stations were joined for a few days by the domestic Hungarian network, transformed into a multi-headed clandestine operation. In the first period of unrest, when it appeared that Imre Nagy was in control of events, stations such as Free Petoefi Radio (named after the intellectuals' club largely responsible for bringing down the old regime) co-ordinated its output with the official Radio Kossuth. But as Soviet troops moved in, Radio Free Kossuth was born, to merge very shortly with the Petoefi station. This was the signal for other stations such as Free Borsod Radio, based in the Miskolc University of Technology, to go on the air in several languages as well as Hungarian to arouse international support. During the deceptive lull in the fighting, the Miskolc station hopefully changed its name to the more official-sounding Radio Station of the National Council of Northern and Eastern Hungary. But words and titles were not enough. Although more 'free' stations such as Rajk and Salgotarjan kept up their calls for resistance to Soviet intervention until the last tragic moments, finally, at 13.34 on 4 November, a last appeal was heard on the frequency of the Petoefi transmitter in Szolnok:

Peoples of Europe, whom we had helped for centuries to withstand the barbaric attacks from Asia! Listen to the tolling of Hungarian bells warning of disaster. Come. Save our souls! Civilized peoples of the world! We implore you in the name of justice, freedom and the binding moral principle of active solidarity to help us. Our ship in sinking. The light is failing. The shadows grow darker every hour over the Hungarian land. Listen to our cry, civilized peoples of the world, and act. Extend your fraternal aid to us. SOS! SOS! May God be with you!

Then there was silence.

All these clandestine stations, however brief their lifespan, and though finally ineffective against tanks, did have a profound effect on the morale of the 'freedom fighters', playing, too, an important

E

co-ordinating role at a time of considerable confusion. Without them, resistance would surely not have been so fierce or so bloody; nor would the Czechs and Slovaks have used radio so effectively in 1968. In 1956 the freedom stations' influence spread into Romania also, in particular into the Hungarian-speaking area of Transylvania where many citizens seized the opportunity not just to acclaim the revolt of their ethnic brothers but also to raise the old issue of secession, thus pouring salt on the most sensitive spot in Romanian national pride. Bucharest Radio went on the air to deny explicitly reports from Radio Free Kossuth and Miskolc that the Transylvanians were in a state of unrest—with the customary, if contradictory rider that 'it is superfluous to reply to such inventions'. But the Hungarian reports were true.

Official Romanian sensibilities were further offended by a mysterious station called Radio Romania Viitoare (Future Romania Radio) which re-emerged, after an apparently false start in 1955, in the opening stages of the Hungarian uprising, broadcasting anti-Russian slogans and appeals for the independence of Bucovina and Bessarabia, both annexed by the Soviet Union after the Second World War.

In Czechoslovakia, the almost miraculous continuation of pro-Dubcek broadcasts on apparently unsilenceable transmitters defying the Soviet order to accept the new regime was a key feature of the resistance to the Soviet-led invasion during the night of 20-21 August 1968. During the period immediately after the Soviet invasion, several local transmitters continued to broadcast anti-Soviet material from emergency undergound regional government headquarters. It was said at the time that either those responsible for Russian contingency plans and operations on the ground were remarkably inefficient in tracking down observably powerful transmitters, or else the resistance broadcasters were remarkably astute in keeping one jump ahead. Certainly the effect of their message on world opinion as well as on the Czechoslovak people as a whole—who often heard these stations at second hand via western broadcasting services—was as important for morale, indeed for basic self-respect, as wartime broadcasts were to those who suffered in despair under Nazi rule or occupation.

But very soon the Russians were shedding doubt on the authenticity of these Czechoslovak transmissions. Moscow Radio put out reports early in September that, while some clandestine stations did carry on inside Czechoslovakia for a short while, most had been operating on West German territory, using wavelengths that had 'temporarily gone off the air'. Moscow accused the BBC of supporting 'forgeries' and of being in 'direct contact with West German psychological warfare army units'. The Russian case was that NATO had simply applied to a real-life situation the lessons learnt from an exercise held only a short while before which simulated exactly the sort of conditions that arose in Czechoslovakia. This case finds no support, not surprisingly, in the west.

Whatever the truth, the Russians were quick to set up a black operation of their own. Radio Vltava came on the air on 21 August, using transmitters sited in Dresden to put out a daily nineteen-hour barrage of pro-Soviet propaganda. At the end of November the newly-installed officials in Prague were themselves protesting at the virulence of the tone, claiming that this could only be harmful to their plans to return to 'normal'; these protests had some effect, since the operation was slowly downgraded, even changing its title to Radio International Berlin, and finally came off the air altogether in the middle of February 1969. The counter-effort was as unproductive as the original operation had been productive.

Moscow has, since the war, sponsored a whole series of stations ostensibly run by the banned communist parties of a number of European countries and of Iran. These transmit an estimated 200 hours a week under the banners of Radio España Independiente, Radio Portugal Livre (both from transmitters near Timisoara in south-west Romania), Our Radio (in Turkish), the Voice of Truth (in Greek) and Radio Iran Courier. The Iranian station (run by the 'Tudeh' Party) began at the end of 1957 as an overt programme of the East German International Service operating from Leipzig, later adding Azerbaijani and then Kurdish to its Persian Service. In 1963 it included Arabic broadcasts, but they were later hived off to a separate Voice of the Iraqi People. Additional programmes for Greek, Turkish and Italian workers in West Germany are beamed from transmitters located between Burg and Magdeburg over the border in the DDR.

In support of Moscow's clandestine operations, the Czechs began to put out propaganda to Italy in 1951, in a programme entitled *Oggi in Italia*, whose source remained a mystery for the first three years. Prague then admitted to being the 'onlie begetter.' But constant pressure from the Italians (and disapproval from the BBC with whose Italian signal the Czech programme interfered) obliged them to close it down in March 1971. A parallel programme, *Ce Soir en France*, was put out mostly from Czechoslovakia but has also been traced to locations in Hungary and Poland.

A more recent extension of genuine clandestine radio emanating from communist sources has sprung from the Sino-Soviet dispute. 'Sparks' (Huohoa in Chinese) is a KGB operation, staffed by Chinese ex-members of the '28 Bolsheviks' group from the Sun Yat-sen University in Moscow. It beams anti-Maoist propaganda across that long and disputatious border. A similar operation, sharing transmission facilities with Sparks, calls itself the Radio of the Chinese People's Communist Party, thus rubbing in their refusal to identify Mao Tse-tung's clique and his less-than-authentic Party with the 'true' followers of Marxism-Leninism.

The Chinese get their own back, not only, it is said, through support of a Kazakhstan nationalist station, but also by a barrage of open propaganda supplemented by such tricks as broadcasting backwards. It has been suggested that this is to deceive the Soviet jammers and allow dedicated listeners to tape the transmission and play it back the right way round. A more likely explanation is that the Chinese are deliberately plaguing the Soviet monitors, forcing them to delay their assessment of the Chinese polemic until they have unravelled the message.

Chinese clandestine activities are the cause of much of the confusion in the entire radio situation in the Far East. Another cause is, of course, the pace of political change. Propaganda planners have to make rapid priority switches, as when the American withdrawal from South Vietnam involved phasing out the CIA's black Voice of the Patriotic Militiamen's Front. Other defunct stations include the two anti-Sukarno operations in Indonesia, the Voice of Free Indonesia and Radio Sulawesi (Celebes). Radio Free Japan, a Chinese-run station which was thought to originate from the mountains near Tokyo, closed down in 1956 and was replaced by increased white broadcasts from Peking. Foreign monitoring services have trouble in keeping track of, or even fixing at all, a whole range of fluctuating radio stations.

Some of these, it is clear, are based in China, like the Voice of the People of Burma, the Voice of the Malayan Revolution and the Voice of the Thai People. Others have somewhat precarious territory of their own to operate in: the Voice of Pathet Lao uses transmitters concealed in caves and other protected places in the liberated zones of Laos. The Vietnamese Liberation Radio is the voice of the South Vietnamese Provisional Revolutionary Government and operates on a large scale from five high-powered Chinese-built stations in Cambodia and also from Hanoi. The PRG transmits in English, Khmer, French, Laotian and Vietnamese and has a full 'Home Service' in addition to its foreign operations. The pro-Sihanouk Voice of the National Front of Cambodia borrows the Vietnamese transmitters, and Sihanouk himself is also given airtime on Radio Peking. The CIA once tried a phoney copy of this station, which included broadcasts by a suitably squeaky-voiced 'Prince Sihanouk', but it was exposed. A communist but pseudo-neutral station of the 'South Korean' Voice of the Revolutionary Party for Reunification almost certainly broadcasts from North Korea. On the anti-communist side there is the Voice of the East, run by the South Koreans for their compatriots in Japan. And that is not by any means a full list of the clandestine radios in the Far East.

Before we leave the area, it is worth focussing on one example to point up some of the typical motives and frustrations of many of the small stations in the Far East. Burma has been under the strong military isolationist rule of Ne Win since 1962. By a policy of making neither friends nor enemies in the world outside, he has consolidated his own position and weakened that of his predecessor, U Nu. But that has not prevented U Nu—represented by three of his generals—putting out hostile propaganda from a radio station in Chiengmai in northern Thailand. The difficulties which this National United Liberation Front Radio is up against are immense. Despite financial backing from the Americans who are interested in the oil off the south Burmese coast, the signal is very weak and is powerfully jammed. On 4 June 1973 the NULF put out a pathetic report:

Listeners, parents and people, from the 6th of April our NULF station suspended its broadcasts. We wanted to build our station in a liberated area which was closest to our people. We wanted to receive the love of the parents and people from close to. To do so the members of our NULF station had to cross a series of mountains and jungles. However, members of our station are happy and they do not mind climbing mountains and jungles. We are now broadcasting on the way. It is not easy for us to cross mountains and jungles with our broadcasting equipment. We will broadcast from this camp as much as possible and then move on to a new camp in a liberated area.

A measure of their audibility and effectiveness was provided when U Nu announced his resignation as leader of the opposition party—he is now lecturing on Buddhism in America. This important news was monitored from the NULF by the BBC and given over the air on its Burmese Service; only then was it picked up by the official Burmese media and given its due prominence. The NULF broadcast went unheard and ignored in Burma.

From China, another clandestine voice, the Voice of Burma, organ of the Maoist Burmese Communist Party, penetrates the homeland on a far stronger signal. Technically it provides a better service than the amateurish attempts of the NULF's ageing generals and their low-quality staff. But the Voice of Burma suffers from its alien connections and from the same vices as Peking Radio itself: it is dull, esoteric and remote. Ne Win, it seems, has little to fear until and unless the uncontrolled border areas become the scene not just of a war of words but of guerrilla warfare backed by foreign powers. But for the Burmese opposition waiting in the wings the moral appears to be that, no matter how long-term their objective, a radio station must be maintained in order to have any hope at all of reaching that objective.

This is a view shared by many opposition groups or minority peoples all over the world. Radio resistance, or just the propagation of a forlorn message into the ether, is a common enough feature in any disputed area or troublespot. In Cyprus, for example, the Turkish Cypriot community organizes a complete radio network simply to encourage unity in the face of hostility from the more numerous Greeks—a necessary precaution in view of the events of the summer of 1974. The situation at the time of writing is uncertain. Up till mid-1974 no less than five Turkish-language stations were transmitting from the Turkish sectors of the island—Radios Bayrak and Canbulat, Doganin Sesi, Gazi Bafin Sesi and Lefka Sancak. They support the cause of the minority population of the island, and while claiming to be editorially independent of the Turkish Cypriot administration, rely on it for their financial backing, a relationship similar to that of the BBC with Her Majesty's Government. Radio Bayrak, the chief station on Cyprus, also runs an international service in Greek and English, claiming audiences in Lebanon and Israel as well as in the two 'master' countries, Greece and Turkey. Turkish listeners in Cyprus also have the option to turn to two stations broadcasting from the southern coast of the mainland: the Voice of Paphos Veterans and the Voice of the Falcon. All five island-based stations were set up after the 1963 inter-communal troubles. Apart from an ephemeral pro-Makarios Voice of Free Cyprus during the confusion in 1974, it appears that no parallel move has been made by the Greeks.

In Ulster the battle of the airwaves has never rivalled the battle on the streets with guns and bombs despite the apparent ripeness of the province for intensive propaganda. In the seventh edition of an annual publication of information for short-wave enthusiasts, *How To Listen To The World*, Lawrence E. Magne lists nine separate stations, four extremist Protestant and five Catholic/IRA/Marxist. All are small-scale and irregular operations. Most, he claims, are located in the opposing quarters of Belfast. Radio Free Derry, the oldest clandestine station in Northern Ireland, run originally by the Socialist Resistance Group but since taken over by the Official IRA, broadcasts from a low-powered 25-watt transmitter in the Bogside area of Londonderry. Magne says that the Provisional IRA Freedom Radio may also operate either from the Bogside or Creggan areas of Londonderry, and/or from the Andersontown district in Belfast. Andersontown also houses the Voice of Free Belfast, the station of a socialist organization called People's Democracy, while Workers' Radio, the organ of the Official IRA which started on Easter Monday 1972, appears to be located in the Lower Falls area. Magne places Republic Radio, otherwise called Radio na Poblachta, which occasionally puts out Marxist propaganda and forewarns listeners by placing announcements in Dublin newspapers, near the capital of the Irish Republic. All four Protestant stations are in Belfast: the Ulster Vanguard Movement's Voice of Ulster, operating on a mere ten watts of power; the Ulster Defence Association's Radio Free Nick which broadcasts rude messages to Catholics and scratchy Orange discs and, so Magne claims, has to close down every three to four hours to let its transmitters cool off; the Gnomes of Ulster, so called because of the anarchist Kabouters (Gnomes) who functioned in Holland in the nineteenth century; and finally Radio Antrim which broadcasts pop music and pro-Unionist propaganda and is described by Magne as a 'political neo-pirate station'. Indeed, that description does well for all nine.

The British security forces in Northern Ireland, however, pour cold water on this colourful story. There have been, they say, only two known Official IRA stations—Radio Saorse (Gaelic for Freedom) in the Lower Falls area of Belfast operating in about 1970, and Radio Free Derry in the Creggan estate in Londonderry in 1969–70. The British army also detected a Protestant Loyalist station, perhaps called Radio Shankill, whose announcer was styled 'Orange Lily'. Of the others on Magne's list, no sign. It is not impossible that the security forces have simply failed to detect what may have been such fly-by-night operations that only vigilant hams could be expected to pick them up. Even so, that does not invalidate the army theory that radio in Northern Ireland is a non-event. And no use is made of black radio by the authorities.

Why is it that the clandestine radio stations, however many there are involved in the bitter and inconclusive struggle in Northern Ireland, operate strictly on the fringe of affairs and have minimal influence on the course of events? To some extent this is a reflection of the chaotic 'Irish' element in the communal conflict, an element which would undoubtedly dominate as far as the uncomprehending outside world is concerned were it not for the fact that the fight is also real and deadly and causes fearful suffering. Both the IRA and Protestant extremists are an amalgam of fragmented groups who would find it hard to maintain a consistent line of propaganda. But above all, the radios are on the fringe because there is no essential need for them. Other means of communication exist, the area is small, the aims of the participants are well enough known, even if the tactics must sometimes need some explaining to the faithful and to outsiders alike. All this means that the dangers inherent in running an illicit radio station outweigh the marginal advantages it would bring.

But there is a recent case of a civil war, where the fighting was also bitter and the aim of one side was freedom and secession from the other, and where radio played an absolutely key role. That is the struggle of the FLN against the French in Algeria.

Fortunately, the role of radio in the Algerian war has been chronicled by one of the most incisive and brilliant observers of the death agony of colonialism, Frantz Fanon. In a chapter in his monograph, *A Dying Colonialism*,[4] Fanon writes that the Voice of Algeria, the voice of the Front National de Libération, 'created out of nothing, brought the nation to life and endowed every citizen with a new status, *telling him so explicitly*' (author's italics). It is worth letting him tell the story in some detail. The Voice of Free, or Fighting, Algeria is the best illustration of the direct involvement of underground radio in a political and military struggle where conditions were uniquely favourable for pointing up its effectiveness.

In pre-1945 Algeria, radio was an almost exclusively European preoccupation. Ninety-five per cent of sets were owned by them and Radio Alger was what Fanon calls 'a re-edition or an echo of the French National Broadcasting System operating from Paris [and] essentially the instrument of colonial society and its values'. This was a contributing cause to cultural and political separation, reinforced by the Algerian belief that there was something immoral in radio which caused strains in a good Muslim family with its 'sex allusions' and 'clownish situations'. Most Algerians were not involved in the so-called civilizing process of which radio was, and is, a key part. Radio Alger was the occupiers' radio. In reverse, the remote European settlers would claim that 'without wine and the radio, we should already have become Arabized'.

After 1945, nationalist revolution began to spread through the Maghreb, and Algerians began to develop an interest in radio even if only to hear international broadcasts from other Arab countries and from further abroad. In response, the French authorities started to Algerianize Radio Alger and to encourage the sale of sets, indirectly helping the ordinary Algerian to keep abreast of events when open resistance broke out at the beginning of November 1954.

The nationalists soon realized, however, that Radio Alger gave a partial account and that they would have to counter the French-sponsored propaganda. 'Confronted daily with "the wiping out of the last remaining guerrilla bands", the civilian could fight off despair only by an act of faith, by an obstinate belief.' He was prey to rumours, often dangerously optimistic. The press—especially the 'democratic' French papers such as *Le Monde* and *L'Express*—went some way to filling the need for objective news, but it soon became too dangerous to buy them openly at street kiosks. Besides, a high proportion of the Algerian population was illiterate. Radio was therefore the only answer. Writes Fanon:

The acquisition of a radio set in Algeria, in 1955, represented the sole means of obtaining news of the Revolution from non-French sources. This necessity assumed a compelling character when the people learned that there were Algerians in Cairo who daily drew up the balance-sheet of the liberation struggle. From Cairo, from Syria, from nearly all the Arab countries, the great pages written in the *djebels* by brothers, relatives, friends, flowed back to Algeria.[5]

But, as Fanon emphasizes, it was not enough to listen to the Voice of the Arabs, however important that was as an introduction to the habit of identifying with the nationalist cause through the radio. At the end of 1956 the Voice of Free Algeria announced its existence, the signal not just for a rush to buy any and every radio set, but also for a new unity between the leaders of the revolution and the ordinary people in whose name they were fighting the French colonists. 'Since 1956,' writes Fanon, 'the purchase of a radio in Algeria has meant, not the adoption of a modern technique of getting news, but the obtaining of access to the only means of entering into communication with the Revolution, of living with it.' There could be no clearer statement of the effectiveness of radio. The Voice of Free Algeria reversed the popular prejudice against radio as an alien medium, and it became an essential tool of the fighter and the agitator.

The French recognized radio's potency by banning the further sale of sets except on presentation of a voucher issued by the security forces, and then by jamming the Algerian broadcasts. The myth of radio was doubly reinforced. Even when it just crackled and whined, it was still the voice of truth. And the more the French tried to stop people listening, and hunted down the fugitive transmitters, the more credible became the persistent, elusive and sometimes less than audible Voice. It was a matter of pride to have picked up and listened to its signal. Fanon compares the popular reaction with that of the citizens of occupied Europe listening to the BBC, in particular the French listening to the voice of Free France. But, he suggests, the special character of the switch from hatred towards an infidel medium to dependence on the voice of their own national struggle made radio even more profoundly influential in the Algerian case. It created a new national speech and a new national consciousness, and produced, as Fanon says, a fundamental change in the people.

It is a big claim to make that radio itself was responsible for such important developments. But even allowing for Fanon's emotional as well as rational commitment to the Algerian cause, he cannot be accused of myth-making. In its early stages particularly, when the problem was to arouse nationalist consciousness and when military resources were too small to make a large or immediate impact, the Algerian revolution was indeed dependent on the particular medium which could reach the people and speak to them in a language that they understood and accepted as friendly. Whereas the French radio confined its counter-appeals to selling the prospect of material gains, the Voice of Algeria identified itself with the much more powerful concepts of nationalism, freedom and pride, using the prevailing current of history. It is a case where the particular circumstances combined to give radio its maximum effectiveness—an effectiveness which, for once, can be recorded in some detail.

Some of the generalities, if not the specifics, of the radio situation in Algeria from 1956 until independence can be applied to the early years of the Voice of the Arabs. Nasser's cause, and the strident voice of Ahmed Said, were, as we have seen, susceptible to a radio campaign and coincided with a burgeoning of Arab self-consciousness and self-confidence. But the Voice of the Arabs could not, of course, play the detailed support role that the Voice of Free Algeria provided for the FLN fighting forces.

The only recent, identifiable success comparable to the Voice of Algeria—despite the failure of the cause it represented—is Radio Biafra. Its manipulation of anything that could hide or postpone the inevitable military defeat was recognized at the time as exceptionally skilful. It begun on a note of dramatic ineptitude by announcing five 'phantom' recognitions of Biafra by foreign countries the day after seccession. But it soon made a strong impact on the local audience, despite the fact that Radio Enugu, its main component, was obliged to play an elusive role after the capital's fall. Later, Radio Biafra's voice was listened to throughout Nigeria and by interested parties around the world. Some of the credit must go to an adviser who achieved wider fame as the author of *The Day of the Jackal* and *The Odessa File*. But Frederick Forsyth alone was not responsible for Radio Biafra's success. Much depended on the forceful personalities of speakers and commentators like Okonkon Ndem, formerly of the federal radio network, 'often known as Biafra's Lord Haw-Haw . . . whose Shakespearean imagery and resonant voice became well known throughout the country',[6] and on the powerful voice of the Biafran leader himself, Colonel Ojukwu.

The function of Radio Biafra, which broadcast primarily in English but also in three local vernaculars, was to boost internal morale. It also played a clever game of disseminating misinformation. Here the tricks learnt from the world war were applied with great sophistication. But Radio Biafra also put stress on a third aspect, which took it a stage further than its predecessors in the field. It relied heavily on public relations work. In particular it relied on the expertise of advertising boss William Bernhardt, and his dynamic

firm, Markpress. Radio became part of an integrated worldwide
promotion campaign. Radio Biafra's short-wave broadcasts were
partly aimed at assiduous monitors in Lagos and elsewhere. Its message—notably the charge of genocide—was also planned to fit in with
the spate of hand-outs, articles, press conferences and lobbying
organized by Markpress. While morale-boosting at home and misinformation to the enemy remained the first preoccupations of the
radio station—because that is the particular strength of the medium
—there is no question that its PR role added a powerful new dimension. Not only was radio the 'principle weapon', writes St Jorre, 'it
also became a symbol of nationhood. Whenever Federal troops made
a breakthrough, it was always the Biafran radio station that was first
moved to safety.' The parallel with Algeria is obvious.

The main criticism of Radio Biafra was that it overdid its propaganda and made itself too easy a target for denials. In the long term,
whether it can be accounted a success depends on one's viewpoint: as
an example of the effective use of radio it was frequently brilliant;
as a tactical weapon in a wider military and political struggle it could
achieve very little, despite the failure of the opposing Federal Radio
to overcome the hostility towards propaganda expressed by General
Gowon, and what St Jorre calls an 'appallingly inefficient' Ministry
of Information in Lagos. It cannot be denied that in a war deeds can
always drown out words.

Radio is most powerful when it is identified with a specific cause,
but above all when that cause is likely to lead to success. Here the
narrow focus of clandestine radio gives it an edge over government
stations which broadcast in good times and bad and, on the whole,
have to soldier on under the banner of 'my country right or wrong'.
But single-purpose clandestine stations can look very stupid indeed
when they back a loser. The CIA's anti-Cuba operations are a case
in point. Arguably it is still too early to brand the ongoing émigré
station run by La Frente Cubana Revolucionaria as a failure. But
certainly the back-up operation to the Bay of Pigs was quite unable
to compensate for the fiasco of the invasion.

The Basque radio station has to cope with an erratic mixture of
failure and success, but it has contributed to morale among members
of a beleagured minority group. Instructions and communiqués are
issued over Radio Euzkadi from José Maria de Leizaola, 'President
of the Basque Government'. Unfortunately the signal is transmitted
from Caracas in Venezuela with what Magne describes as 'telephone
quality'. To make up for this, the Basques have on occasions imitated
their South American revolutionary colleagues and captured for brief
periods the facilities of local radio stations.

Radio Euzkadi, like all voices of oppressed minorities, has a
straightforward morale and information function. But it is less easy

to see what Abie J. Nathan had in mind with his 'Peace Ship' project. A rich American-Israeli, Nathan decided to spread the message
of peace in the Middle East by taking a ship with transmitting
apparatus to a point in the eastern Mediterranean where Arabs and
Jews could pick up a programme from which the bias of the two
sides was absent. A test broadcast in May 1973 announced:

> Good evening everybody. By everybody, I mean all you beautiful
> people in Lebanon, in Syria, Jordan, Israel, the UAR, or wherever
> you are . . . Now we start the programme with Tony who will give
> you just music, music . . . love and peace with music to begin the
> evening; and then we will give you some more music, and then we
> will give you some more music. Now and then we will talk to you
> about the news and what is happening in the world.

That, at least, was the soft-sell theory. But bad luck intervened.
After financial problems and gales had delayed the project, the
Peace Ship came on the air only days before the outbreak of the
October war. (Thus the Peace Ship turned out to be the mirror image
of the USS *Courier* which was about to go into full service as a
Mediterranean relay in 1945 when the European war ended; it then
crawled across the Atlantic and through the Panama Canal just in
time for the Japanese surrender.) Ignominiously, Nathan's ship of
hopefuls was obliged to return to the less bellicose shores of the
United States: proof that the only message that gets through is the
one the audience wants to hear.

Another problem faced by all small-scale operations is that they
cannot call on the enormous resources, not least the numbers of
skilled and dedicated broadcasters, that, for example, Delmer had
behind him in the war. It is impossible for Radio Euzkadi, or the
Peace Ship, or the numerous little operations from Ulster to Burma,
to have remotely the same impact as Delmer's *Soldatensender Calais*
and many of the post-war clandestine operations with full national
support. Only exceptional circumstances such as existed in Nigeria
during the civil war or in Algeria in the years leading up to
independence provide the opportunity for radio to change the
course of events. Even then the Voice of Algeria never had the
chance to deliver the sort of sucker punch that British wartime
Intelligence could pack. And Radio Biafra was always vulnerable to
the temptation to oversell its optimism or react too strongly against
its more real despair.

In the Vietnam war and the Middle East wars between Arabs and
Israelis, clandestine radio appears not to have fulfilled the potential
suggested by the world war, or even by Algeria. In the case of the
Middle East, the short duration of the fighting, the hopelessness of

creating an effective fifth column in either of the opposing camps, and the discrediting of the Voice of the Arabs in 1967, meant that the BBC and Moscow Radio picked up a large share of the listenership to non-domestic radio. Neither of these is likely, or intends, to create the sort of subversive atmosphere that is the aim of clandestine operations. In Vietnam and the rest of Indochina, the CIA's dirty-tricks department did its best to create diversions but there is little evidence that its impact impinged on the military and political fortunes of that disastrous war. Similarly, though on a smaller scale, the British attempt to influence Arab opinion at the time of the Anglo-French-Israeli incursion into Egypt in 1956 was quite incapable of countering the harmful propaganda effect of attacking in the first place.

The British effort was based in a small station under their control in Cyprus. It was a remarkable example, possibly the only one, of a clandestine operation in reverse. It was billed as the Voice of Britain. In reality it was the voice of the Conservative government. And it was designed to correct, indeed subvert, the non-governmental though official voice of the BBC.

From the moment on 30 October when the British government commandeered the commercial Cypriot Shark al Adna station, things began to go wrong. First of all, it was not a legitimate commercial station at all, but a British undercover operation. It had been functioning for five years, and was known to the Lebanese as the 'Cavalry of St George', from the British coins sporting the patron saint's image which were still in circulation there. This should in theory have simplified the British army's takeover. But the reverse happened. The entire Arab staff of the station resigned rather than broadcast overt anti-Nasser propaganda. Its director, now a clergyman in the West Country, 'feeling that this was not the sort of station I had been engaged to run', came back to England.

At short notice a government troubleshooter, recruited from the BBC, ironically, had to assemble a new staff to put out ten hours of material in Arabic each day, twice as much as the BBC's own Arabic Service was broadcasting. Then it was discovered that the same transmitters on Cyprus were broadcasting the Voice of Britain *and* relaying the BBC, by now regarded as a hostile station because of its insistence on giving due weight over the air to the critics of the Suez venture. Between the attack on Port Said and the cease-fire, therefore, the BBC found itself without its medium-wave relay and obliged to rely on the less penetrating short-wave signal. Incredibly, despite the obvious political failure of the government's policy, the Voice of Britain was not wound up until March the following year.

The criticisms that followed, notably from the Labour Party, were as bitter as might be expected. Barbara Castle argued the point that the temporary relay contaminated the trustworthiness of the BBC. This was true except for those who appreciated the more subtle argument that the BBC, by maintaining its position not just against government pressure but also against active and audible competition, had proved precisely the opposite. Fortunately for the Corporation, a large number of Arabs did see this point and remained faithful to the BBC.

The varied fortunes of the many types of clandestine radio show, therefore, how dependent they are for their success on the political specifics of the context in which they are used. Where clandestine radio backs up positive action, and where listeners are sensitized to the message, it is indeed a potent weapon. Whenever it is used at a safe distance, or as a substitute for action, it is ineffective. Under no circumstances is radio an alternative to committed supporters, to outside help (or non-intervention), or to guns and the other paraphernalia of instant power.

But, in a general sense, is clandestine radio likely to be used more, or less extensively in the late seventies and onwards than it was during the world war and in subsequent conflict situations? With the 'liberation' part of the anti-colonialist drive already achieved in most of Africa and parts of Asia, though not in central Asia, do, for example, black and grey radios have a role in situations of economic exploitation or pseudo-independence? The answer is surely yes.

In some cases, circumstances do not permit the establishment of an opposition radio station. One of the Chilean junta's first moves was to start up an External Service to combat 'communist slander', and this, one might think, was an open challenge to opposition forces to counter government propaganda with their own. But so tight is the junta's control that, as yet, no such operation has begun. On the other hand, active conflict situations where there is no radio war are rare. The Middle East continues to be a radio battleground. The Kurds are using radio successfully in their freedom struggle. In Indochina the contending parties are only beginning to develop the radio weapon. In Africa, black states and guerrilla groups are likely to grow in strength sufficiently to mount their own counter-propaganda operations. Even nationalist groups in the Soviet Union —and it is not improbable that the Ukrainians and others will broaden their struggle for independence—could well turn to radio once the campaign reaches the stage when it could be used productively; in other words, when the risk of provocation leading to official repression rather than to popular revolt reaches an acceptably low level.

There is no immediate prospect of clandestine confrontations on the scale of those of the Second World War. It is not difficult, however, to outline a wide range of scenarios where radio battles will be fought as part of local political and military struggles. The *New York Times* reported the Imam of Yemen as remarking, apropos of a coup d'état, 'It seems all you need to make a government these days is a radio station and a declaration that you have made a government.' That was in 1962. But it is a statement which today Radio Free Yemeni South, not to mention the rival Adeni Voice of the Revolution and numerous other stations in this area and around the world, take literally.

So long as conflicts analogous to those in the Middle East, Indochina or Southern Africa still occur throughout the world, the role of clandestine radio will not decrease. The black radio and the 'freedom station' are necessary tactical weapons. There is, in fact, unlikely ever to be a coup or a revolution, a liberation or a campaign of repression, where radio is not at the centre of things.

11 *Propaganda Fide*

Books about propaganda always include, and often start with, a reference to the religious origin of that word which has since come to sound so nefarious. 'Propaganda fide' lends an aura of ancient respectability to a practice that has seen many refinements since the days of Pope Gregory and his missionary overseers. Today, the Roman Catholic church is as intent as ever on propagating the faith, but the College of Cardinals has at its disposal a wide range of techniques which never existed in the seventeenth century. Vatican Radio is one of them.

The Holy Church was quick to sense and to seize the possibilities of radio; the global extent of the Catholic community magnified the problem of communication and control, and radio could help to solve it. Moreover, in the thirties, the centre of the church was in particular danger of being cut off from the periphery, at a time when Mussolini's fascists were hostile to its domestic and international influence. While the radio's message was primarily religious—exemplified by its Latin section—it was undoubtedly a weapon of church politics as well, and considered as such by the government across the Tiber.

From its first broadcast in 1931, when Marconi went to the microphone to introduce Pope Paul XI, Vatican radio has provided a highly professional service. Walter Emery mentions an audience of up to 9 million, although Vatican officials fight shy of quantifying their audience at all.

The responsibility for running the station was from the start given over to the Jesuits. At present, the twenty-eight Jesuit fathers attached full-time to Vatican Radio are in charge of the majority of the language and regional sections. The station reached its maximum (to date) of thirty-two languages in 1964, although programmes in most languages last only fifteen minutes or less in one transmission daily. Total weekly output amounts to about 100 hours, low by international standards; the Dutch, for instance, put out four times as much, the Italian government almost double. Vatican Radio's output is slightly less than the Hungarian government's, but slightly more than Yugoslavia's.

But Vatican Radio compensates by the specific nature of its message and the devotion it can expect from its audience. Not that religious news and services are the only fare on offer. Since 1957, Vatican Radio has run a balanced news service, and its music programmes, often taped and rebroadcast locally, act as attractive bait for cultured listeners.

For Catholics, especially in places where the church is unable to reach them physically, Vatican Radio is a kind of lifeline. Certainly at the church's headquarters in Vatican City their radio service is seen as indispensable, as the fortieth-birthday statement underlined:

Today it is difficult to imagine how the Holy Father could fully accomplish his universal prophetic mission without it, so effectively does the radio fulfil the needs of the evangelical mandate . . . Through the microphones of Vatican Radio, every sector of the Church, in every part of the world, at whatsoever stage of development, can communicate daily with all other sectors, edify them by its living example and inspired activity and, in time of trial, feel close by offering them consolation and hope.

But the Roman Catholic church is not the only representative of Christianity to have discovered radio. A similar faith in the medium is echoed by Lutherans, Adventists, indeed Christians of all denominations and non-denominations.

In all, the World Radio and TV Handbook 1974 lists forty separate religious broadcasting organizations. Seven worldwide operations are based in the United States: Adventist World Radio, Trans World Radio (which is non-denominational and has transmitters on the Caribbean island of Bonaire), the Evangelical Alliance Mission, the West Indies Mission, the Far East Broadcasting Co. Inc. (from Manila), World Radio Gospel Hour, and the Herald of Truth Broadcast. Miami is the US headquarters of La Voz de los Andes—the voice of the World Radio Missionary Fellowship. The Lutheran Voice of the Gospel transmits on a powerful signal from Addis Ababa and has a reputation for good news coverage and features, and for religious soft-sell. Other organizations are listed in Australia, Japan, Korea, Hong Kong, Burma, the Lebanon, and elsewhere.

In addition, there is a World Association for Christian Broadcasting, an offshoot of the World Council of Churches which acts as a pressure group and also trains broadcasting staff, situated in Geneva; not far away, in Fribourg, is an organization which assists and co-ordinates communication among Catholics, the International Catholic Association for Radio and TV, founded as long ago as 1927; and finally, International Christian Broadcasters, which sprang from the earlier World Conference on Missionary Radio in 1966. All in all, religious broadcasting is big business. Total weekly output amounts to around the 1,000-hour mark, similar in scale, therefore, to all the clandestine stations of the world put together.

Religious broadcasting is also heavily dependent on American money. The Christian message is something Americans are accustomed to pay for if they want to see it regularly circulated. Many local radio stations throughout the United States are founded by, or sell airtime to, churches, missionary groups, or Christian cranks. The international business is an offshoot of that. And the money from churchgoers and other benefactors seems in no danger of drying up.

Without American backing there would have been no Radio Omega, that semi-clandestine station using Radio Free Russia's transmitters for its programmes in the Russian and Baltic languages. But the subversive role of the Christian message when broadcast into atheist states is something of which all programme planners in western stations are aware. The BBC's Father Rodzianko, for example, was a colourful figure who had quite a following among the Orthodox faithful in the Soviet Union.

The message which comes back from the other side is an anti-religious one, but little is made of atheist propaganda by communist outlets, probably for two reasons. Christianity as a force for motivating behaviour is fading away on its own; any attempt to help it disappear is likely to be counter-productive, which brings us to the second reason, namely that atheism is a negative message, liable to give more currency to the positive doctrine it attacks than the reverse.

During the war, religion was used as a weapon of psychological warfare. The Germans put out pacifist propaganda in the name of the 'Christian Peace Movement', and the British replied with their 'Christ the King' station. The latter's chief speaker was an Austrian Roman Catholic priest, Father Andreas, whose main theme was the bestiality of the Nazi anti-Semitic campaign and the anti-Christian elements of Nazism. According to Sefton Delmer's account, this was a straight rather than a black operation, putting out no deliberate inventions or rumours; the only black part was the rumour spread by Delmer's agents that it was a clandestine *Vatican* station.

Religious broadcasting is not confined to the Christian community, although Christianity does dominate the international airwaves. One rival, though confined to listeners in the Middle East, is Radio Cairo's channel, given up entirely to Islamic teaching—the Voice of the Holy Koran. It breaks off only for one hour a day to put out the Palestine Liberation Organization programme. With the exception of the communist services, foreign stations make full use of Arab devotion to the Koran as bait for their political programmes. I remember walking into a remote house in the centre of the Tunisian island of Djerba and hearing holy texts intoned through a small transistor hung on the wall. Its owner explained that he kept the set tuned on that channel to be sure of hearing the text each morning. The source was the BBC in London.

In March 1974, Libya undertook to finance the construction of a radio station in Niger. Its intention is to propagate the Islamic message in Africa, and it will be known as the Voice of Islam. This will reinforce an already observable trend towards a revival of the Muslim religion south of the Sahara.

But all religious propaganda by radio is directed at the faithful. It is not and cannot be a medium for proselytizing, except incidentally, being too distant, too easily switched off and, by itself, not nearly insistent enough. Besides, as Jacques Ellul says:

> Propaganda is effective not when based on an *individual* prejudice, but when based on a *collective* center of interest, shared by the crowds. That is why religious propaganda is not very successful; society as a whole is no longer interested in religious problems. At Byzantium, crowds fought in the streets over theological questions, so that in those days religious propaganda made sense. At present only isolated individuals are interested in religion.[1]

No amount of money poured into expensive worldwide religious radio stations can hope to do more than stem the tide.

Present enthusiasm for new churches and new faiths, notably as the west discovers the religions of the east, might belie the generality, but Ellul is describing the rule not the exception. Radio came too late to play a really positive role in revitalizing Christianity. Only among the collectivity of Arab Islamic brotherhood, where a Holy War can still be whipped up for a mixture of political and religious motives, does the medium fulfil its potential.

12 Interference

Signals beamed across national frontiers are by no means always audible when they reach their destination. Sometimes the loss of signal is due to natural causes: holes in the ionosphere through which short waves disappear, sun-spots, the aurora borealis, electrical storms, unsuitable land formations. In other cases, the signal is inaudible because it is jammed.

Deliberate interference usually takes the form of a loud noise. It can be like a petrol-engine generator, or a rotary whine, or, as a recent technique is described by a member of the BBC's Monitoring Service, an 'oscillating woo-woo'. The effect can also imitate static, the crackling sound caused by electrical interference. In any case, jamming makes a horrible noise, demanding extraordinary powers of perseverance on the part of the listener hoping to pick up some of the original message beneath it. Less ear-cracking, but just as effective techniques which have been used by the Russians are constant morse code signals (sometimes the call sign of the jamming transmitter, for example a continuous MK for Murmansk) and the broadcasting of the Moscow Second Programme, Mayak, from short-wave transmitters, over the incoming signals from abroad.

In the early days of radio, before the Second World War, foreign interference was largely unintentional, due to the overspill of domestic or armed forces signals on to neighbouring countries using the same or a very close wavelength. Rapid development of short waves increased the range of the signal and at the same time the problem. By the beginning of the war, about half the sets in Europe could pick up short waves. Many attempts were made to regulate the frequency spectrum internationally, with the result that some of the more anarchic features of broadcasting were eliminated. They had only limited success, however.

Both before and after the outbreak of war, the Axis powers were the most active as far as jamming was concerned. But a considerable discrepancy could be observed in the relative efficiency of Germans and Italians. Italy was renowned as an erratic jammer, coming on early and leaving late, straying off wavelengths and sometimes affecting her own. But in Germany 'Broadcast Defence' became one of the regime's most painstakingly organized tasks. The *Deutschlandsender* would sometimes interrupt its own programmes to use a transmitter to jam the BBC. Outside the period of peace provided by the Molotov-Ribbentrop Pact, Moscow was also assiduous in jamming Nazi broadcasts. On one occasion Russian engineers interrupted Hitler's speech in which he was making his famous threats before the Munich meeting in the autumn of 1938 . . . with a curious result:

> While engineers in London thought the effect very successful, a Russian psychologist, who was unaware of his country's part in it, hailed the combination of brooding thunder in the background with the vivid cries of Hitler and his followers as Goebbels' masterpiece in mass-terrorization.[1]

As war approached, however, the main worry was not that frequencies were difficult to organize or that there would be widespread jamming, but that radio would be put out of action altogether by the bombing of transmitters. It was feared that radio signals would act as directional beacons providing a ready-made guide-path to enemy planes. In fact the phoney war lasted long enough for BBC engineers to develop a system of scrambling the signals by 'synchronization' of a number of transmitters and so confuse the direction-finding apparatus. Sadly for the Germans, they never succeeded in discovering this formula and, to the end of the war, had to close down their transmitters whenever and wherever there was a bombing raid. This led to one coup of which the American Office of War Information and the British were particularly proud. On 30 January 1943, Hitler was due to make a speech commemorating the tenth anniversary of Nazi power in Germany. It was decided to bomb Berlin at that precise moment and interrupt the speech as a demonstration of Allied power. In fact Goebbels replaced Hitler at the microphone, but the RAF carried out the raid as planned. The speech went off the air to the muffled sounds of explosions and shouts in the background.

That kind of deliberate interference can hardly be practised in peacetime. But there are many other ways, apart from jamming the signal, of stopping or at least dissuading people from listening to 'undesirable' broadcasts. One of these is the manufacture and distribution of specially prepared radio sets designed to receive only those signals which have no subversive effect. The Nazis pioneered the 'People's Receiving Set'. Although it was not the only one on the market, it was so much cheaper than its more sophisticated rivals that it sold correspondingly well. Reputedly the Germans also handed out suitably adapted sets in Latin America and the Middle East, and it appears that the British did the same. The Americans used this technique later in the Vietnam war. The *Wall Street Journal* reported in March 1966 that 10,000 cheap little transistors, specially constructed to receive only American and South Vietnamese stations, were dropped into enemy-held territory both north and south of the demarcation line.

Another way to interfere with free reception is to install 'wired' radio whereby a signal is received by an authorized station and relayed by telephone wires to loudspeakers in homes and public places. It is intended to act as a substitute for short-wave sets which receive signals both desired and not desired by the authorities. Wired radio has appeared all over the world from the Middle East to the Soviet Union to China. It is usually a totalitarian cousin to 'Music While You Work' and, once removed, to Muzak. As a planned means of limiting reception to approved programmes, it has been more of a feature in tightly-controlled societies than in countries where restrictions of this sort would also affect the right to hear commercials and soap operas.

Today the Chinese make massive use of wired radio, claiming that its resurgence in the late sixties was a popular triumph against the sabotage attempts of the renegade Liu Shao-chi. In the Soviet Union, wave receivers overtook wired receivers in 1963, and the transistor has since galloped ahead. Despite the continued use of wired radio in rural and remote areas, the extensive use of short waves for domestic radio (as in all large countries) encourages the easier and, what is more important, cheaper, use of ordinary short-wave sets. The use of wired radio in the main population centres of the Soviet Union is now largely confined, as in the west, to factory entertainment, with the bonus of ideological inserts. Alexander Solzhenitsyn wrote in *Cancer Ward*:

> Compulsory loudspeakers, for some reason generally regarded in our country as a sign of cultural breadth are on the contrary a sign of cultural backwardness and an encouragement to intellectual laziness . . . The permanent mutter—information you hadn't asked for alternating with music you hadn't chosen (and quite unrelated to the mood you happened to be in)—was a theft of time, a diffusion and an entropy of the spirit, convenient and agreeable to the inert but intolerable to those with initiative.[2]

In the early sixties, South Africa, as we saw, adopted a deliberate policy of introducing a nationwide frequency modulation (FM) system in addition to wired radio in some African townships. Following the Sharpeville shootings, the South African government became more than usually sensitive to foreign criticism, and this hastened the introduction of a national system which would encourage the sale of relatively simple transistor sets tuned to FM but only adaptable to short waves at great expense. This has dulled the impact of long-distance foreign propaganda aimed at the black audience.

An example of indirect censorship by diplomatic pressure was observed in Greece. During the regime of the Colonels the Voice of America's Greek transmitters, which were given new power in 1969 and which beam programmes into eastern Europe, were a useful card in the junta's hand. According to Spyridon Granitsas, the Colonels threatened to cancel the facilities unless the Voice accepted some degree of censorship over its Greek-language programmes. He cited as an example the text of a statement from former and current Premier Karamanlis on 30 September 1969, which was publicized by other foreign radio stations but not by the VOA.[3]

Of course not every country is friendly enough to house another country's sensitive propaganda equipment and at the same time liable to be the 'victim' of subversive broadcasts from that same source. Many international broadcasters with worldwide commitments do, however, face delicate negotiations to ensure that the siting of their transmitters does not impair their freedom to broadcast from them. The VOA has been prepared to make more concessions here than the BBC. Nevertheless, the BBC did implicitly undertake to be specially careful to frame the text of relevant news items in such a way as to avoid provoking President Makarios and so protect the relay station on Cyprus.

The most common way to 'interfere' with free reception is counter-propaganda. It is implicit in the counter-attraction provided by all domestic broadcasting everywhere. But some counter-propaganda is directed explicitly at foreign stations. Recent Russian attacks on the BBC are a case in point. After the obvious Cold War rhetoric, the Russian media hardly bothered to mention the BBC or any other foreign broadcaster when jamming temporarily stopped in 1963. The reason would appear to be partly a kind of truce and partly a wish to avoid giving unnecessary publicity to programmes that could now be heard. But during 1968, as the Czechoslovak experiment gathered momentum, so too did Russian attacks on western stations, reaching a crescendo at the time of the invasion, which was sustained well into the following year. In September 1968, Moscow Home Service described the BBC's Russian Service as:

. . . a veritable museum collection of émigrés, who have not quite forgotten the Russian language which was their mother tongue at some time and in most cases a long time ago. One common characteristic has brought them all together: their readiness to bite and to revile their motherland.

The newly appointed Director-General of the BBC, Charles Curran, was vilified as a mad anti-communist. Several more or less fictional biographies were published or broadcast, including the 'fact' that he had earlier been dismissed from Bush House for incompetence. Radio Peace and Progress, after repeating this canard, carried on:

> Then he worked for a provincial fishermen's magazine in Aberdeen. Then came a lawsuit for libel in which he was defendant, after which he became Director-General of the BBC.

The high spot of the campaign was the publication in *Izvestia* and the weekly *Nedelya* of an investigation by V. Lyadov and V. Rozin into the BBC's connections with British Intelligence. Photographed documents with lists of journalists, including the editor of the *Observer*, complete with code numbers, were printed to accompany the articles. But no conclusive proof was offered, certainly none that would be accepted by western journalistic standards. Fleet Street ridiculed the allegations. Keith Blogg in the *Evening News*, following up Soviet accusations that the BBC put out tunes as signals to British agents abroad, suggested coded meanings for some of the pop favourites of the time. 'Build me up Buttercup': Your monthly allowance is hidden in the cow meadow; 'The Good, the Bad and the Ugly': Two of your contacts are suspect; 'Breaking down the Walls of Heartache': You will replace our man in Peking; 'Race with the Devil': They're on to you. Goodbye!

But when the jokes were over, the BBC had to take the threat seriously. The BBC name would be blackened. Some people would believe the accusations. More important, the Soviet authorities would have made it more dangerous than before to listen to the BBC —the very act could be construed as contact with foreign Intelligence. Over the years, however, the stridency in the Soviet campaign evaporated, and some of the harmful effects were undone. But from time to time vicious attacks are still launched. In the autumn of 1972, the Intelligence connection was resurrected briefly, and comparisons were made on Moscow Radio between the 'fabrications of Goebbels' and the Russian Service broadcasters 'who act with a complete lack of elementary decency as did their spiritual father Goebbels'.

But dissuasion may not be enough. The ultimate sanction is the imposition of legal penalties for listening to foreign radio. The Germans frequently executed people found listening to enemy broadcasts during the war. Even earlier there had been instances of severe sentences on those who used information gleaned from foreign broadcasts to counter the barrage of Nazi propaganda. In his diaries, Goebbels complained angrily that the Italians had failed to forbid listening to foreign broadcasts until February 1942. 'As it was, the enemy stations did a lot of harm in Italy.'[4] For the Allies, the frequency of reports about punishment of illegal listeners in the Axis media was an important guide to the effectiveness of their own output.

As early as 1924, it was written into Soviet law:

It is forbidden to record and disseminate the output of foreign radio stations, including public broadcasting stations.

During the Second World War, all private radio receivers in Russia were confiscated. This provision lasted until the end of 1945. Later, at the height of the Cold War, the Russians again took a strong line against anyone who undermined national solidarity by paying attention to foreign radio propaganda. Again, penalties were imposed for disseminating the untruths so learned rather than for the act of listening itself. It is still rash for Soviet citizens to make too much fuss about their devotion to foreign programmes, although the KGB now makes a distinction between listeners to the BBC, the Voice of America and Deutsche Welle on the one hand, and to the much more subversive Radio Liberty on the other. But official attitudes change.

As far as China is concerned, it would appear that the tiny minority who have access to foreign programmes, and who want to listen, are still running a big risk and would at the very least be subject to severe pressure to indulge in self-criticism. It is equally illegal for the Chinese in Taiwan to listen to Radio Peking.

In 1966, the South African government announced that fines and imprisonment would be imposed on anyone caught taking part in a programme put out by any 'hostile' radio station and transmitted to the Republic. The Postmaster General assumed the power to 'name' any radio station in the world which he considered 'guilty of injuring the morals, religion or morale of any section of the South African population'. And the ban included any support or endorsement of such a station's activities. In 1972, the Bill re-emerged before Parliament and a maximum sentence of seven years was included in one of its clauses. While this does not penalize listeners, it is an effective way of discouraging South Africans from appearing on any radio station other than the domestic ones.

There are two reasons why indirect interference is now generally preferred all around the world to the relatively crude method of jamming. One is cost, and the other the technical inadequacy of superimposing noise. Of these, cost is the most important in the eyes of the jammers. Precise figures are difficult to come by from the communist world, but some estimates have been made in the west. In 1956, when the Poles ceased jamming altogether, they did in fact give an estimate themselves. It had cost them, they said, an annual total of $17.5 million, which, at the time, was the equivalent of the total annual budget for the worldwide operations of the Voice of

America. In 1962 western reports suggested that the Russians were using about 2,000 transmitters for jamming, and that another 500 or so were in operation in eastern Europe. An estimate for 1973 quoted in *The Economist* put the number of transmitters used for this purpose in the Soviet Union and eastern Europe at 3,000. Total construction costs have been put at $250 million and the annual operating cost at around $185 million. These figures are taken from American sources. *The Economist* estimate agreed with the figure for construction costs, but suggested an annual running cost of $100 million. Edward Barrett, a former official of the USIA, claimed that it costs five times more to jam any given programme than to transmit it.

Jamming is expensive for a technical but simple reason. The incoming signal starts at one point, but it ends up over a huge area. If it is transmitted on a number of frequencies, it has to be combated by both sky-wave jamming, in other words by using the same medium as that used by the broadcaster, and by ground-wave jamming, which interferes with signals in the immediate vicinity of the jamming transmitter. This requires, in a country the size of Russia, innumerable transmitters directed against a single signal. It also requires large teams of monitors to follow the signals around the frequency spectrum and, if jamming is selective, to listen out for the hostile parts. An indirect cost is incurred in the transfer of manpower (estimated to be up to 10,000 technicians in Russia) as well as equipment, which would otherwise have been used to boost domestic broadcasting services.

When this cost is set against the incomplete efficiency of jamming it becomes doubly difficult to justify it in economic terms. There is in fact no way of preventing some of the signals getting through. Both broadcasters and listeners can seriously minimize the effects of jamming. At the transmitting end, the most effective technique is saturation broadcasting, a technique at which the Voice of America is particularly adept. Examples include Ed Murrow's 'Sunday Punch' on 5 November 1958, when fifty-two VOA transmitters on eighty frequencies were concentrated in an eight-hour barrage against the Soviet Union attacking the Soviet decision to resume nuclear testing. Later American evaluation suggested that half the signals got through loud and clear. A similar operation was mounted at the time of the Cuba crisis. Less spectacular super-broadcasts have been staged by a number of countries from time to time; for instance, the BBC rapidly increased the power of its Czechoslovak transmissions to 500 kilowatts at the time of the 1968 invasion.

Careful siting of the transmitters can also reduce the effect of jamming. Deutsche Welle, for example, moved its transmitters to Sines in Portugal to get less interrupted reception in the Soviet Union.

VOA takes great care to surround its targets as far as possible and to come in from all angles simultaneously. In addition, broadcasters use techniques to improve the penetrating quality of the human voice. Electronic devices like the 'Clipper' can increase their loudness and also increase what is known as 'top', that is to say the upper frequencies to which the ear is more sensitive. Speakers can be selected for their powers of penetration more than for their sweet tones. For the same reason, morse code has been used in emergency situations to cut through the generally very different noise of jamming. During the war the BBC used to transmit morse messages and news in the early hours of the morning, laboriously repeating each word, to guarantee reception by those who were preparing underground newssheets. The Chinese have been known to combat Russian jamming by putting out staggered programmes; the same material is transmitted six times over, beginning at intervals of four or five minutes. The Americans had long before pioneered another technique: 'cuddling up'. By transmitting on frequencies very close to those of the Soviet domestic output (which was blatantly illegal), they hoped to dissuade the jammers. The ruse had little effect. Russian jammers were not so easily put off and carried on jamming, despite interruptions to their own programmes.

Nowadays most cuddling up is unintentional. The airwaves are so crowded, particularly in Europe, that programmes both domestic and international tumble over each other, to the despair of the regulating agency, the International Telecommunications Union. Despite a Master International Frequency Register, in existence since 1961, the rapid rise in demand for frequencies (up thirty per cent between 1961 and 1973) outstrips the ITU's capacity to keep sufficient distance between them. The Register only just succeeds in preventing total anarchy. It cannot prevent declining audibility through overcrowding. Just to give one small example: when the first two British commercial stations, London Broadcasting and Capital, went on the air in the autumn of 1973, the quality of their medium-wave signals was audibly poorer after dusk when Continental signals and east European jamming could reach across the Channel and get in the way. Even on VHF it was not always possible to escape police radio transmissions. In fact the medium-wave situation all over Europe is likely to provide the first instance of a complete breakdown in audibility.

So much for what the broadcaster can and cannot do. As for the listener, his best method of breaking the noise barrier set up by deliberate interference is, wherever possible, to move out of range of the jamming transmitters. Not infrequently he can do this by moving out of the town where the more localized ground-wave jammers are sited and into the countryside. Apart from this, there are a number of improvements in terms of filters, pre-selection devices and directional aerials that he can apply to his set. A little knowledge of radio engineering can do wonders in finding the precise spot on the dial to pick up the desired signal and reduce the impact of interference. A set which can receive the higher range of frequencies is also more likely to find one that the jammers have kept free for their monitoring colleagues. If all else fails, the ardent listener can learn another language. There appears to be no case of jamming of any broadcast in a language that is not native to the receiving country.

In the not too distant future the technology of transmitting and jamming international signals may be pushed a big step forward. The new factor is television. It is estimated that any time from 1980 onwards it will be technically possible to beam television signals by satellite into domestic sets. Already, plans for educational community television are well advanced in India and in Canada. One satellite will be used to cover the entire area of each country acting as a relay station and, positioned high above the earth, it will replace perhaps hundreds of local TV relay transmitters and the expensive overland connections joining them up with the supply source. It is perfectly possible for the type of 'dish' aerial used at satellite ground stations to be adapted for any ordinary set in the home—a miniaturization of the equipment already developed for community reception. The power necessary for each satellite would only be in the order of one kilowatt for an area the size of the British Isles. The cost of aerials and converters for the household television would be around $350. There is already international agreement on the wavelengths which would be allotted to international television broadcasting. Politics aside, the main drawback would be the $300 million or so needed to build and launch each satellite.

But politics cannot, of course, be put on one side. In 1972 the Russians presented a draft resolution to the United Nations whose purpose was to get all states to undertake to exclude from satellite TV programmes all material detrimental to international peace or publicizing war and racial hatred, material interfering in other states' affairs, and material undermining local mores. The draft also provided for counter-measures to be recognized as legal under international law. But above all, it insisted that direct broadcasts to foreign countries should be made illegal unless made with the direct consent of the target states. Not surprisingly, this draft soon became known in the west as the 'Jammers' Charter'. The American reaction was to repeat the formula about not broadcasting material incompatible with international peace—a safe enough generality—and to stress the need to expand the free flow of information and ideas. The deadlock was familiar.

The Soviet tactic was then to move the whole issue into the sphere of the UN Committee of Peaceful Uses of Outer Space. Already the UN had had some success with agreement on Outer Space law, and the Russians were anxious to argue their case in relation to the very delicate questions of co-operation in this broad field, because no country can afford a battle here. Interference with someone else's space communications is too easy, too deadly, and too open an invitation to retaliation. This much had been mutually agreed at a 1971 meeting of the ITU.

The Americans, however, continue to see international TV broadcasting as simply an extension of radio broadcasting. They believe the same rules, or rather lack of rules, should apply. But in fact they will be forced to recognize the Russian principle that some international agreement should be signed. The card they have in their favour is that satellite television is attractive to the Soviet Union because it is the cheapest method of domestic broadcasting in the wide spaces of that sparsely-populated country. And if Russian sets are adapted to receive signals from Moscow, the door is open to signals from wherever. So far the issue has not been settled. Perhaps technology will come to the Russians' rescue and they will find a way to differentiate between domestic and foreign signals. What is more likely is that the sheer cost of beaming TV programmes by satellite, compared with long-distance radio signals, will dissuade the Americans, who alone may be expected to try, from taking the risk of having them jammed or the satellite itself taken out of commission. They are unlikely to upset the network of outer space communications for the sake of an expensive and indefinable propaganda advantage.

So far the assumption appears to be that jamming is the prerogative of communist countries. And in fact there are few non-communist countries that make it a regular practice to jam other countries' radio programmes. It is ironic perhaps that the country which was the first to use radio for international propaganda should now be its principal victim. Not that the Soviet Union was also the first country to jam hostile broadcasts. This honour is generally agreed to be Austria's, and it occurred in 1934, at a time when the Dollfuss government was desperate to combat Nazi propaganda aimed at the eventual incorporation of Austria into the Reich, and at the development of the Austrian Nazi Party. An attempt by Romania in 1932 to jam Soviet propaganda was technically unsuccessful. By the late thirties the practice had spread. The Italians jammed Ethiopian radio broadcasts as well as the BBC's Arabic Service. The rival factions in the Spanish civil war jammed each other. By the time the world became involved in war, almost everybody was doing it. *Almost*—the BBC resolutely stuck to the principle that all versions of the truth should be given an airing, even in wartime. In a statement issued in 1940, the BBC declared:

> Jamming is really an admission of a bad cause. The jammer has a bad conscience . . . He is afraid of the influence of the truth . . . In our country we have no such fears and to jam broadcasts in English by the enemy might even be bad propaganda.

The postwar battle began with the mutual jamming of Spanish and Russian broadcasts and picked up momentum as the Cold War developed. The Russians began to jam the Voice of America in 1948 and the BBC in April 1949. The mixture of genuine exacerbation and fantasy exhibited by both sides in the early days of the Cold War is typified by the Soviet Foreign Minister's defence of jamming given at the UN. Vishinsky declared that one of the reasons was that the Russian people had to be prevented in the name of world peace from rising up in wrath to attack the United States, as they assuredly would if they were to hear the American broadcasts. The eastern European satellites, now entering their benighted period of blind obedience, followed the Russian example. Not only the Voice, but also the BBC, Deutsche Welle and, of course, the new CIA-financed operations from Munich, were blotted out in an ever more cacophonous battle in the ether.

There have since been four periods when Soviet jamming has been restricted to Radio Liberty and a selected number of stations outside the big-league western opposition. The first of these periods lasted a mere six months during 1956 between the visit of Kruschev and Bulganin to Britain and the Hungarian and Suez disasters in October. In 1960 the British Prime Minister, Harold Macmillan, induced another temporary shutdown of Soviet jamming, but his efforts were undone (as was the summit conference) by the U2 spy-plane furore. In fact full jamming was not resumed at this point. The Russians now attempted to rely on selective jamming of particularly 'offensive' broadcasts or items. On the whole this was a counter-productive approach despite the fact that they were careful to let in those parts of western broadcasts which, in the interests of 'balance', revealed the seamy side of 'Free World' life. The ruse was too obvious. Besides, it made listening to the censored bits that much more attractive.

Recognizing the inefficiency of partial jamming, not least the way it encouraged rumour, the Soviet authorities decided to try once again to drop it altogether in the summer of 1963. This third break lasted five years until August 1968, when that and a number of other liberal measures went out of the window. One of the consequences of stamping on the Czechoslavak vision of socialism with a human face was a retreat into fear in the face of hostile propaganda. Jamming was now applied not only to Radio Liberty but to the Voice of America, the BBC, Deutsche Welle, Radio Peking and several others. Later the Russians started jamming Kol Israel. But they left free the Russian-language broadcasts from France, Sweden and Canada, whose output was considered sufficiently non-controversial.

This period finally came to an end in September 1973, partly as a gesture of good faith at the opening of the Geneva Conference on European Security. The gesture did not, however, include the free reception of broadcasts from Russia's Enemy Number One, the People's Republic of China. Chinese broadcasts in Russian languages are still solidly jammed, as are Albanian broadcasts in Russian, Yiddish and Bulgarian. The inaudible polemics continue as bitter as ever on both sides.

Russian jamming appeared to be temporarily reimposed on Deutsche Welle in January 1974 when the West German station began to broadcast readings from Alexander Solzhenitsyn's *Gulag Archipelago*. Chilean broadcasts began to be jammed from Cuban transmitters soon after the 1973 coup against President Allende. This long-distance operation has apparently interfered with some of Chile's domestic broadcasting. Yet another exception to the Soviet decision to stop jamming is Kol Israel. In this case, the Russians appear to have learnt a positive lesson from the days of selective jamming. They sometimes allow free reception of the Voice of Zion for the Diaspora, but just in certain limited areas when they want to encourage the emigration of a particularly awkward group of Jews. If true, this is also a compliment to the effectiveness of Israeli appeals.

The eastern Europeans have tended in the last ten years or more to make their own rules. For example, Romania stopped jamming altogether in 1963, and Hungary did the same the following year. The Poles, as we saw, dropped the habit in 1956. The Bulgarians, as they usually do, have roughly followed the Soviet line. This is not to say that any eastern European country, or the Soviet Union itself, would hesitate to reintroduce jamming should political circumstances demand it. Permission to listen to foreign broadcasts has for a long time been one of the most sensitive barometers of east-west relations, and will continue to be so.

But jamming has not been exclusively a communist concern since the war. The Rhodesians selectively jammed the Francistown transmitters, sited only eight kilometers from their border, for the three years of British propaganda which followed UDI. This was one of the reasons why the operation was closed down and the facilities handed over to Botswana in 1968. Spain keeps up its jamming of the communist Radio España Independiente and the Basque Radio Euzkadi. *The Economist* reported that the Greek government was try-

ing to ban the Greek-language broadcasts of Deutsche Welle.
Israel interfered with some Cairo Radio transmissions during the
October war. But since the coup in Chile, the Chileans have become
the biggest anti-communist jammers, including stations such as the
leftist Radio Sweden in their ban.

Innumerable clandestine stations are jammed all round the world,
although the jamming potential of the transmitters of Radio Cairo
and Radio South Africa—which alone on the African continent
could be used effectively—has never been brought into play. The
British tried their hand at jamming Athens broadcasts to Cyprus in
1956. The French jammed the Voice of Free Algeria. The Americans
have yet to resort to jamming, except locally and tactically, although
pressure has been brought to bear to extend its use. As Thomas C.
Sorensen, one-time Deputy Director (Policy and Plans) of the USIA
wrote: 'The US has never seriously contemplated jamming, although it has been suggested by the military from time to time.'[5]

But if jamming is only partially effective, and if it costs so much,
and if it is represented as a sign of cowardice and tyranny by the
other side, why has it gone on for so long? Indeed why does it continue? In 1956, the Poles made their position clear. Jamming, they
declared is 'a method which has brought us no credit'. And stopping
it 'is a victory for the principle, correct in our opinion, that the
foreign radio stations should be countered by factual arguments'. Besides, the cessation of jamming would save 'enough electric power
to supply a town of several thousand people'. And a Polish
engineer claimed to feel relief that the end of jamming would
refurbish the image of his colleagues associated in the public mind
with the 'dirty work' of jamming. It would seem that to continue is
merely perverse. But that is not the Russian view.

For the Russians, foreign radio propaganda is not just interference in their internal affairs, it is illegal and dangerous. And whether
their counter-measures are illegal or not (they clearly are under
United Nations rules), the Russians argue that they are only using
one illegal act to combat another. But their case sounds more like
special pleading when one remembers the long history of Soviet radio
propaganda, which not only began as far back as the First World War
but was quick to make use of technological progress, turning powerful transmitters against Romania in 1926, and a full propaganda
programme against Germany from 1930 onwards. Today the Soviet
Union is the second largest international broadcaster after the
United States.

So the Russian legal position is shaky. But in reality the whole
question of the legality of both propaganda and jamming is to all
intents and purposes academic. Three resolutions were passed at the
United Nations in 1950 which underscored the right for everyone to

have free access to information, but this was the year when the Cold War was bursting out into its full fury, when Radio Free Europe got under way, when the CIA was established, and the Korean war broke out. Realpolitik was the name of the game, not legality. It is scarcely surprising that the Yugoslav delegate pointed out the impossibility of separating information and politics, voicing here a basic tenet of Marxism-Leninism: 'Today,' he said, 'there is no neutral news and no neutral information.' Everyone on both sides—and in 1950 the Yugoslavs were right in the middle—knew what the score was. The Americans were only interested in promoting resolutions which showed the Russians up in a bad light and which could then be exploited for propaganda purposes. They were quite aware of the impossibility of proving that propaganda directed at the communists was tantamount to intervention or to using force against a sovereign state, or even to incitement to criminal action. One might as well outlaw 'hostility' and, anyway, when everybody does it, it's all right.

The Russians have been able to jam and get away with it, but this has given the west an extra propaganda weapon. It was humiliating enough to the Russians back in the twenties when Moscow Radio first started broadcasting in English (provoking protests in the British Parliament) to find that no-one listened and that the signal was almost inaudible anyway. (The protests faded away as a result.) As the audience in the west has never been on a scale to cause the governments worry, western governments have never been strongly tempted to jam, which makes it all the more easy for them to rub in not just the illegality of the Russian action, but also their weakness and their lack of confidence in the ability of the Russian people to reject the anti-communist message.

But the western view of propaganda has always been too simple, deliberately simplified, in fact, precisely for the purposes of propaganda. The entire structure of Soviet power depends on the ability to make unchallenged decisions within their sphere of influence. Not just for political, but also for economic reasons, there has to be unanimity. Since 1917 the Soviet Union has had to struggle against far greater odds than any western country—today this includes the self-inflicted wounds of the Stalinist excesses. But whatever the arguments, the basis of Soviet thinking on the subject remains the same. To them hostile propaganda is far more of a threat than it is to the prosperous west whose techniques of government and propaganda depend at least on the illusion of having a balance of multiple opposing forces. To the west, allowing foreign propaganda to function—at least from a safe distance, and radio is hardly the same as bomb-throwing—is part of the fundamental political credo. To the countries between Berlin and Vladivostock the very opposite is true. What to one is an affirmation of a human right, to the other is an irresponsible invitation to chaos.

In the report of the Presidential Study Commission on International Broadcasting, the American position was clearly stated:

Poverty and ignorance alone substantially deny many peoples their right to knowledge. But others are robbed of this right by interference, more or less stringent, practised by their governments—governments which plainly believe that a free flow of information and ideas among their peoples could lead to criticism and calls for internal reform.[6]

What the report does not acknowledge is that the second part of the equation is directly related to the first. The Russians claim that the restrictions on information that they impose are designed precisely to enable their country to escape from the vicious circle of poverty and ignorance from which it suffered throughout its entire previous history. 'Criticism and calls for internal reform' are to them the very recipe for setting back all the progress made so far—progress already interrupted by foreign activity in the form of more than one military intervention.

In fact the Soviet Union's greater confidence in its ability to withstand outside pressure and the new spirit of détente makes it likely that the recent decision to suspend jamming of most foreign stations will remain in force for much longer than earlier suspensions. Two decades after the Poles, the Russians are probably deciding that it is unnecessary to insist on such rigid controls. One effect will be, however, to focus attention more sharply on Radio Liberty and, as far as eastern Europe is concerned, Radio Free Europe. It will also underline the difference between Russian tolerance of western government radio and their jamming of Radio Peking.

The trouble with Radios Liberty and Free Europe is that their claim not to be subversive is, as we have already seen, simply implausible. The Russians dub them 'radio saboteurs'. Despite the switch from CIA financing to open government support, the stations remain in being with the sole purpose of undermining and overthrowing communism. That much is recognized in the Presidential Study Commission's report. But the report denies any explicit aim to use national minority friction. This the Russians do not accept. Although, for obvious reasons, they are unlikely to say so openly, they are in fact aware of the real danger that the Soviet Union might disintegrate. Much as they would like to see multilateral disarmament in the radio war, they would readily settle for any deal whereby the two émigré stations were taken off the air and disbanded. The

F

west, of course, is aware of this view. One of the reasons why RL and RFE have been reprieved is that the stations represent such a good card in the American negotiating hand. In the long run a deal is inevitable. But in the meantime, the signal will go out and the jammers will faithfully continue to track it down.

It is not improbable that after Soviet jamming of all western stations has ceased, some transmitters will remain in service to jam the Russian-language broadcasts from China. There is some ground for believing that the Soviet Union is more fearful of attacks from the left than from the traditional right. Dissension on the left often has a more lasting quality of bitterness than the open and expected enmity between the opposite extremes of the political spectrum. And jamming between the Soviet Union and China is mutual. This will make it more difficult to reach an agreement to cease jamming simultaneously. Neither will want to be the first to give it up.

But the Sino-Soviet radio battle does serve to point up the absurdity of using arguments of international law to criticize or defend jamming. No-one knows better than the jammer himself that his labours are only partially effective and desperately expensive. It will only be undertaken when the alternative seems very serious indeed. The view that the Russians have jammed so much and so often since the war because they disputed the west's right to interfere in their internal affairs is an understatement. They have been concerned about the very survival of their own form of socialism. They take no risk, however small, which could threaten the system which they see as uniquely able to lead them eventually to communism, abundance and all the rest. Only recently have there been signs that they believe they are getting there. Clearly the Chinese still pose a threat, and that is why the Russians will continue to jam Radio Peking.

13 *The Broadcasters*

The link between radio propaganda and the listener is a voice. However well-planned the propaganda, dull delivery can ruin it; however perfunctory the message, it can arouse an audience if delivered with conviction or with passion. Not only the performer, but also the producer who shapes and edits programmes can influence the outcome. Even the news is more or less persuasive depending on the reader and the sub-editor. The first decision which strategists of international radio have to take is whether to go for personalities to achieve maximum effect or to go for teamwork.

Today, virtually all international broadcasting organizations have come down on the side of teamwork and all-round professionalism, with only minimum emphasis on 'star' performers. The object is to create a 'BBC sound' or a 'Moscow style'. Although some names are known and have a following, the very fact that the faces and characters behind them live and work in a country, and generally a political system, that is remote from their audience deprives them of the sort of fame earned by performers on the domestic media.

During the war this was not so. William Joyce—Herr Fröklich to the Germans—was a character whose fame in Britain, even in the United States, was unrivalled by any other radio star. But he was not famous under either of those names. The nickname created by a *Daily Express* reporter became his own adopted identity: Lord Haw-Haw, the pompous, ranting, unmistakable 'Humbug from Hamburg'.

Born in 1906 in New York City of an Irish father and an Irish-English-Scottish mother, Joyce had a Jesuit education in Ireland and moved to England in his teens. He was a student at London University, then became involved with the British fascist movement, becoming their director of propaganda. But he quarrelled with Oswald Mosley after being caught with his hand in the till and left for Germany with his newly-acquired second wife to sample the real thing. For the Germans Joyce was a godsend. His mocking upper-class accent, his resentment of British society, but above all his ardent and unfeigned enthusiasm for the Nazi cause, coupled with experience in propagandizing this cause in England, made him an obvious choice as the star turn in the Nazi radio campaign against the British. With the microphone of the Hamburg station at his disposal, and a handsome pay packet as an earnest of German faith in his talents, Joyce went on the air in April 1939, five months before the outbreak of the Second World War.

At first his identity was a mystery. Some people suspected he was Lieutenant Norman Baillie-Stewart, a British army officer arrested and imprisoned as a German spy in 1933, released after five years and allowed to go to Austria. Although Baillie-Stewart did broadcast to Britain and to the United States for the Nazis, he was not 'Lord Haw-Haw'. (Had he been, he would not have returned to Ireland after the war—if Sefton Delmer's account is correct—and settled down with an Irish wife to make his living as a commercial agent for German firms.)

It was not until April 1941 that *Picture Post* identified Lord

Haw-Haw as William Joyce. By this time he had become a household word. His voice was a refreshing contrast to the heavy German accents of his colleagues, and to many people a stimulating change from the sanctimonious voices in the BBC, and by January 1940 Lord Haw-Haw had thrust himself into thirty per cent of all British households where there were radio sets. Some of what he had to say was incisively accurate, always allowing for Nazi twists, particularly his attacks on the British class system, on tax-evaders and profiteers. He could be quite witty, for example in his comic dialogues between Schmidt and Smith and his mockery of leading British figures. When Duff Cooper opened up his Silent Campaign to stop loose talk, Lord Haw-Haw conjured up the image of a stuffy Englishman accusing his friend of helping the German Air Force by saying 'Good Morning' on a fine day.

Reception of the Hamburg station was excellent, and he could be heard just as clearly when he moved into the Radio Luxembourg studios after the Germans had overrun them. Moreover, the signal came through on a wavelength that nestled close to the BBC. Only the smallest adjustment of the dial was needed to change from Alvar Liddell to Lord Haw-Haw, who regularly made his appearance just as the BBC bulletin was ending. Incredibly, *The Times* continued to carry the hours when German broadcasts were on the air for some months after the outbreak of war. The BBC itself was slow in realizing how profound an impact Lord Haw-Haw was making on the British. This attitude changed somewhat after the publication of an opinion poll showing how many people listened to him and the extent to which many of them agreed with his message. But fortunately for all concerned, Lord Haw-Haw himself was slowly becoming his own worst enemy. His tone at first had been reasonable, full of regret that the British were failing to understand the virtues of Nazism and of uniting against the real enemy, the Bolsheviks, Jews and plutocrats. But he failed to adapt to the change in the British mood when the phoney war was over and Britain faced her 'finest hour'. He became cocky—an unforgivable sin in British eyes. He began to rant and rave. Goebbels, though an admirer of Joyce, was a more sophisticated propagandist. He wrote in his diary (entry of 23 May 1942):

Our broadcasts in English are, after all, very effective . . . However, an aggressive, superior and insulting tone gets us nowhere . . . The English speaker, Lord Haw-Haw, is especially good at biting criticism, but in my opinion the time for spicy debate is past . . . During the first year of war the people still listen to the delivery; they admire the wit and spiritual qualities of the presentation. Today they want nothing but facts.[1]

This was the beginning of the end of Lord Haw-Haw, even in German eyes.

In Britain he had lost his credibility and most of his following by the time of the Battle of Britain in the summer of 1940. Duff Cooper, the Minister of Information, reported that His Lordship's audience had shrunk to a fraction of its former size. But there was evidence of a revival of Lord Haw-Haw's popularity during 1941, and as late as the summer of 1944, a spate of rumours about damage by doodle-bugs, as the flying bombs were called, was attributed to Lord Haw-Haw.

In April 1945, as the Russians were overrunning Berlin, Joyce made his last recording, the tape of which has only just been dis-covered in the Radio Luxembourg archives. It was never broadcast. Joyce was audibly drunk, maudlin, his upper-class accent slipping into an Irish-Lancastrian brogue. Later that year he was hiding in a forest near the Danish border with his wife. Two British officers searching for firewood nearby heard him speaking. So familiar was the voice that he was at once recognized, seized and arrested. After some legal debate as to whether his birth in the United States should absolve him from a charge of treason, he was hanged in Wandsworth jail in January 1946.

Richard Crossman criticized Lord Haw-Haw as too obvious a propagandist. It is true that Joyce made a virtue out of his Nazi enthusiasm which, by definition, ruled out good taste and measured reason. But the fact remains that every propagandist of the no-holds-barred school has had to compare himself, or see himself compared, with the original star turn. Propagandists ever since have been dubbed 'the American Lord Haw-Haw' or 'the Lord Haw-Haw of the BBC'. A Japanese-American, Charles Yoshii, alumnus of the University of Oregon and propagandist for the wartime Tokyo Radio, was called the 'slant-eyed Lord Haw-Haw'. Fred Kalten-bach, the homespun butcher's son from Waterloo, Iowa, pro-Nazi broadcaster, punster and wisecracker (he would start his programmes for America: 'Lend or lease me your ears!') was known as Lord Hee-Haw.

Kaltenbach was one of a large team of American Nazi sym-pathizers who, before and during the time of the United States' active involvement in the war, attempted to drum up support for Nazi ideals and to counter the special relationship between Britain and America. There was roving reporter Edward Leopold Delaney of Glenview, Illinois, known as Ed Ward; Douglas Chandler, an ex-journalist from Baltimore who styled himself 'Paul Revere'; *Kultur* vulture and 'Philadelphia hostess and socialite' Constance Drexel; characters known as 'Mr OK' and 'Mr Guess Who'. There was Gertie (Gertrude Hahn) who put on a long-running act as a switch-

F*

board operator on the *Pittsburgh Tribune* and would read out letters from her boyfriend Joe, the *Tribune* correspondent in Berlin; she came on as a kind of Hitlerite flapper. Jane Anderson was a more serious personage, a former journalist and Franco agent. But she was taken off the air for gloating about drinking champagne and eating Turkish delight just when Goebbels had launched a campaign to prove that Germans could cope with shortages. Not all members of this motley team escaped retribution. Kaltenbach died in the Soviet Union, for example, and Douglas Chandler was given life imprisonment in the United States.

American victory in the war makes it impossible to assess the impact of the Nazi short-wave campaign. But there is firmer evidence of a Nazi success in the broadcasts to France leading up to the invasion and occupation. Notoriously, French defeat was in large measure due to moral collapse preceding the military débâcle. One small but identifiable cause was the personality of the 'traitor of Stuttgart', Paul Ferdonnet. 'In Ferdonnet,' wrote Tangye Lean, 'the Germans had a first-class speaker who drove home his simple, unvarying points with force and conviction. Many Frenchmen thought him better than anything to be heard on the home (French) radio; certainly he was incomparably superior to the English Lord Haw-Haw.'[2] A special trick of Ferdonnet's was to exploit French sexual fears, putting out 'regretful' reports that the English were raping the wives of French soldiers fretting at the front. After the German occupation, however, Ferdonnet retired from the scene, leaving the organization of Radio Paris in the less spectacular though not ineffective care of Friedrich Sieburg.

The Japanese never rivalled the Nazis' sophisticated efforts to get through to foreign audiences. They tended to employ their own nationals, often with accents so impenetrable that even the monitors had difficulty in following them. The Italians, on the other hand, collected a professional team for their American transmissions, including one much-appreciated young lady with a Kentuckian mother and a seductive voice, Evgenia Ernesta Andreani. But their star was a man whose microphone appearances became a literary and legal *cause célèbre*, the brilliant poet and crank, Ezra Pound.

Pound was persuaded down to the studios in Rome for highly personal reasons. For one thing, he was in despair at American philistinism and regarded Italy as the guardian of a sacred cultural heritage. That was where he was living when war broke out. For another, he was a passionate advocate of the economic theories of Clifford Hugh Douglas, author of *Economic Democracy*, which put forward the idea that 'the real unit of the world currency is effort into time—what we may call the time-energy unit'. The moral that Douglas (and Pound) drew was that the money system was inefficient, indeed a racket, responsible for such scandals as the destruction of the US food surplus in the 1930's while people were starving. They saw war as the inevitable result of the money system, the basis of which was usury; but Germany and Italy had prospered without the aid of bankers, who put the poor in debt and gathered the riches for themselves. This led Pound to the third reason for his propaganda campaign on behalf of the fascists: what he called at the end of his life 'that stupid, suburban prejudice of anti-Semitism'.

Pound was always careful to stress that he made very little money out of his broadcasts apart from his expenses—350 lire, out of which he had to pay for the journey between his home in Rapallo and Rome. And he prefaced his twice-weekly talks with an announce-ment, made on his behalf in the studio, that he had not been asked to say anything against his conscience or 'incompatible with his duties as a citizen of the USA'. At the microphone Pound affected a folksy western drawl, a kind of self-conscious rustic accent in which he car-ried on a rambling monologue, elaborating on his well-worn themes, though seldom directly attacking the Allied war effort. He was silent for a month after Pearl Harbour, but picked up again in his familiar style, as this extract from his broadcast on 23 April 1942 shows:

> Of course for you to go looking for my point—points of my bi-weekly talk in the maze of Jew-governed American radio trans-missions—is like looking for one needle in a whole flock of hay stacks. And your press is not very open. However, if some lone watcher or listener on Back Bay or on top of the Blue Ridge does hear me, I suggest he make notes and ask Advocate Archibald [MacLeish] whether it does win anything to have the people pay two dollars for every dollar spent by the government. I ask whether the spirit of '76 is helped by a-floodin' the lower ranks of the Navy with bridge-sweepin's; whether war is won by mercantilist ethics and, in any case, whether men like Knox and Stimson and Morgenthau can be expected to fill the heart of youth with martial ardour and spirit of sacrifice.

Not surprisingly, he converted no-one with this half-demented drivel. But he believed in it himself. 'Not a traitor but a phrophet' was Pound's explanation to his postwar American captors. He was, he claimed, battling for enlightenment against narrow jingoism. After a spell in a six-foot-by-six-foot cage in a deserters' camp near Pisa, he was brought to the United States to face charges of treason lodged against him back in 1943. His defence was that he had been protest-ing against the system that caused wars rather than this particular war. But the Washingtom court was more impressed by the report of four psychiatrists who found him 'eccentric, querulous and egocentric'. In February 1946, Pound was judged unfit to stand trial and was sent to a mental hospital, the first year of which he spent in a barred cell in the prison ward. Later he was treated like any other patient, and was finally released fourteen years before his death at the end of 1972.

Pound was by no means the only eminent man of letters brought to the microphone to fight the propaganda war. The BBC used, among others, Thomas Mann and Salvador de Madariaga. Tangye Lean had this to say about the former's contribution:

> Mann invited comparison with Victor Hugo in exile from the Second Empire in the Channel Islands where he wrote *Les Châtiments* in denunciation of Louis Napoleon and the disasters he brought on the French. The invective of both novelists was more than an exile's rancour; it united indignation at the setback of their countries' tradition with austere pity for their prostration.[3]

But Mann's appeals to the Germans to awake to reason had something of a remote ex-cathedra feeling about them. The really brilliant propagandist from the world of letters, despite being a cosmopolitan Jew remote from the ordinary populace and an almost eccentric individualist, was not a recruit of the BBC but of Moscow Radio—Ilya Ehrenburg.

Born in Moscow in 1891, Ehrenburg spent a wandering life, better known in the bistros of Paris than in his native country. Before the 'Great Patriotic War', and after it, he was under the Soviet authorities' fire as a deviationist. And yet he became the most popular of all the Soviet propagandists, particularly to the Russian soldiers, with whom, ostensibly, he had almost nothing in common, but with whom he still managed to develop an extraordinary rapport. By no means all Ehrenburg's propaganda work was done over the radio, but his fame as a writer—rather in the same way as J. B. Priestley in Britain—preceded him as a broadcaster and set up a positive reaction in the audience. It is a great advantage for a propagandist to be known as an individual in his own right and not just a mouthpiece. The present stress on teamwork does not entirely compensate for the paucity of regular broadcasters of public notoriety.

The advantage of having a well-known figure at the microphone is even more evident when the individual is a political figure. National leaders apart—and Hitler, Goebbels, Mussolini, Churchill and Roosevelt were all effective radio orators in their different ways—most politician-propagandists were those whose national base had been removed from them and whose only weapon was propaganda until the time came, or did not come, for them to return to the front line of their political battle. Leaders and representatives of governments in exile and many other political factions and parties were active during the war from 'enemy' territory. Undoubtedly one man stands out above all the others, the Free French leader, Charles de Gaulle. Though Churchill later claimed that the 'Cross of Lorraine was the heaviest cross I had to bear', and de Gaulle's relationship with his hosts was always one of love-hate, no-one has questioned his value to France both as a symbol and as a propagandist. From his first broadside on 18 June 1940, de Gaulle launched a frontal assault on the collaborators and occupiers. His prophecy that 'whatever happens, the flame of resistance must not go out, and it will not go out', was to a great extent self-fulfilled. It is possible to exaggerate the importance of the Free French programme, which was a very small part indeed of the BBC's French Service—or rather a semi-dependent insert into the BBC output. But there is no question that de Gaulle himself, and above all Maurice Schumann, later to become France's Foreign Minister, depended as much on their success as broadcasters as on any other single factor for laying the foundations of their political roles in a liberated France.

Unorthodox characters, from de Gaulle down to the humblest newsreader, were the rule rather than the exception in the wartime international radio services of both the British and the Americans. It would take too long to repeat their stories here; there are too many of them and they are now little more than names, often remembered with gratitude and affection by hard-pressed listeners. At the time, men like Benno Frank, the son of an American diplomat who had spent some of his early years in the household of General von Kleist and was known to his German listeners as Captain Angers; or Michel Saint-Denis and Jean Oberlé of the BBC's French Service; the Arab star Mohammed Abdul Wahab, lured away from the Italian Arabic Service when the British began their propaganda counter-offensive just before the war; Lindley Fraser, Richard Crossman and Hugh Carleton Greene from the BBC's German Service—all of these and countless others developed their own styles and appealed to particular listeners. Some earned nicknames, like the cultured ex-military attaché in Rome who 'spoke English with a slight neapolitan accent and Italian with a slight English accent', Colonel Stevens. He was known as Colonnello Buonasera, from the invariable and emphatic way he introduced his talks on the BBC. (These, however, were not written by him but by regular members of the Italian Service staff, notably the Triestino journalist Aldo Cassuto.) And then there were the strange characters manning black radio operations in all the belligerent states.

As far as propaganda radio is concerned, those were the days. The tensions of war, the personal predicaments and convictions of so many of the broadcasters, and the gravity of the task, combined to create an intense hothouse atmosphere which has never been re-peated. Radio subsequently lost many of the personalities who only came to the microphone because of the circumstances of war, and the regular broadcasters never found in the Cold War the same stimulus for their passionate involvement, or the same conditions in which that intense level of broadcaster-listener relationship could be created or maintained.

But there are one or two exceptions, and the Cold War is purely incidental to their success. For example, the only character to really stand out from the Voice of America ruck with its many mouth-pieces of USIA and State Department policy is not a political commentator but a disc jockey. Willis Conover with his *Music USA* programme has a devoted following, especially in the Soviet Union.

The BBC's Russian audience are fans of a man much closer in character to Ilya Ehrenburg than to Conover, a man whose Jewish cosmopolitan background, incisive yet idiosyncratic mind, and broad knowledge of the world and its languages must indeed remind the older listeners of their wartime hero. Anatol Goldberg is in fact an admirer and biographer of Ehrenburg. He was born in St Peters-burg in 1910 on 7 May, a day that was to seem prophetically appropriate, since it later became 'Radio Day' in honour of the Russian 'inventor' of radio, the engineer Popov. Goldberg left Russia as a small boy and remained in Germany until 1936, protected from Hitler's persecution of the Jews only by his Lithuanian passport. In 1938 Goldberg became a founder member of the BBC's Monitoring Service—not to monitor any of his main languages—Russian, German, French, Chinese and Japanese—but as a Spanish-language monitor. When the Soviet Union marched into the eastern half of Poland in 1939, and the British authorities were obliged to recognize Russia as a real political force, the monitoring of their broadcasts was begun, and Goldberg joined the team.

But it was not until 1946, when the BBC began to broadcast to the Soviet Union, that his slow sceptical voice was first heard in his home-land. His *Sunday Notes* first went on the air on 10 October in that year and have continued uninterrupted ever since—the second longest-running series of radio talks ever, certainly a worthy rival of Alistair Cooke's *Letter from America*, which began in March 1946. Anatol Goldberg's reports from first of all the Paris Peace Confer-ence, and almost all subsequent summit meetings and conferences, helped to build up a devoted following. But he has never been a cold warrior. 'I have welcomed every improvement,' he told me, 'and de-plored every setback. What matters is the constructive development of the Soviet Union.'

The Russians themselves acknowledged this when they permitted him to broadcast a report of the signing of the nuclear test-ban treaty in 1963 live from Moscow back to the Soviet Union via the BBC's Russian Service. But that was to be an illusory symbol of thaw. After 1968 and the Soviet-led invasion of Czechoslovakia, the Russian authorities once again felt it necessary to warn off listeners not just by resuming jamming but by dubbing Goldberg as a hostile Goebbels figure. Goldberg philosophically takes the long view, quoting the landowner in *Dead Souls* who, in reply to Chichikov's question: 'How do I get rich quickly?' says: 'If you want to get rich quickly, you won't get rich at all.'

The BBC's External Services still have a quota of exceptional, polyglot intellectuals, though fewer and fewer. Possibly the most remarkable is George Campbell, a Highlander who has 'collected' almost every important language in the world and many which are totally unimportant, if one can so call Cherokee and Cherkessky-Kabadin. The Chief Commentator, Maurice Latey, is also no mean intellectual. He is a 'Corporation Man', having entered the Empire and German Services straight from Oxford in 1938. Rising to senior positions during the Cold War, Latey has earned himself a reputation for being uncompromisingly anti-communist, but he takes this as a compliment if by that one means that he has helped prevent Stalin's policy of 'social engineering in a completely isolated society' from coming to fruition. Latey is part of the 'old guard' of Bush House, whose tendency to follow up any harsh comment on, for example, South Africa, with a 'but the Russians are just as bad' encourages the view among the 'young Turks' that objectivity can become an obsession.

BBC broadcasters and heads of service have learnt to accept the occasional poison-pen attacks of Soviet critics. They are partly comforted by the knowledge that they are ultimately tolerated as official and, in a sense, well-meaning, communicators. This is not at all how the Russians and east Europeans see the staff of Radio Liberty and Radio Free Europe. Because both these stations put out programmes that amount to an alternative domestic channel in each of the target countries, they are seen as little more than espionage operations, examples of blatant psychological warfare. And in fact, a great many RL and RFE broadcasters do provoke a correspondingly passionate response in their audience. Their styles and personalities are well known, and hated or loved as the case may be. A great many leading anti-communists have either worked on the staff in Munich or been offered airtime. Communist antagonism towards them sometimes spills over on to the staff of the official West German stations, Deutsche Welle and Deutschlandfunk, as when a Ukrainian magazine accused the head of DW, Felix von Eckhardt, of being an ex-Nazi propagandist and in the same breath accused RFE of

employing fascist sympathizers.[4] General Dietmar, incidentally a top
Nazi broadcaster, applied unsuccessfully after the war to join the
BBC's German Service. Many Nazis did indeed see the Cold War as
an opportunity to carry on their anti-communist crusade.

But it is not just the communists who attack the men of Munich.
RL and RFE have been notorious hotbeds of intrigue and self-loath-
ing. The exile mentality of the majority of the staff, and the intermix-
ture of politics and espionage in their work as broadcasters, set up a
we/they split not just between themselves and the audience, but
among themselves. As Robert Holt said in 1958:

> The official character of RFE is still that of the 'Voice of the
> Exiles'. This means, of course, that exiles must be employed and
> also that they be given more independence than they would have in
> an official foreign radio operation like the foreign service of the
> British Broadcasting Corporation.[5]

But this freedom is granted only to a proportion of the staff, and even
they are subject to American control. Morale suffers when exiles in
junior positions are of a political persuasion that differs from the
desk chief's or from their American masters'. And everyone has
their own way of 'restoring freedom' to their 'imprisoned country'.
Staff members have accused each other of being communist agents,
so violent does the faction-fighting become. These battles are
reminiscent of those fought in some of the BBC's most quarrelsome
wartime sections—the Greek, Polish, Hungarian and Spanish ones
for example—but they lack the unifying factor of faith in ultimate
victory over the enemy.

It is indeed difficult for any broadcasting service to keep off its pay-
roll all those people who have undesirable pasts or who are prepared
to use the medium for their own personal ends. Not so long ago, a
Brazilian of the BBC staff revealed himself to be a more enthusiastic
opponent of his government than the BBC was prepared to allow.
One night, when only a technician was with him in the studio, instead
of reading the news, he broadcast a personal statement. Since the
studio manager understood not a word of Portuguese, the substitu-
tion was only discovered later. The Brazilian was sacked.

It is amazing that this does not happen more often. There were
hardly any incidents recorded during the war of a BBC 'switch
censor' having to be called upon to cut off a deliberate attempt to
broadcast unauthorized material. Bruce Lockhart tells of a rare case
in 1944 when the House of Commons voted in support of British
intervention on the side of the Greek government against the communists. For one member of the divided and unhappy Greek section,
this was too much. He added to the relevant news item: 'The vote of

confidence is not the end for Greece. The people of England will express their real will at the next election.'[6] He too was sacked.

The worst tensions come when a team of broadcasters are faced with a test of loyalty, either between their host country and their country of origin, or between rival factions back home. Arab nationals at the BBC were confronted with the first test in 1956. They declared they could only continue if the BBC stuck firmly to the provisions of the BBC charter and maintained its impartiality and its independence of government. This was done and the crisis passed. Although Arab pressure was applied during the subsequent wars—the Egyptian newspaper, *Al Ahram*, appealed to BBC and VOA announcers in an open letter to stop working for 'hostile anti-Arab radios' in October 1973—relations between the Arab staffs and their employers have remained friendly.

A classic example of the second kind of test came during the Nigerian civil war. Nigerians in all those broadcasting services which put out programmes to west Africa were obliged to work alongside each other, Ibo beside non-Ibo, and accept the policy of the station for which they worked, or else quit their job.

Conflicts of loyalty apart, it can be a lonely job working in a foreign country, one of a small team of broadcasters whose only common ground is a sense of the suspicion that exists between themselves and the country they have left and which they now address from a safe distance. It is worse for the exiles and the émigrés than for those who can return. Inevitably, they are drawn into émigré politics. But they will have little say in shaping the policies behind the words they are asked to say at the microphone. A few reach the higher levels of editorial planning and responsibility, but most are little more than mouthpieces. The lucky ones are those whose target country, which is usually, but not always, the country of which they are citizens, is indifferent to the broadcasts aimed at it. When two countries have friendly relations, such as Britain and Italy, neither minds that each is broadcasting what in the final analysis may be considered propaganda by the other. There is, in fact, close co-operation between Radiotelevisione Italiana (RAI) and the BBC. But since the whole point of this kind of broadcasting is to maintain a service until such time as it might become politically essential—for example if fascism were to return to Italy, or if either country, for whatever reason, introduced strict censorship of the media—the foreign broadcasters are running the long-term risk of offending their own country.

In the case of Greece in 1967, the Greek staff of the BBC faced precisely this dilemma. Unlike their Voice of America partners, the BBC opted to attack the dictatorship of the Colonels when they made their coup, despite the fact that Greece was, and is, a member of NATO

and therefore officially a 'friendly' country. At once the broadcasters were at risk. It can, on the other hand, be argued that they
were less at risk than political opponents of the new regime in Greece
itself. Nevertheless, they were forcibly transformed by the coup from
virtually unknown and ignored broadcasters into politically active
propagandists. Just to make the international broadcaster's life more
interesting, the situation can also be reversed. When General Spinola
came to power in Portugal on the back of an army coup in April
1974, the staff of virtually every Portuguese-language foreign radio
station suddenly became personae more or less gratae.

In the case of the foreign staff of the various communist radio
stations, official and clandestine, the choice that the broadcasters have
made is generally based on a clear-cut ideological position. Some are
the victims of persecution (like their equivalents who have *fled* from
communism), but most join for positive, not negative reasons. Taking Radio Peking as an example, about sixty per cent of the short-
term staff are recruited through Maoist-oriented Marxist groups
around the world, and the other forty per cent find their way to China
after curiosity or contacts have sent them for an interview at the
nearest Chinese embassy. Security checking is no more than routine
in the latter case. The potential broadcaster's political convictions are
not considered important—unless he or she is a Chinese speaker, in
which case the motive for applying is investigated with great
thoroughness. The Chinese can afford to recruit their foreign-
language staff in this relatively casual fashion because, in Peking,
the broadcasters are isolated absolutely, seeing ordinary Chinese outside the radio building only under close supervision. Contracts are
for two years, though sometimes renewed, and the job consists very
definitely in translating and broadcasting, no more. Texts are given to
foreign staff in English, French or Spanish and then checked against
the original Chinese; the first and last stages of the preparation of
the text are done by the Chinese themselves. Since the Chinese
language is so very different in structure and expression, the problem
of agreeing an exact version frequently leads to acrimony between the
foreign staff and the Chinese supervisors who are usually literal-
minded and always cautious, if not frightened, of their superiors.

But some of the foreign staff are long-term. They are either people
who were caught up decades earlier in the revolutionary struggles,
ex-agents, businessmen and so on; or else they are permanent
refugees from persecution, like many of the Latin Americans at
Radio Peking. Over the years they divide into those who are more
Maoist than Mao, living in the simplest workers' garb and eventually
absorbing Chinese thinking to the extent of talking to outsiders in
that curious slogan-language which visitors notice on official
tongues, or else they become lonely cynics. It seems that the Chinese

prefer the second category. With these they can relax their natural suspicion of the foreigner and accept that he cannot be like themselves. Of the others, like the American Rittenberg who spent many years in China and joined the Party, becoming a leading light in the English-language service of Radio Peking, the Chinese remain indelibly suspicious. Indeed, during the Cultural Revolution, Rittenberg fell into disfavour, as did his superior, Lao Meng. Whatever their political convictions, it is a hard and sometimes unnerving life for all the foreign broadcasters in Peking.

In general, the staff of the communist international stations have less editorial responsibility than their colleagues in non-communist stations. With the exception of China, this is not a case of special discrimination. It is a reflection of the strictness of the directive principle that applies in all the media which carry political news and analysis. When the structure of the station is based on a system whereby policy is made at the top, fleshed out with supporting argument in the middle ranks, and the broadcasters themselves are left with the task of translating and speaking the text, the work is dull. Of course there are performers outside the obvious political sphere who present music or cultural programmes with only their consciences and an inbuilt awareness of political realities to guide them. The same is true, only to a lesser degree, outside the communist world. And this, finally, is why so little is heard on any international radio that either reflects exceptional individual talent or departs from the orthodoxies of the broadcasting country. All that is needed is a uniform recruitment policy and the programmes will take care of themselves.

International broadcasting today is no longer the direct product of skilled propagandists. Few 'personalities' remain. It is unnecessary to carry on the debate that raged during and for some time after the last world war. The psychological warriors were much exercised by the question: 'What makes a good propagandist?' But their replies were inconclusive and the debate itself became more and more confined to the purely military sphere. It is generally recognized that psychological manipulation by the message or the voice does not work unless it is part of a co-ordinated political and military campaign. For peacetime radio it is too obvious, and therefore an embarrassment.

Today, from Washington to Peking, more emphasis is put on the intelligibility of the message than on the psychology of propaganda. In the BBC the subject of training broadcasters in the 'science' of propaganda never arises. The fact is that anyone can do it, and does. Athens students found themselves in the role of radio propagandists when they set up a pirate radio during the November 1973 riots; a Romanian rugby player who decides on the spur of the moment to defect is likely to shop around the Voice of America, RFE and the BBC and, if he is accentless and there is an opening for him, he too will be a propagandist; a student falls in love with a Russian girl, stays on, and that could be the voice which Africans tuning in to Radio Peace and Progress pick up on their breakfast show. Not all recruitment is so random of course, and the security services in all countries vet every applicant, however cursorily. But within the limits set by the Official Secrets Act (and its international equivalents), the prejudices of security officials, and natural competence to speak at a microphone, anyone can be and is a radio propagandist.

14 Monitoring

Speaking on the Voice of Kurdistan Radio, General Barzani appealed to the United Nations . . .; an announcement is expected imminently on Uganda Radio . . .; in Greece, the coup d'état is reported to have failed, but martial music is still being played . . .; all links with Santiago have been cut, but radio reports suggest . . . How many times has the world been alerted to some shattering event by variations of these phrases? In more ordinary times, the consumer of news is usually unaware of the channel by which it reaches him; but newsmen themselves know very well how dependent they are on the world's monitoring services.

Ever since international broadcasting began, governments and professional communicators have listened in to each other's messages. At first this was a haphazard process. The BBC began to monitor in any kind of systematic way when it was required to find out what the Italians were telling their Arab listeners and how they were inducing them to doubt the benevolence of the British presence in the Middle East. A large-scale Monitoring Service was set up in 1939.

The Americans were slower and less thorough with their monitoring, as they have been in all aspects of international propaganda. Even when they joined the war, there were only minimal facilities for learning what the enemy had to say, despite the efforts that both Germany and Britain (and others too) had been making to persuade the American people to see their point of view and either keep out of or enter the war. The task was largely left to the Princeton Listening Center, which tuned in to Europe every day from a little white-frame house in a quiet Princeton side street. Later on, Stanford University undertook a similar task on the far side of the American continent. The American government lent its support to a comprehensive service after the war had broken out in Europe; only then did the Office of War Information begin to undo what O. W. Riegel, an American expert on propaganda, called the 'disastrous effects of the blindness, stupidity and "too little too late" behaviour of the democracies on the propaganda front.'[1]

In Germany, the monitoring service had a chequered career for quite other reasons. Situated in a building known as the 'Seehaus', the German monitors formed what became known as the 'Sabotage Club'—both because of their reputation for anti-Hitler views and for the damage they were said to do by circulating the transcripts of enemy broadcasts.

By January 1942, Goebbels had connected the evidence of defeatism in high places with the output from Seehaus, and his diary makes several mentions of his attempts to restrict circulation of what he regarded as subversive material. Believing that 'the Seehaus Service has become a veritable fountainhead of defeatism', he took vigorous steps to prevent any but a very few high-placed officials from being on the daily circulation list.[2] He instructed that special permits be issued for those, such as foreign correspondents, who needed access to the sort of information only obtainable from the monitoring reports. On 27 January 1942, Goebbels wrote:

Whether or not I already have full authority for so doing, I am intervening vigorously and have especially forbidden the distribution of material to higher officials and officers since they are the most easily demoralized by such a news service.

But he was resisted equally strenuously; and it appears that the output of the BBC and other enemy stations continued to be eagerly consumed in all branches of government and the armed forces. The diary provides evidence in May the following year that the Seehaus reputation was still valid. 'The damage to the dams,' Goebbels wrote on 20 May 1943 with reference to the dam-buster attacks, 'has not been quite so serious as at first feared. The reports by Berndt [his most trusted lieutenant] which caused me such a headache the first day are now proved to have been tremendously exaggerated. It is quite obvious that Berndt got his information from the BBC. This fact illustrates once more how impractical and irrational it is to forward alarmist reports of this kind to the higher leadership.'

Today the Americans, the British and, as a junior partner, the West Germans, combine to listen to the greater part of the world's radio output. Some gaps exist for technical reasons; for example, the

BBC Monitoring Service complains of inadequate coverage of parts of Central Africa and of the Arabian peninsula. But even when coverage is technically feasible, the monitors do not listen to all the output all the time. The cost of hiring enough people to listen to the tens of millions of words broadcast every day, making a reasonable selection, and publishing even a fraction of them, would not only be prohibitive but unnecessary, given the political irrelevance of a large part of it. The BBC has investigated the value of extending its coverage to television; but as a news source, television is neither as fast nor as thorough as radio.

The BBC's Monitoring Service is housed in a converted nineteenth-century château, away from the electronic and other distractions of London, in a park just outside the town of Reading, forty miles from the capital. The staff at Caversham Park is now just over 400, less than the maximum of 550 reached at the end of the war, but still capable of producing daily reports of up to 100,000 words a day. These reports are sent to government departments, newsrooms, universities and, again in return for a fee, to anyone else who might need them for research or information. Intelligence services around the world are avid consumers of monitoring reports, today just as much as during the war.

In America, the organization responsible for monitoring is the Foreign Broadcast Information Service, a part of the CIA. Its Intelligence connection makes it marginally more wary of publishing the material it selects than the BBC, but this does not impair the regular exchange system with the British. Between them and Deutsche Welle, they capture everything of importance that goes out over the airwaves, feeding it to each other as it comes into their receiving stations around the world. In addition, the FBIS and the BBC, together with their respective governments, consult constantly over whom they should be listening to, and when.

Meanwhile, other organizations are also doing monitoring of their own. Radio Liberty and Radio Free Europe listen in to many of the internal radio stations in the Soviet Union and eastern Europe (around fifty in the latter alone). They depend on this information to give substance to their criticisms of events in the area, to operate their system of cross-reporting of the events in each of the target countries, as well as in the preparation of their research reports. In turn the Russians and east Europeans monitor incoming broadcasts and a wide variety of foreign domestic channels. The Presidential Study Commission which investigated RL and RFE made the specific point that the radios' output is monitored and that:

> . . . transcripts are circulated daily or weekly in high party and government circles. These reports are confirmed by frequent ver-

batim references in Eastern media. In two speeches, for example, Czechoslovak Party leader Gustav Husak has referred to 'reading' monitorings of RFE, while former Polish Party leader Gomulka is reported by his former private secretary to have been a regular reader.[3]

Most governments do some monitoring of their own; at a minimum, their wireless departments in embassies all over the world are listening in and gathering information for assessment by diplomats and foreign service officials.

One organization that conspicuously does not monitor foreign broadcasts, in spite of feelings in many quarters that it should do so, is the United Nations. In 1958, President Eisenhower proposed to the UN Assembly that:

. . . [it] should reaffirm its enunciated policy and should consider the means for monitoring radio broadcasts directed across national frontiers in the troubled Near East area. It should then examine complaints from these nations which consider their national security jeopardized by external propaganda.

But no action followed this or other appeals for UN action.

There would, of course, be some advantage in bringing the more blatant examples of scurrilous propaganda out into the full glare of international publicity—governments are notoriously prone to deny charges against them or at least muddy the waters by denying their own responsibility. On the other hand, it is difficult to see what the United Nations could do apart from recording and possibly censuring extreme cases. First of all, there is the unsolved problem of whether international propaganda is illegal or not. Secondly, UN intervention is as likely to stir up a hornet's nest of charges and counter-charges as it is to pacify enmity. The victim would point to 'offensive' statements in the broadcasts of the complaining country, or of its client or master. Debates would be predictable and sterile, and probably no country would feel it worth while to waste time on stimulating further international discord.

The great advantage of any monitoring service is its speed. Eventually the news of a coup d'état, civil war, or invasion will filter out via eye witnesses or visiting journalists. But at the very moment that it's all happening, the only clue as to the course of events is generally provided by reports put out over the radio by one side or another, or perhaps both, backed up by radioed news flashes from correspondents. The sudden flare-up of fighting in Cyprus in the summer of 1974 showed that the value of radio in such situations is as great as ever.

The monitor is trained to listen for and to react to the unexpected news flash with speed. As the first words are picked up out of the air, they are taken down, if necessary translated, given an instant valuation, and fed into the wires. Perhaps as little as a couple of minutes later the first inklings of a story are emerging in the tape machines of thousands of newsrooms and government departments. As the story unfolds, the details follow in just as quick succession.

Since radio itself is a rapid and more or less continuous medium, it is not only customarily first with the news, but its reports have also been known to pre-empt the slower-witted censor. For example, Moscow Radio once put out the full report of an East Pakistani communist leader, which the Soviet authorities later deemed to be embarrassing. Only extracts were then permitted to be released. But the damage had been done. The BBC monitoring report carried the full and uncensored text.

And in a routine way, news editors around the world use foreign broadcasts, domestic and international, as an instant check for their own output as well as a source of news. As a Hungarian journalist described it:

> When the Hungarian stations' monitoring service searches the ether for fresh information, it is also performing an act of self-defence by noting the content of the main news of the foreign stations, which is most important to us, for it serves our news editor with a basis for preparing his own programmes; he edits the news broadcast by the Hungarian stations according to how other editors do theirs.[4]

Monitors point with pride to some notable coups of their own. At 1404 GMT precisely on 28 October 1962, Moscow Home Service broadcast the message of Kruschev's decision to withdraw the Russian missiles from Cuba, effectively ending the imminent and very real prospect of the total annihilation of the world in a thermonuclear war. The message was received instantaneously at Caversham, it was flashed to the FBIS in America, and there it went immediately to the White House. Almost at once President Kennedy reacted, realizing that the crisis was over, although, as he said, 'I have not yet received the official text.'

A parallel situation arose years earlier when Italy declared war. Mussolini made the announcement fifteen minutes prematurely. The BBC, eavesdropping on the message intended for the Italian people, immediately put it out over all their services, including the German Service. There was no denying a distinct propaganda advantage over the Nazi information apparatus. And as a coda to this story, Goebbels admitted that he first heard of the Italian surrender in September 1943 'via the London radio', which he described as 'an occurrence that undoubtedly is unique and without precedent in history'.

At the time of the Polish riots in 1970, Radio Free Europe claimed a success due not so much to speed of reaction but to attentive listening. Strict censorship was imposed in Poland on news about the events taking place in the Baltic coastal cities, but local media did give some reports of disturbances. These were monitored in Munich. Immediately, the entire Polish population was informed of developments, and from then on kept informed, over the RFE transmitters. Later surveys confirmed that this was the way most Poles first heard about the events.

Though the speed with which news can be reported is a spectacular asset of a monitoring service, its daily round is no less important. The output of all radio channels, domestic and international, when intelligently selected, provides one of the most reliable and complete pictures of the events and policies of a foreign country. In wartime, monitoring reports provide Intelligence services with basic information for assessing an enemy's future moves. It was apparent from this source alone that Germany planned to invade the Soviet Union in the summer of 1942, as there was a growing tendency to renounce the propaganda truce agreed to in the signing of the Nazi-Soviet Pact. There are innumerable other examples.

In both war and peace, monitoring reports also play the incidental role of informing governments what foreign correspondents based in their country are saying about them. It is not unknown for correspondents to be expelled for sending unfriendly despatches that have been picked up by curious officials of the host country, even though these despatches were intended for quite other ears. The expulsion in 1973 of John Bierman, the BBC's man in Teheran, was a case in point.

The Intelligence role of monitoring underlines the imperative need for accuracy. Despite recent technical advances, conditions under which messages are received are less than perfect—there is likely to be interference, and double-checking means losing vital time—but decisions are taken on the basis of the reports. The audibility problems of wartime monitors remain much the same today.*

First reports of the 1972 Bolivian coup provided a testing example. Three radio stations were monitored in Caversham, the government's, the opposition's, and the miners' station. All gave different versions of the events, and it was up to the monitors to make sense of them. Similarly, when Italy surrendered in 1943:

Three different bulletins in Italian were picked up simultaneously on the same wavelength from three, geographically and politically,

* see Appendix D

entirely different stations—Allied-controlled Palermo, Badoglio's transmitter at Bari and German-controlled Milan—which all shared one channel; it rested with the 'Special Listening Service' and the monitors to disentangle which was which.[5]

Purely aural problems of identification can get entangled with problems of political interpretation.

A mistake can give rise to a whole chain of unfortunate consequences. An exaggeration in translation, or the misinterpretation of an idiom, can influence foreign reaction. When, for example, Moscow and Peking are charging each other with heinous crimes, often using oblique language or referring to incidents or dogma whose minutiae have a meaning out of all proportion to their apparent significance, the monitors' ability to present an accurate rendering is crucial.

It is in fact impossible to conduct a radio war, or even polemics over the air, without an efficient monitoring service on both sides. During the world war, one of the BBC's most successful gambits was to play back to Germany recordings of Hitler's promises of victory by such-and-such a date. Moscow Radio frequently proves its points by quoting (not always in full or in context) what has been said by the BBC, or the Voice of America, or, especially, Radio Peking. It is monitoring alone that prevents these international polemics becoming a dialogue of the deaf. Extracts from opposition broadcasts are used in evidence by all international services, even though it is often regarded as bad propaganda to give added currency to 'incorrect' views. A number of international stations run programmes on the lines of the BBC's *Listening Post*, where extracts from foreign broadcasts are compared and commented upon.

But the very effectiveness of the world's monitoring services does raise one awkward question: to what extent are the radio voices of governments broadcasting expressly for other governments in the target countries? Knowing that whatever they say will be assiduously listened to, noted down, and transmitted to all interested parties, it is tempting, especially for those governments which directly control their radio stations, the vast majority, to use international radio as an extension of diplomatic communication. It is a good way, and an instant one, to fly a political kite, to propose a plan which may or may not be carried out, to strike a posture that may or may not be genuine, even to create an incident in a foreign country. In fact, this is a use of radio that has been accepted as a convention by both receivers and transmitters. Through the opposition monitors, who are trained to watch for precisely such things, an impression can be given of an official line or intention which never in reality exists. Radio becomes an instrument of diplomatic bluff.

But to ordinary listeners, all this is likely to be hidden in the mass of regular programmes. The process of propagandizing the masses across the frontiers continues unaffected by the subtleties of government information and misinformation. But the monitors provide professional analysts with voluminous and rapidly-available material, from both domestic and international sources, which makes their job both easier and harder: easier because radio is for the most part a unique source of authentic information; harder because it is also a medium of government-to-government propaganda, and this kind of propaganda is intended as much to mislead as to inform.

15 Conclusion

Radio propaganda can be merely osmotic, its influence percolating into the mind persistently but painlessly. The BBC is the most professional exponent of this type. At the other end of the scale, radio propaganda can be an explosive weapon, an artillery barrage, the punching arm of an aggressive diplomacy or a freedom struggle. The sounds of Zeesen, of Cairo, or Radio Biafra, all represent this type.

The effectiveness of both sorts of propaganda is only measurable against the yardstick of the expectations of the propagandists themselves. The British risked going for a long-term effect, even in wartime. Hitler, Nasser, Ojukwu, despite their entirely different political views, all had in common a desire to persuade the masses to believe in their cause, as many as possible as quickly as possible, in order to achieve specific political ends. In all three cases, although the Voice of the Arabs took on a new lease of life when Arab fortunes changed, political and military failures obscured the real impact of their propaganda. But, until the moment of setback, that propaganda was evidently doing its job of changing not just opinions but behaviour.

Radio propaganda is only effective in these terms when it reflects, both in technique and message, the traditions and the psychology of the country or group it represents. The voice, in other words, must echo, not distort, the message from the brain. Broadcasting institutions as a whole follow national patterns. As Asa Briggs says, 'few other institutions reveal more clearly the differences between national traditions, national ways of life, and national policies.'[1] But not all international services conform to this general rule which applies to domestic services.

Whereas the BBC External Services and the Voice of the Arabs are identifiably in harmony with national traditions and ambitions, and act as extensions of the internal radio services, the Voice of America's foreign broadcasting is conspicuously at variance both with the commercialism expressed in the domestic media and with the mixture of isolationism and interventionism which characterizes American foreign policy. It suffers from spasms of objectivity which only exacerbate the ulcers caused by high-pressure selling of Freedom and Democracy.

In a not dissimilar fashion, Moscow Radio, in the business of promoting a world proletarian doctrine, confuses the listener by its extreme nationalistic fervour—a true reflection of the political confusion in the Kremlin, but all the same an ambivalent voice. The fact that Moscow now probably regrets having started the international radio war prevents it from exploiting the political advantage of being the First Country of the most appealing of international political systems.

Radios Peking and Tirana, on the other hand, fail on the grounds that they simply ignore the basic ground rules of propaganda techniques. Propaganda may be an inexact science, but there are some ways of going about it that turn the most attractive message into an indigestible concretion of slogans and speechifying. Radio propaganda must be radiogenic. This can mean a melodious, comprehensible reflection of everyday speech patterns—to achieve an imaginary dialogue over the air—or, alternatively, a vivid evocation of events and emotions calculated to arouse enthusiasm and passion and bring the masses into line, marching behind the leader. In either case, the object is to keep people switched on when they can so easily, if bored or confused, switch off.

It is the unscrupulous passion-provoking kind of propaganda that has given the word a bad name. Because of its capacity to be used in this way, radio has been a tool irresistible to dictators and national leaders with aggressive ambitions at home or abroad. Propaganda of this sort is by its very nature disruptive, because it is intended to disrupt. On other hand, when it is turned against a system or a government of which we disapprove, we are likely to admit that it is disruptive, but in a beneficial way. Only those who take an uncompromisingly legalistic view would argue that all virulent, emotional propaganda used for 'hostile' ends should be condemned and forced off the air through international sanctions. It is justifiable to give a shake to conservative governments, whether of the left or right, and arguably no less justifiable to give a violent shake to ultra-conservative governments. Legally, propaganda becomes more dubious the more violent it grows; but, politically, propaganda is blameworthy according to whether the forces it attacks are regarded as good or bad—regardless of whether the tone of the propaganda is violent or moderate.

Black radio, though a small part of radio propaganda outside wartime, has no function other than to disrupt and confuse, though again it can only be judged in political terms on the content of its message, not on its inherent moral qualities. Its effectiveness, in relation to white radio, is so much a matter of subjective judgment that it is useless to make definitive pronouncements. On the whole, the more it is deployed merely in tactical situations, to provoke an ambush or to turn an orderly withdrawal into a chaotic defeat by issuing false orders, the more identifiably effective it is. As a means of mass communication, black stations have never had any profound influence.

The major propaganda stations set out to be disruptive in a very different way. Their aim is to make available an alternative voice. If all politicians tend towards conservatism, even in states founded on revolution, then any alternative source of information and any expression of an alternative point of view makes governing that much more difficult. To the governed, radio propaganda, presenting news and opinions of a kind that the domestic media fail to provide, gives an opportunity to see all points of view. It therefore militates against political stagnation. What is doubtful is that it reaches more than a minority, except in rare cases. The majority, who 'deliberately (if unconsciously) seek out only those views which agree with their own', are generally resistant to messages that 'fail to fit into their own picture of the world and their own objective circumstances'.[2] As W. Phillips Davison also emphasizes, people on the whole only believe what they find comfortable to believe.

It is precisely because most people are resistant to propaganda from a remote, alien source that its two extreme forms, the osmotic and the ultra-violent, are most successful in getting through. In the first case, the victim should ideally be unaware he is being propagandized. In the second, he cannot prevent himself being manipulated by the message.

Although most people in Europe and North America, if they come across radio propaganda at all today, are able to recognize it for what it is, not so long ago, in the thirties and forties, and even in the fifties, its influence was widely feared to be both pernicious and irresistible. Perhaps now there is a tendency to underestimate its power.

Propaganda, particularly by radio which is the quickest and most influential means of mass communication, is indeed extremely pervasive. By sheer repetition alone, the unthinkable can become the acceptable.

If a man had stood up in Hampstead in 1913, and shouted at the top of his voice that the Jews are all tainted with venereal disease and lusting to corrupt the wives and daughters of Hampstead residents, he would probably have been regarded, quite literally, as mad . . . In 1938, because everybody knows that such attacks are frequently made, the speaker will not be regarded as mad even though not a word of what he says is taken as true. He is just a Fascist doing his bit.[3]

The way many people became aware of the frequency of such attacks was by listening to German international radio.

A parallel negative effect of propaganda—and again radio propaganda in particular because its message is unverifiable, coming from a remote source—is its capacity to start rumours. In the Second World War, there were any number of rumours of the 'Russians passing through Britain in August with snow on their boots' kind, whose origin was in all probability foreign radio stations. There was, for example, a flood of Pearl Harbour rumours in February 1942, such as that Hawaii was occupied by the Japanese. Lord Haw-Haw spread all kinds of misapprehensions among the British, causing the government no small concern. Today, in Kampala as in Bucharest, rumours circulate on the basis of half-understood radio reports, often fuelled by an atmosphere of fear or social unrest. Wherever news is spread by word of mouth, whether through tradition or circumstances, the power of international radio propaganda is enormously increased. The BBC, conscious of its role as the final source for checking whether a piece of news is or is not true, and therefore unusually careful to verify both sources and facts, nevertheless receives numerous reports that it is quoted as verifying the most unlikely occurrences.

It would seem that people are both resistant to alien ideas and, at least in the short term, gullible enough to believe them. Propagandists of the manipulating school see this as an opportunity to convert confusion to their own advantage. The Nazis, in particular, believed that by encouraging this confusion, bombarding their audience with highly-charged and sometimes contradictory news and ideas, they could keep people gullible over the long term. So far neither they nor anyone who has followed their techniques has had the chance to test whether this works over a long period of years. All we know is that it can be remarkably effective in the short term.

In the case of this extreme form of propaganda, there is no trace of politically disinterested desire to keep people informed and dispel ignorance. But for the most part, even in the case of Radio Peking, for example, international radio services at least include as one of their aims the innocent function of telling a potentially wide audience things about which they would otherwise know nothing. This is not always a question of circumventing censorship, although the disinterested news-service role becomes a political issue where foreign governments actively interfere with its free reception, but generally and genuinely a contribution to the spread of knowledge.

In this innocent category must be put the teaching of languages by radio. Although used in the broadest sense as a political vehicle, as bait for other programmes—and in a narrower sense the material can be full of ideological nods and winks—language teaching by radio is a positive and beneficial way to break down international barriers. Other aspects of education are more suspect; history merges into nationalist special pleading, science into technological advertising, and the many religious stations are by definition partial. But language teaching is far bigger business over the international airwaves than any other form of direct instruction.

Another positive effect of international radio propaganda is the influence it has on the standards of all communications media. It provides a challenge which cannot be ignored. The Bulgarians, for instance, were obliged to make their domestic services more entertaining in order to compete with Radio Free Europe, the BBC and others. All around the world, the presence in the ether of countless foreign stations waiting to pounce on dissatisfied listeners is used as an argument by professional broadcasters to pressure their governments for more resources to meet the challenge.

Where governments impose tight censorship, this challenge takes on a new dimension. Those who defend absolutely the 'free flow of information' argument see only good arising out of the international battering at the gates of censorship. In the case of the communist countries, where censorship has now become more of an instinctive reaction than a necessary defence against foreign machinations, the obligation to widen and improve their own coverage of events is surely justified interference in their internal affairs. The graver problem, as we have seen, concerns the imposition of alien ideas by the rich and powerful on the poor and weak.

At the heart of this problem is the fact that international radio stations appeal to the elite of the underdeveloped world and only incidentally to the masses. Throughout history, it has been the ruling class in the poor countries which led the people towards dependence on the great powers, not just the industrial capitalists, but the cultural capitalists too. The Americans, the British, the French, the Russians, all have their own ways of continuing this dependent relationship. The French External Service, for example, supports cultural and economic links between the former mother country and colonies largely by relaying to Africa suitable parts of the domestic services. We have seen something of how the others defend their national interests. But the common factor is that they aim their broadcasts primarily at the influential and politically active.

The theoretical justification for this is provided by a number of writers on the subject of propaganda, for instance Hans Speier:

> Since in modern societies the mass of the population cannot overthrow, or actively influence the policies of, despotic regimes without armed domestic or foreign support and without organized leadership, the population at large is no rewarding target of conversion propaganda from abroad. Any notion to the contrary may be called the democratic fallacy of democratic propagandists who disregard the differences in political structure between the regimes under which they and their audience live.[4]

Others deny that it is a 'democratic fallacy' to assert the power of public opinion even in 'despotic' conditions. John Foster Dulles changed his mind on this point. During the Second World War, propagandists on both sides were deeply concerned about influencing the masses, on whom morale and therefore their country's ability to fight depended. Bruce Lockhart declared:

> However entertaining and occasionally useful it may be to score off the enemy, propaganda is not and should not be a duel of dialectics between the political warriors of the rival propaganda organizations. It should be addressed to the masses.[5]

On the German side, radio propaganda was consciously and almost exclusively directed at the masses. Neither Hitler nor Goebbels suffered from democratic fallacies, but both believed in the power of well-mobilized and manipulated public opinion, backed by force.

But this debate is in some ways a false one. Radio is above all a medium available to everyone and, in a physical sense, incapable of being directed to one audience rather than another. The question is usually one of whether a radio station aims primarily or only secondarily at one particular sector of its potential audience. And since international radio's purpose is information rather than entertainment, to provoke rather than to distract, it follows that special effort is made to broaden the appeal to reach the masses rather than to narrow it down to reach the elite.

In the Russian case, this means reaching an audience beyond the committed. In the BBC's World Service, this means modifying its middle-class tones. The Voice of America has never been short of advice on how to reach the masses without boring the intelligentsia. Whether it accepts all or none, it continues along its middle path. But in no case is there any real solution to the problem that each service has a limited number of hours at its disposal and limited resources, and yet an unlimited audience. No External Service can hope to cover the same range of audience (with the huge range of languages which this implies) that domestic services usually try to achieve.

But even if an international radio station would like to measure the effectiveness of broadcasting to different audiences and draw up its plans on a cost-effective or scientific basis, and so widen its coverage, there is no way of obtaining the necessary information. All propaganda is difficult to measure and assess. Radio propaganda presents added problems, and international radio propaganda is impossible.

It is, however, possible to make certain broad and confident statements about the effectiveness of propaganda as such. Jacques Ellul, despite a constant tendency to qualify and contradict himself, is uncompromising on this point:

All those who have lived in a strongly propagandized environment and have been subjected to the effects of propaganda (while trying to remain unaffected), all those who have seen propaganda in massive action, are agreed that propaganda is effective. Those who deny it live in countries that are still liberal and not subjected to intense propaganda. Today, hardly any Germans, Russians, or Algerians question the effectiveness of propaganda.[6]

What is confusing is the attempt to measure the relative impact of different types of propaganda, the different media that carry it, and, above all, the relative impact of the medium and the message. To what extent are some doctrines or ideologies more amenable to propaganda techniques than others? The questions are so broad that no-one has come up with satisfactory answers. All that can be said is that some techniques are better suited to the presentation of a particular message than others.

There are, however, three unsatisfactory but common ways of judging the effectiveness of international radio propaganda: subjective opinion based (sometimes) on theoretical analysis; 'proof stories' based on personal observation; and the findings of audience research.

Here are two examples of subjective judgment on the impact of western programmes beamed into the Soviet Union and eastern Europe:

Western propaganda directed to these countries, even when transmissions are not jammed, has often been singularly inept, and it is probable that its main results have been the introduction of beatnik mannerisms, a thirst for modern jazz, and the cult of pop singers and American film stars.[7]

> The Commission . . . is confident that the radios [RFE and RL], by providing information and interpretation, will continue to be of help in future negotiations and co-operation between the Soviet Union and the United States in such areas as strategic arms limitation, trade, European security, and environmental protection.[8]

One sounds like over-contemptuous dismissal, the other like special pleading.

Proof stories abound, and are told by VOA directors to convince Congress, and to boost their own morale, as they are by staff members of all External Services. Certainly, if every one were true, the influence on governments and individuals of radio propaganda of all kinds could hardly be doubted. They were especially popular in wartime, indeed often the result of deliberately planned tests. The call from London for Frenchmen to assemble and fly a tricolour flag on Bastille Day in 1942 was obeyed by thousands—in Lyons and Marseilles by a hundred thousand, so it was said. This story finds an echo in the presence of thousands at Boris Pasternak's funeral at Peredelkino, when the news had been announced over western radio only.

Other proof stories emerge from listeners' letters, used by External Services everywhere to substantiate their opinion of the impact they are having in different countries and among different classes of listener. The Czechs brandish a total of over 100,000 letters a year as proof of success; the BBC crows over its 1,000 letters a week addressed to its Bengali Service at times of crisis. Analysis of these letters is the prerogative in most External Services of special Audience Research Departments.

In the cases of Radio Liberty and Radio Free Europe, extensive interviewing of refugees and temporary visitors to the west is combined with analysis of letters to investigate the vexing problems of measuring an audience, and drawing conclusions for programming purposes, in countries to which there is no physical access. Generally, surveys conducted in the target countries are used as back-up to the mailbag. But these surveys are notoriously (even to the researchers) suspect. The samples, for reasons of cost, are too small, as the head of the BBC's Audience Research Department complained:

> As far as external broadcasting is concerned, the sheer size of many countries prohibits audience research on a nationwide scale; what might be a typical audience in one area is not necessarily representative of the country as a whole.[9]

Nor is the method of asking questions of selected panel members any more satisfactory. The listener who joins such a panel is unlikely to be typical of the mass of listeners, if only in his enthusiasm and his availability to do the job. The answers to questionnaires are probably under-critical. Gradually, sampling techniques and statistical analysis are becoming more reliable, but their results are unlikely ever to do more than offer a sop to those, such as politicians, who demand a body-count in the war of words.

Audience research does, however, reveal certain patterns. The average age of listeners to all External Services is going down, for example—not surprisingly, given overall demographic trends. As a result, more programmes are created with young audiences in mind. And the number of listeners to foreign stations jumps dramatically in times of crisis.

Detailed evidence apart, it is generally agreed that the total numbers listening to foreign radio stations is rising, partly as a result of the increasing number of radio sets around the world, and partly because of the inadequacy of many countries' local media, especially in the Third World, which fail to satisfy ever more numerous discriminating audiences.

For all these reasons, it would be unwise, even if it were remotely possible, for international radio services to be the object of an embargo, albeit a simultaneous embargo, on the grounds that they are vehicles of propaganda, and that propaganda is disruptive. It would require an over-naive faith in the intentions of politicians, whether of the left, right, or centre, to imagine that the world would be a better place if all information sources were under exclusive national control. The suggestion that a United Nations International Radio Service would satisfy the need for alternative sources is no answer. While there is a good argument for the United Nations having a voice of its own, to act as a publicizing agent, it could be no kind of a substitute for the many-tongued voices of individual stations, governmental and non-governmental. Besides, the editorial problem, beyond the minimum task of reporting debates, would be horrific. Having spent some time drafting reports on a few of the most innocuous meetings of one UN agency, I would not choose to be in the firing line when it came to 'balancing' the output of a universal radio station.

Besides, the small-scale experiences which the UN has had in this field are hardly promising. A station once went on the air in the Congo, replacing Tshombe's pop music and urgent messages over his own Radio Katanga. The South Africans accused it of transmitting 'anti-white racialist propaganda', but after a few months of putting out what was in fact harmless talk, it came off the air. The UN is better employed outside the propaganda field, whether monitoring or broadcasting, to conserve its resources for solving more concrete problems which are amenable to legal and political solution.

Radio propaganda by countries and pressure groups, by independent corporations and companies, by freedom fighters and secret services, is here to stay. It is too useful a weapon to those who wield it, and too important a source of alternative information to those who, for any reason, are deprived of what they feel they need. No technical revolution is likely to replace radio as the principal medium of international communication—television and satellites will at most be complementary in the foreseeable future.

Nevertheless, some of the uses of international radio are identifiably harmful. Only a small minority would agree that the Voice of South Africa is a benign institution. And many governments and individuals feel threatened by other countries' transmissions and favour an embargo, if only against the messages aimed at themselves.

But the political cost of banning all radio propaganda is an increase in conservatism. Politicians would then be able to govern in their own way, rather than be forced to react to the pressures of public opinion. They would be freer to manipulate the media they control, whether directly or indirectly. It is a particular feature of the extreme right to try and create an attitude of acquiescence on the part of both the elite and the masses; but, whatever the label attached to political groups or parties, all tend towards conserving their established positions. Radio propaganda is one means of keeping politics on the move. It may risk spreading anarchy or courting repression, but it is also a prerequisite for progress.

APPENDIX A
Radio and TV sets in 1973

	Population	Radio Set Ownership		Television Sets
		Radio Sets	Wired Sets	
WESTERN EUROPE	401,200,000	174,600,000	1,042,000	92,900,000
USSR and EUROPEAN COMMUNIST GROUP	357,400,000	83,900,000	45,200,000	65,800,000
MIDDLE EAST and NORTH AFRICA	163,600,000	21,500,000	3,000	4,200,000
AFRICA (excluding North Africa)	280,300,000	21,200,000	113,000	449,000
ASIA and the FAR EAST	1,926,000,000	164,800,000	52,300,000	31,400,000
PACIFIC and OCEANIA	22,000,000	10,200,000	—	4,300,000
NORTH AMERICA	237,500,000	362,800,000	25,000	109,000,000
WEST INDIES	9,500,000	3,300,000	44,000	976,000
LATIN AMERICA	285,200,000	54,400,000	5,000	19,500,000
TOTAL 1973	3,682,700,000	896,700,000	98,732,000	328,525,000

reproduced by kind permission of the BBC

APPENDIX B

External Broadcasting: estimated total programme hours per week*

	1950	1960	1970	1973
United States of America	497	1,495	1,907	2,060
Voice of America	497	640	863	882
Radio Liberty	—	411	497	602
Radio Free Europe	—	444	547	576
USSR	533	1,015	1,908	1,952
Chinese People's Republic	66	687	1,267	1,326
West Germany	—	315	779	806
United Kingdom (BBC)	643	589	723	751
Egypt	—	301	540	613
Albania	26	63	487	490
Netherlands	127	178	335	370
Spain	68	202	251	361
Cuba	—	—	320	354
Australia	181	257	350	348
Poland	131	232	334	340
East Germany	—	185	274	322
India	116	157	271	321
France	198	326	200	306
Portugal	46	133	295	297
Japan	—	203	259	257
Czechoslovakia	119	196	202	234
Israel	—	91	158	191
Romania	30	159	185	190
South Africa	—	63	150	184
Bulgaria	30	117	164	179
Italy	170	205	165	168
Canada	85	80	98	164
Ghana	—	—	186	161
Hungary	76	120	105	111
Yugoslavia	80	70	76	86

* Not featured in this list, supplied by the BBC's External Broadcasting Audience Research, are Taiwan, North and South Vietnam, North and South Korea, and other international commercial and religious stations. Certain countries (e.g. France and Egypt) transmit part of their domestic output externally on short waves; these broadcasts are mainly excluded also.

APPENDIX C

Extracts from the *Internal Policy Guidelines* of Radio Free Europe and Radio Liberty.

Radio Free Europe

111 D *Restraints*

The correct tone is as important in adhering to RFE policy as correct content of broadcasts. The following restraints continue, therefore, as in the past, to be observed:

1. Avoidance of vituperation, vindictiveness, belligerency, stridency, pomposity, emotionalism, arrogance, pretentiousness and condescension.

2. Avoidance of programming the content of which is or could be legitimately construed as inflammatory or unrealistic. Even straight news or press reviews can be inflammatory if improperly handled in tense situations.

3. Avoidance of blatant, propagandistic argumentation.

4. Avoidance of sweeping generalizations and evaluations.

5. Avoidance of any comment or broadcast of any material which would amount to or could be reasonably construed as incitement to revolt or other violence.

6. Avoidance of tactical advice, by which is meant recommendations for specific action in particular cases, except in unusual circumstances, and then only to calm moods in tense situations. The people of East Europe, provided they know the relevant facts, are better qualified to judge the efficacy and consequences of their actions than anyone outside the countries. Such advice is likely to be resented and, if acted upon, could cause harm to the people involved.

7. Continued discussion of key issues is essential, but monotony or needless repetition should be avoided. Boring repetition is the key to the failure of communist information media.

8. No programs will be broadcast which are based upon or use rumors or unsubstantiated information. If, under unusual circumstances, a constructive purpose will be served by calling attention to a prevalent rumor, it will clearly be identified as such.

9. RFE will not jump to conclusions, either by attaching undue weight to East European government or other pronouncements which experi-

ence has shown the governments may not carry out to the letter, or by unduly discounting them.

10. RFE will not encourage defections from any East European countries, either in programming or in personal contacts with East European travelers in the West. Any radio programs on the life of defectors in the West and interviews with such defectors will carefully avoid encouraging others to follow their examples. No information on 'how to defect' will be broadcast.

11. RFE will not in any way lead the East European peoples to believe that in the event of an uprising or other turmoil the West would intervene militarily. RFE will not speculate about an uprising in East Europe, nor about contingencies arising therefrom.

12. RFE will not broadcast any material which could be characterized as petty gossip, slander, or attacks on the personal lives or families of government or party figures, or on individuals as such. This is not meant to exclude the discussion of the public acts of public officials.

13. In the event of emergency conditions affecting East Europe, nothing will be broadcast by any RFE broadcasting department prior to consultation with the Director of RFE.

Radio Liberty's Basic Techniques

The following principles apply to all Radio Liberty's broadcasts:

1. *Effective broadcasting consists of presenting the truth, hard fact and cold analysis.* RL organizes all the facts of a political event or an economic or cultural development cogently and skilfully so that they lead to a reasoned conclusion. RL regards this technique as more effective for radio broadcasting than unsupported assertions or statements which could be questioned as inaccurate or interpreted as no more than personal opinion.

2. *A question mark is a good ending for a script.* While reasoned conclusions are useful, as outlined above, Radio Liberty's chief task is to stimulate its listeners to think for themselves. If RL relates all the facts, properly organizes and presents them, and challenges the listener to draw conclusions for himself, those conclusions will stay in the listener's mind, and the script is not so likely to be forgotten.

3. *RL avoids direct comparisons which can be odious and counterproductive.* Soviet citizens know better than Radio Liberty how much they must pay for goods and services. . . . Radio Liberty relates representative wages and costs of citizens of other countries, translating them into ruble equivalents—pointing out the purchasing power of such wages in terms of how much clothing, food, and consumer goods a week's salary of a worker in western Europe can buy, etc., and lets its Soviet listeners draw their own conclusions. The same general approach applies to our discussions of human rights and freedom of the individual,

freedom of travel, freedom of exchange of information and ideas, and the welfare of all citizens in democratic countries. . . .

4. *The more brutal the facts, the less emotional should be the presentation.* Dramatic writers and actors must become emotionally involved in their roles to project them successfully. This applies to Radio Liberty presentations of dramatic works, poetry, and certain non-political material.

But political broadcasting is more effective when understated. Should RL become too emotional in describing political oppression and economic hardships of Soviet citizens, we could give the impression that we relish recitation of these facts because they show the evils and failures of the Soviet system. This becomes 'anti-Soviet propaganda' in the minds of many listeners . . . RL also refrains from sarcastic or spiteful references when discussing Soviet leaders or other figures who may have the respect of certain categories of RL listeners.

5. *RL avoids polemics with Soviet media.* As a general rule, it is counter-productive to engage in polemics with Soviet media because a considerable part of polemics involves disagreement and criticism (as well as explaining the opponent's position) . . .

When Radio Liberty itself is attacked, replies to Soviet media should be kept to a minimum. The quality and nature of Radio Liberty's regular output should serve as an unspoken refutation of any slanders in the Soviet press, rendering them incredible to any listener . . .

6. *RL does not engage in pejorative use of terms or phraseology acceptable to Soviet listeners or use obsolete terminology.* Large numbers of RL's Soviet listeners still view 'communism' as a distant goal which if it could be achieved, would be to their benefit. Many of RL's listeners are members of the CPSU, i.e., 'communists'. Many Soviet citizens believe the 'October Revolution' was a progressive event. Some listeners sincerely believe that 'communist' partisans in other countries are working for freedom and progress.

. . . Radio Liberty also avoids using terms which no longer apply: 'the communist monolith' (it is no longer a monolith), 'the communist Bloc' (it is no longer a solid Bloc), 'communist Satellite countries' (the East European countries are no longer slavish satellites), 'East vs. West' and 'capitalism vs. communism' (these convenient phrases do not reflect the real diversity in both the communist and non-communist worlds), the 'Free World' (we should specify democratic countries), etc.

APPENDIX D

Extract from *The Ears of Britain*, an unpublished wartime memorandum by Anatol Goldberg, formerly of the BBC's Monitoring Service.

The difficulty of hearing correctly was formulated by Goethe, on the basis of his experience in dictating, as follows:

> Man only hears what he knows. He can only perceive what he feels, imagines or thinks. Also the case may occur where the listener substitutes for the word he has heard that which his personal inclination, his passion or his need suggests—the name of a beloved person or a tit-bit he craves for.

After six years of monitoring there is little one could add to this. 'Man only hears what he knows.' Since professional monitoring generally presupposes that the text of the broadcast is not available in advance, perfect knowledge and therefore perfect hearing in every single case is impossible.

It is unnecessary for a good monitor to have abnormally good physical hearing, though it must naturally be sound. What he needs in the first place is knowledge. Ideally, in addition to the language, he should also be familiar with all the political, historical and geographical factors mentioned in the broadcast. This is obviously a tall order, since no one can be expected to know all the details in every case. The monitor must therefore learn how to obtain information quickly. Moreover, knowledge is useless unless it is combined with common-sense. The monitor must be able to judge whether or not what he believes he hears is possible. If, logically and factually, a passage does not make sense, he should assume with almost absolute certainty that he has misheard it, no matter how good reception is and how distinctly it may sound to him.

This, however, is not all. The ear is an imperfect instrument, and hearing also means guessing. To be able to guess, man must have imagination. To be able to guess correctly, the monitor must have the right type of imagination, joined to knowledge and common-sense.

It is surprising how little these facts are realised outside the relatively narrow circle of persons professionally associated with listening. Generally, it is taken for granted that monitoring means translating what has been heard at this end. This is wrong. Monitoring means trying to establish what has been said at the other end.

The virtual impossibility of monitoring purely phonetically can easily be demonstrated by the following experiment. Let us assume that some one who does not know Japanese is given a recording of a Japanese speech and asked to put down all the words as they sound to him, in Latin script. No matter how good reception is, how clearly the text is spoken or how often it is played back—a large proportion of the sounds transcribed will be wrong. It will be observed that the vowels are easier to transcribe correctly than the consonants, and certain consonants, easier to handle than others. The final result, however, will bear very little relation to the original Japanese text.

This experiment is by no means remote from real life, for it is precisely this situation that faces every monitor whenever a name is broadcast which he does not know. If it is a name of a place of some size or that of a more or less prominent person, he may establish it with the help of maps and reference books. If, however, it is a name of an obscure little village or of a person hitherto unknown to the world, the monitor is powerless, since in such a case the absence of knowledge is inevitable and neither his common-sense nor his imagination can help.

Of the multitude of incidents which have revealed the impossibility of monitoring without knowledge supported by common-sense, I shall quote only a few, to show the process that takes place in the monitor's mind.

A colleague and I were listening to a broadcast of an anti-Fascist meeting from Moscow. In accordance with the current Soviet practice, the meeting began with the election of an honorary presidium: the Chairman read out the names of the proposed members, and these were approved by acclamation. He began as usual with the names of Stalin, Molotov, Kalinin, Voroshilov, and other prominent Soviet personalities. Then my colleague and I, independently, heard him pronounce the name of the well-known Soviet writer Ehrenburg. It sounded very distinct. Nevertheless it was quite obvious that although we had clearly heard 'Ehrenburg', the speaker could not have *said* Ehrenburg. An honorary presidium is on such occasions usually composed of persons holding the highest appointments in the USSR Communist Party or State. Ehrenburg, to the best of my knowledge, held none.

We had recorded the whole transmission, and I played back the relevant passage over and over again; it was no use. The name continued to sound like Ehrenburg. Another colleague was called in to listen. He heard the same as we did and thought it was a sensation. I then decided to approach the problem from a different angle. I looked carefully at the composition of the presidium and tried to think who of the prominent Soviet personalities was not there. Then the name of Malenkov, one of the Secretaries to the Central Committee of the Communist Party, occurred to me: he had been a member of the honorary presidium on all similar occasions in the past. I listened to the record again: this time the name sounded like Malenkov. 'Man only hears what he knows.'

One should have thought Hitler's name was familiar enough. Nevertheless we registered five cases where it had been misheard. Once in an English broadcast it was heard as 'Admiral Pepper', in French as 'Leclerc', and in German as 'Bosfors'—whoever that may be—'Syria' (Syrien) and 'Lo and behold' (Sieh da). As far as 'Admiral Pepper' and 'Bosfors' were concerned, the monitors naturally knew that they had misheard something but for some reason or other were unable to think of Hitler in that connection. With 'Leclerc' and 'Syria' they had certainly used both their knowledge and their common-sense but had done it along the wrong lines, associating the context with the part played by the French troops in the Italian campaign and the then topical events in Syria. In the case of 'Lo and behold', however, the monitor had hardly any reason to doubt that he was right: for why should a propaganda talk from Moscow not end with the words: 'Sieh, da ist der Krieg!' (Lo and behold: there is war!)? Grammatically and logically, this was quite plausible. It was, however, established that the words actually said were: 'Hitler ist der Krieg' (Hitler means war).

Another good example of how many additional forms one word could take, was provided by a speech of Cordell Hull's broadcast from the USA. In it the word 'future' was heard by various monitors in three different contexts as 'peace', 'cyclic' or 'sacred' and, finally, as 'history'.

I have mentioned that, in addition to knowledge and common-sense, it is essential that the monitor should also have imagination of the right type. This has been very aptly described by one of my colleagues as 'floating'—as distinct from 'rigid'—imagination.

A person with a 'rigid' imagination will find it very difficult to monitor accurately: if his imagination is rigid and scanty, it will prevent him from hearing things; if it is rigid and excessive, it will make him hear things which have not been said. Naturally no human being is completely free from either of these defects, and every monitor occasionally finds that his imagination is being affected by rigidity.

When a monitor listens, his mind follows a definite logical track. If he mishears a passage, it automatically sets out on a wrong track. The effect becomes apparent only when he comes to the next sentence on the record: the sounds he perceives no longer fit into the track along which his thoughts are moving. A monitor with a scanty and rigid imagination plays back the sentence innumerable times; it is no use. His mind remains in bondage, he is unable to abandon the track he has erroneously chosen, he cannot hear the words and gives up. Nor does a monitor with an excessive and rigid imagination succeed in freeing his mind from bondage and abandoning the wrong track, but *he* does not give up. Instead he resorts to violence: unwittingly, by hook or by crook, he makes the sounds correspond to words which do fit into his track, and hears things which have not been said. A person with a floating imagination, however, switches his mind back to the root of the trouble —the sentence he has originally misheard. He rejects his previous interpretation of it, listens to it again, re-examines it from new phonetic and logical angles and continues doing so until he brings his mind on to the right track and hears both passages correctly.

Once a Russian monitor showed me an item from Moscow dealing with the funeral of Lenin's brother, at which a number of speeches had been made. His transcript contained the following sentence: 'On behalf of (indistinct) workers, a speech was delivered by Comrade Stalin.'

I was curious to find out who the indistinct workers were and listened to the record of the bulletin. To me the word he could not hear clearly sounded as 'medical'. I told him so and asked him to listen again. His reaction was: 'I admit it sounds like "medical" but, surely, this must be wrong. Why should Stalin represent the medical workers of all people?' His argumentation was perfectly correct. He had used both his knowledge and his common-sense; what had failed him was his imagination; in that particular case it had been rigid and insufficient. He had heard 'Stalin' and was therefore unable to hear 'medical'. I had heard 'medical' and therefore knew that the name could not be Stalin. Once this conclusion was reached, the speaker at the funeral could easily be identified as Parin, the Soviety Deputy People's Commissar for Health, which made good sense, especially in view of the fact that Lenin's brother had been a doctor.

As far as excessive and rigid imagination is concerned, I am unfortunately in a position to quote a highly compromising example from my own personal experience. It also shows the effect on monitoring of the most dangerous of all emotions, the craving for the sensational. Like all persons professionally associated with news, the monitor is naturally interested in providing information of exclusive importance, more particularly so since, being completely dependent on what other people choose to broadcast, he can do very little to obtain it through his own initiative. This often causes a feeling of frustration which makes him doubly keen on any sensational item he happens to pick up. However, while being doubly keen, he should also be doubly cautious, since excitement can easily lead his hearing astray. On one particular occasion at the beginning of the war, I failed to resist the passion for the sensational. What happened then cured me for the rest of my life.

One morning after the invasion of Poland, I was keeping a watch on the Deutschlandsender, the principal German long-wave station, at a time of the day when it was normally off the air. Suddenly I heard a muffled voice say:

Achtung! Achtung! Die Russen sind nicht weit. Achtung! Achtung!

Die Russen sind nicht weit. (Attention, attention. The Russians are not far away.)

This mysterious announcement made me lose my wits. Since at that time everybody was speculating about the possibility of friction between Germany and Russia, the muffled voice appeared to me as coming from obscure Nazi quarters—dissidents, perhaps?—which were using the main German radio channel during one of its silent periods to warn the German people about the Russians' dangerous proximity resulting from the invasion of Poland.

The muffled voice then added, rather incongruously: 'Es liegen keine Nachrichten vor' (Nothing to report) and signed off with a promise to return in a few hours' time on a different wavelength.

The announcement had not been recorded and could therefore not be checked. For this reason it was decided to keep back my sensational discovery until such time when confirmation could be obtained. The mystery was soon cleared up by a colleague who had heard the muffled voice before. It had said what it had been saying with monotonous regularity every morning shortly after nine o'clock and which had nothing to do with any Russians, far or near. It was an ordinary station announcement: 'Achtung, Achtung. Hier Hochseefunk Norddeich' (Attention, attention. This is the Norddeich High Seas' Radio). The Norddeich transmitter, which shared its wavelength with the Deutschlandsender, used that channel while the latter was silent, for broadcasting messages to ships. On that particular day there apparently were none, which accounted for the by no means incongruous, but, on the contrary, very pertinent statement that there was 'nothing to report'.

NOTES

Introduction
1. George Codding *Broadcasting Without Barriers* (UNESCO publication, Paris 1959), p. 30
2. quoted in Asa Briggs *A History of Broadcasting in the United Kingdom* Vol. 1 *The Birth of Broadcasting* (Oxford University Press, London 1961), p. 309
3. *RL in Profile* from the Office of the Information Adviser (Munich, January 1974)
4. John B. Whitton and Arthur Larson *Propaganda: Towards Disarmament in the War of Words* (Oceana Publications, New York 1964), p. 266
5. in the Preface to Sidney Rogerson *Propaganda in the Next War* (Geoffrey Bles, London 1938)
6. *Fragments of a Journal* (*Journal en Miettes*) tr. J. Stewart (Faber, London 1968), p. 93
7. (Pelican, Harmondsworth 1970), p. 336; originally published by Hogarth Press, London 1964
8. L. J. Martin, 'Effectiveness of International Propaganda', in *Annals of the American Academy of Political and Social Science: Propaganda in International Affairs* (Philadelphia, November 1971), pp. 61–70
9. *German Radio Propaganda* (Oxford University Press, London 1944), p. 477

Chapter 1: The Nazi Model
1. Z. A. B. Zeman *Nazi Propaganda* (Oxford University Press, London 1964), p. 183
2. quoted in Derrick Sington and Arthur Weidenfeld *The Goebbels Experiment* (John Murray, London 1942), p. 139
3. Zeman, op. cit., p. 2
4. Jacques Ellul *Propaganda* (Vintage Books, New York 1973), p. 53
5. Asa Briggs *A History of Broadcasting in the United Kingdom* Vol. 3 *The War of Words* (Oxford University Press, London 1970), pp. 221 ff.
6. *Voices in the Darkness* (Secker and Warburg, London 1943), p. 104
7. *Goebbels' Diaries* ed. P. Lochner (Hamish Hamilton, London 1948)
8. Sington and Weidenfeld, op. cit., p. 150
9. quoted in Sington and Weidenfeld, op. cit., p. 156
10. Briggs, op. cit., p. 328
11. see for example Jerome S. Bruner, 'The Dimensions of Propaganda: German Short-Wave Broadcasts to America', *Journal of Abnormal and Social Psychology* Vol. 36, No. 3 (Washington 1941) reprinted in Daniel Katz, Dorwin Cartwright, Samuel Eldersveld, Alfred McClung Lee (eds)

Public Opinion and Propaganda (Henry Holt and Co., New York 1954); and Harwood L. Childs 'America's Short-Wave Audience', in Harwood L. Childs and John B. Whitton (eds) *Propaganda by Short Wave* (Princeton University Press, 1942)

12. Saul K. Padover, 'Japanese Race Propaganda', *Public Opinion Quarterly* No. 2, 1943 (Columbia University Press, New York)
13. Joel V. Berreman, 'Assumptions about America in Japanese War Propaganda to the United States', in William E. Daugherty and Morris Janowitz *A Psychological Warfare Casebook* (Johns Hopkins University Press, Baltimore 1958), p. 439
14. *The Political Use of Radio*, Geneva Studies, Vol. X, No. 3 (Geneva, August 1939)
15. Briggs, op. cit., p. 8

Chapter 2: The Communist Appeal

1. Vsevolod Skorodumov *On the History and Development of Broadcasting in the Soviet Union* Radio Liberty research report, RL/299/73 (Munich 1973)
2. report of the Presidential Study Commission on International Broadcasting (Milton S. Eisenhower, chairman) *The Right to Know* (US Government Printing Office, Washington 1973), p. 17
3. *Propaganda* (Vintage Books, New York 1973), p. 22
4. Francis Ronalds Jr, 'The Future of International Broadcasting', in *Annals of the American Academy of Political and Social Science: Propaganda in International Affairs* (Philadelphia, November 1971), pp. 71–80
5. Prague Radio commentary, 11 November 1956
6. Radio Free Europe research report, *Eastern Europe/14* (Munich, 25 September 1973)
7. Moscow Radio in English, 3 January 1974

Chapter 3: Voices of America

1. Joseph Morgenstern in *Newsweek* 5 May 1972
2. *A History of Broadcasting in the United Kingdom* Vol. 3 *The War of Words* (Oxford University Press, London 1970), p. 412
3. Edward W. Barrett *Truth is Our Weapon* (Funk and Wagnalls, New York 1953), pp. 72 ff.
4. ibid., p. 19
5. report of the Presidential Study Commission on International Broadcasting (Milton S. Eisenhower, chairman) *The Right to Know* (US Government Printing Office, Washington 1973), p. 42
6. ibid., p. 48
7. Zalai Hirlap, 25 April 1972, quoted in Anthony C. A. Dake *Impediments to the Free Flow of Information between East and West* (a study on behalf of the Atlantic Treaty Association, 1973), p. 27
8. Presidential Study Commission on International Broadcasting, op. cit., p. 56
9. *The Pentagon Propaganda Machine* (Random House Press, New York 1971), pp. 46–7
10. DEW Line, 2, 3 (1969) poster 1

11. US Committee on Foreign Affairs Report No. 2 *Winning the Cold War*: *The US Ideological Offensive* 88th Congress, House Report No. 1352, 27 April 1964, quoted in Herbert I. Schiller *Mass Communications and American Empire* (Augustus M. Kelley, Clifton, New Jersey 1969), p. 12

12. quoted in the *New York Times* 28 February 1965

13. *The Objectives of the United States Information Agency* (Praeger, New York 1968), p. 221

14. *Ambassador's Journal* (Hamish Hamilton, London 1969), p. 97

15. figures quoted in Schiller, op. cit., p. 80

Chapter 4: The BBC

1. *Propaganda's Harvest* (Kegan Paul, London 1941,) p. 37

2. *Radio and Television Broadcasting on the European Continent* (University of Minnesota Press, Minneapolis 1967), p. 4

3. *Comes the Reckoning* (Putnam, New York 1949), p. 160

4. 'Propaganda by Short Wave: London Calling America', *Public Opinion Quarterly* No. 1, 1941 (Columbia University Press, New York)

5. Asa Briggs *A History of Broadcasting in the United Kingdom* Vol. 3 *The War of Words* (Oxford University Press, London 1970), p. 460

6. Daniel Katz, 'Britain Speaks', in Harwood L. Childs and John B. Whitton (eds) *Propaganda by Short Wave* (Princeton University Press, 1942), pp. 111 ff.

7. 'Psychological Warfare' (address to NATO Defence College, Paris 1959) reprinted in Sir Hugh Greene *The Third Floor Front* (Bodley Head, London 1969), pp. 21 ff.

8. Briggs, op. cit., p. 482

9. *The British Press and Vietnam* pamphlet published by the Indochina Solidarity Conference, Indochina Information No. 3, July 1973

10. Terry Baxter, 'The Best of All Possible Worlds', *Time Out* No. 204, 25–31 January 1974

11. 'Speaking Peace . . .?', BBC Handbook, 1968, p. 27

12. *Journalist* No. 5 (Moscow 1968)

13. Moscow Radio in English, 3 April 1974

14. in a 1952 lecture to the British Royal United Services Institution

15. 'Broadcasting to the USSR and Eastern Europe', BBC Lunch-time Lectures, Third Series, No. 2, 1964

Chapter 5: The Third World

1. *International Political Communication* (Praeger, New York 1965), p. 148

Chapter 6: The Middle East

1. W. Phillips Davison *International Political Communication* (Praeger, New York 1965), p. 136

2. *A Dying Colonialism* (*L'An Cinq de la Révolution Algérienne*) (Pelican, Harmondsworth 1970), p. 58; originally published in Great Britain under the title *A Study in Dying Colonialism* by Monthly Review Press, London 1965

3. Winston Burdett *Encounter with the Middle East* (André Deutsch, London 1970), p. 23

4. quoted in Morroe Berger *The Arab World Today* (Weidenfeld and Nicolson, London 1962), pp. 427 ff.
5. 31 March 1971
6. *The Listener* 29 December 1966 (from a Third Programme broadcast)
7. *The Third Floor Front* (Bodley Head, London 1969), p. 38
8. the evidence is presented in condensed form in *War File* ed. Tim Hewat (Panther Record, London 1967)
9. quoted in Berger, op. cit., pp. 427 ff.
10. *Guardian* 24 November 1974

Chapter 7: Africa
1. *Communication in Africa* (Yale University Press, New Haven 1961), p. 149
2. *The Biafra Story* (Penguin, Harmondsworth 1969), p. 226
3. *The Nigerian Civil War* (Hodder and Stoughton, London 1972), p. 357

Chapter 8: East of Suez
1. see Donald R. Brown *International Broadcasting in Asia: A Comparative Study* (paper presented to the Association for Professional Broadcasting Education Symposium, 1970)

Chapter 9: Latin America
1. Francis Ronalds Jr, 'The Future in International Broadcasting', in *Annals of the American Academy of Political and Social Science: Propaganda in International Affairs* (Philadelphia, November 1971), pp. 71–80
2. *The Information Machine* (Syracuse University Press, 1968), p. 183

Chapter 10: Clandestine Radio
1. Secker and Warburg, London 1962
2. *A History of Broadcasting in the United Kingdom* Vol. 3 *The War of Words* (Oxford University Press, London 1970), p. 17
3. *Psychological Warfare* (Infantry Journal Press, Washington 1948), p. 87
4. Frantz Fanon *A Dying Colonialism* (*L'An Cinq de la Révolution Algérienne*) (Pelican, Harmondsworth 1970), p. 80; originally published in Great Britain under the title *A Study in Dying Colonialism* by Monthly Review Press, London 1965
5. ibid., p. 66
6. John de St Jorre *The Nigerian Civil War* (Hodder and Stoughton, London 1972), p. 346

Chapter 11: Propaganda Fide
1. *Propaganda* (Vintage Books, New York 1973), p. 49

Chapter 12: Interference
1. E. Tangye Lean *Voices in the Darkness* (Secker and Warburg, London 1943), p. 172.
2. (Penguin, Harmondsworth 1971), pp. 272–3; originally published by The Bodley Head (London) in two parts (Part 1, 1968; Part 2, 1969)

3. Spyridon Granitsas in E. L. Bernays and B. Hershey (eds) *The Case for Reappraisal of US Overseas Information Policies and Programs* (Praeger, New York 1970), pp. 64–7
4. *Goebbels' Diaries* ed. P. Lochner (Hamish Hamilton, London 1948), entry of 1 March 1942
5. *The Word War* (Harper and Row, New York 1968), p. 228
6. Milton S. Eisenhower (chairman) *The Right to Know* (US Government Printing Office, Washington 1973), p. 8.

Chapter 13: The Broadcasters

1. *Goebbels' Diaries* ed. P. Lochner (Hamish Hamilton, London 1948)
2. E. Tangye Lean *Voices in the Darkness* (Secker and Warburg, London 1943), p. 104
3. ibid., p. 72
4. *Vsevit* No. 1, 1969
5. *Radio Free Europe* (University of Minnesota Press, Minneapolis 1958), p. 43
6. *Comes the Reckoning* (Putnam, New York 1949), p. 333

Chapter 14: Monitoring

1. 'Eavesdropping on Europe at War' (review of *Propaganda by Short Wave*), *Public Opinion Quarterly* Vol. 3, 1942 (Columbia University Press, New York)
2. *Goebbels' Diaries* ed. P. Lochner (Hamish Hamilton, London 1948), entry of 25 January 1942
3. report of the Presidential Study Commission on International Broadcasting (Milton S. Eisenhower, chairman) *The Right to Know* (US Government Printing Office, Washington 1973), p. 30
4. I. Pinter in *Nepszabadsag* 18 January 1973
5. *Ears of Britain* an unpublished wartime memorandum by Anatol Goldberg

Conclusion

1. *A History of Broadcasting in the United Kingdom* Vol. 1 *The Birth of Broadcasting* (Oxford University Press, London 1961), p. 26
2. J. A. C. Brown *Techniques of Persuasion* (Pelican, Harmondsworth 1963), p. 309
3. Amber Blanco White *The New Propaganda* (Gollancz, Left Book Club, London 1939), p. 37
4. quoted in Daniel Lerner (ed.) *Propaganda in War and Crisis* (George W. Stewart, New York 1951), p. 473
5. *Comes the Reckoning* (Putnam, New York 1949), p. 154
6. *Propaganda* (Vintage Books, New York 1973), p. 287
7. Brown, op. cit., p. 126
8. report of the Presidential Study Commission on International Broadcasting (Milton S. Eisenhower, chairman) *The Right to Know* (US Government Printing Office, Washington 1973), p. 28
9. BBC House Magazine *Ariel* 26 May 1972

BIBLIOGRAPHY

Two volumes of bibliography cover some of the aspects of international radio:

Lasswell, H. D., Casey, R. D. and Smith, B. L. (eds) *Propaganda and Promotional Activities: an annotated bibliography* latest edition 1969 (University of Chicago Press)

Smith, B. L. and C. M. *International Communication and Political Opinion: a guide to literature* (Princeton University Press, 1958)

The following have provided useful information on the stated themes:

The nature of propaganda
Brown, J. A. C. *Techniques of Persuasion* (Pelican, Harmondsworth 1963)

Chakhotin, Serge *The Rape of the Masses* (Alliance Book Co., New York 1940)

Doob, Leonard W. *Propaganda: Its Psychology and Technique* (Henry Holt and Co., New York 1935)

—— *Public Opinion and Propaganda* (Henry Holt and Co., New York 1948)

Ellul, Jacques *Propaganda* (Vintage Books, New York 1973)

Fraser, Lindley *Propaganda* (Oxford University Press, London 1957)

Katz, Daniel, Cartwright, D., Eldersveld, S. and McClung Lee, A. (eds) *Public Opinion and Propaganda* (Henry Holt and Co., New York 1954)

Murty, B. S. *Propaganda and World Public Order* (Yale University Press, New Haven 1968)

Steed, Wickham *The Fifth Arm* (Constable, London 1940)

White, Amber Blanco *The New Propaganda* (Gollancz, Left Book Club, London 1939)

Whitton, John B. and Larson, Arthur *Propaganda: Towards Disarmament in the War of Words* (Oceana Publications Inc., New York 1964)

Radio and communications
Barrett, Marvin (ed.) *The Politics of Broadcasting* (Thomas Y. Crowell Co., New York 1973)

Childs, H. L. and Whitton, John B. (eds) *Propaganda by Short Wave* (Princeton University Press, 1942)

Codding Jr, George A. *Broadcasting Without Barriers* (UNESCO, 1959)

Davison, W. Phillips *International Political Communication* (Praeger, New York 1965)

Emery, Walter B. *National and International Systems of Broadcasting* (Michigan State University Press, East Lansing 1969)

Grandin, Thomas *The Political Use of Radio* Geneva Studies, Vol. X, No. 3 (Geneva, August 1939)

Johansen, O. L. and Frost, J. M. (eds) *How to Listen to the World* World Radio and TV Handbook, annual publication since 1967

Martin, L. John *International Propaganda: Its Legal and Diplomatic Control* (University of Minnesota Press, Minneapolis 1958)

Paulu, Burton *Radio and Television Broadcasting on the European Continent* (University of Minnesota Press, Minneapolis 1967)

Schiller, Herbert I. *Mass Communications and American Empire* (Augustus M. Kelley, Clifton, New Jersey 1969)

Thompson, Marian *International TV Programming* unpublished thesis at the University of Wisconsin, Madison 1971

White, L. and Leigh, R. D. *Peoples Speaking to Peoples* (Chicago University Press, 1967)

Propaganda and War

Bulmer-Thomas, I. *Warfare by Words* (Penguin, Harmondsworth 1942)

Daugherty, William E. and Janowitz, Morris *A Psychological Warfare Casebook* (Johns Hopkins University Press, Baltimore 1958)

Delmer, Sefton *Black Boomerang* (Secker and Warburg, London 1962)

Ettlinger, Harold *The Axis on the Air* (Bobbs-Merrill, New York 1943)

Friedman, Otto *Broadcasting for Democracy* (Allen and Unwin, London 1942)

Gordon, Matthew *News is a Weapon* (Knopf, New York 1942)

Graves, Harold N. *War on the Short Wave* (Foreign Policy Association, New York 1941)

Krabbe, Henning (ed.) *Voices from Britain* (Allen and Unwin, London 1947)

Kris, E. and Speier, H. *German Radio Propaganda* (Oxford University Press, London 1944)

Lasswell, Harold *Propaganda Technique in the World War* (Kegan Paul, London 1927)

Lean, E. Tangye *Voices in the Darkness* (Secker and Warburg, London 1943)

Lerner, Daniel *Sykewar* (George W. Stewart, New York 1951)

—— (ed.) *Propaganda in War and Crisis* (George W. Stewart, New York 1951)

Linebarger, Paul M. A. *Psychological Warfare* (Infantry Journal Press, Washington 1948)

Lockhart, R. H. Bruce *Comes the Reckoning* (Putnam, New York 1949)

Martin, Kingsley *Propaganda's Harvest* (Kegan Paul, London 1941)

Meerloo, Major A. M. *Total War and the Mind* (Allen and Unwin, London 1944)

Rogerson, Sidney *Propaganda in the Next War* (Geoffrey Bles, London 1938)

Rolo, Charles J. *Radio goes to War* (Faber and Faber, London 1943)

Siepmann, Charles *Radio in Wartime* (Oxford University Press, London 1942)

Sington, Derrick and Weidenfeld, Arthur *The Goebbels Experiment* (John Murray, London 1942)

Zeman, Z. A. B. *Nazi Propaganda* (Oxford University Press, London 1964)

Current External Services

Barghoorn, F. C. *Soviet Foreign Propaganda* (Princeton University Press, 1964)

Barrett, Edward W. *Truth is Our Weapon* (Funk and Wagnalls Inc., New York 1953)

BBC Handbook, annual publication (London)

Bernays, E. L. and Hershey, B. (eds) *The Case for Reappraisal of United States Overseas Information Policies and Programs* (Praeger, New York 1970)

Black, J. D. *The Co-ordination and Control of Propaganda used as an Instrument of Foreign Policy: a comparative study of present-day governmental practice in the US and the UK* unpublished thesis at the University of London, 1969

Briggs, Asa *A History of Broadcasting in the United Kingdom* Vol. 1 *The Birth of Broadcasting* (1961); Vol. 2 *The Golden Age of Wireless* (1965); Vol. 3 *The War of Words* (1970); all published by Oxford University Press, London

Clews, John C. *Communist Propaganda Techniques* (Methuen, London 1964)

Dyer, Murray *The Weapon on the Wall: Rethinking Psychological Warfare* (Johns Hopkins University Press, Baltimore 1959)

Elder, Robert *The Information Machine* (Syracuse University Press, 1968)

Gordon, George N., Falk, Irving and Hodapp, William *The Idea Invaders* (Hastings House, New York 1963)

Greene, Sir Hugh *The Third Floor Front* (Bodley Head, London 1969)

Hollander, Gayle Durham *Soviet Political Indoctrination* (Praeger, New York 1972)

Holt, Robert *Radio Free Europe* (University of Minnesota Press, Minneapolis 1958)

Lawson, Murray (ed.) *Communist Propaganda around the World* (United States Information Agency, Washington 1962)

Liu, Alan P. L. *Communications and National Integration in Communist China* (University of Michigan Press, Ann Arbor 1971)

Paulu, Burton *British Broadcasting in Transition* (University of Minnesota Press, Minneapolis 1956)

Rubin, Ronald I. *The Objectives of the United States Information Agency* (Praeger, New York 1968)

Sorensen, Thomas C. *The Word War* (Harper and Row, New York 1968)

Thomson, Charles A. H. *Overseas Information Service of the US Government* (Brookings Institution, Washington 1948)

World Radio and TV Handbook, annual publication

The Third World

Browne, Donald R. *International Broadcasting in Asia: A Comparative Study* published in the Association for Professional Broadcasting Education Symposium, 1970

Doob, Leonard *Communication in Africa* (Yale University Press, New Haven 1961)

Frankel, Peter *Wayaleshi* (Weidenfeld and Nicolson, London 1959)

Laurence, John *The Seeds of Disaster* (Gollancz, London 1968)

Miscellaneous

Cornell, Julien *The Trial of Ezra Pound* (John Day Co. Inc., New York 1966)

Dake, Anthony C. A. *Impediments to the Free Flow of Information between*

East and West study on behalf of the Atlantic Treaty Association (1973)

Kenner, Hugh *The Pound Era* (Faber and Faber, London 1971)

Report of the Presidential Study Commission on International Broadcasting (Milton S. Eisenhower, chairman) *The Right to Know* (US Government Printing Office, Washington 1973)

Waniewicz, Ignacy *Broadcasting for Adult Education* (UNESCO, 1972)

Useful bibliographies are contained in the works by Briggs, Childs and Whitton, Davison, Ellul, Martin, Whitton and Larson, Zeman. Of the many periodicals which publish relevant material, *Public Opinion Quarterly* (New York is the most noteworthy. UNESCO, the International Telecommunications Union, the European Broadcasting Union and other UN and intergovernmental agencies are also valuable sources. Radio Liberty and Radio Free Europe's Research Departments publish essential statistics and analyses which are not available elsewhere. BBC and other monitoring reports provide the direct evidence.

Index

Italicized page numbers indicate major references